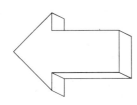

Computer users are not all alike.
Neither are SYBEX books.

We know our customers have a variety of needs. They've told us so. And because we've listened, we've developed several distinct types of books to meet the needs of each of our customers. What are you looking for in computer help?

If you're looking for the basics, try the **ABC's** series. You'll find short, unintimidating tutorials and helpful illustrations. For a more visual approach, select **Teach Yourself,** featuring screen-by-screen illustrations of how to use your latest software purchase.

Mastering and **Understanding** titles offer you a step-by-step introduction, plus an in-depth examination of intermediate-level features, to use as you progress.

Our **Up & Running** series is designed for computer-literate consumers who want a no-nonsense overview of new programs. Just 20 basic lessons, and you're on your way.

We also publish two types of reference books. Our **Instant References** provide quick access to each of a program's commands and functions. SYBEX **Encyclopedias** and **Desktop References** provide a *comprehensive reference* and explanation of all of the commands, features, and functions of the subject software.

Sometimes a subject requires a special treatment that our standard series don't provide. So you'll find we have titles like **Advanced Techniques, Handbooks, Tips & Tricks,** and others that are specifically tailored to satisfy a unique need.

We carefully select our authors for their in-depth understanding of the software they're writing about, as well as their ability to write clearly and communicate effectively. Each manuscript is thoroughly reviewed by our technical staff to ensure its complete accuracy. Our production department makes sure it's easy to use. All of this adds up to the highest quality books available, consistently appearing on best-seller charts worldwide.

You'll find SYBEX publishes a variety of books on every popular software package. Looking for computer help? Help Yourself to SYBEX.

For a complete catalog of our publications:

SYBEX, Inc.
2021 Challenger Drive, Alameda, CA 94501
Tel: (510) 523-8233/(800) 227-2346 Telex: 336311
SYBEX Fax: (510) 523-2373

SYBEX is committed to using natural resources wisely to preserve and improve our environment. As a leader in the computer book publishing industry, we are aware that over 40% of America's solid waste is paper. This is why we have been printing the text of books like this one on recycled paper since 1982.

This year our use of recycled paper will result in the saving of more than 15,300 trees. We will lower air pollution effluents by 54,000 pounds, save 6,300,000 gallons of water, and reduce landfill by 2,700 cubic yards.

In choosing a SYBEX book you are not only making a choice for the best in skills and information, you are also choosing to enhance the quality of life for all of us.

Teach Yourself
HARVARD GRAPHICS 3

Teach Yourself
HARVARD GRAPHICS® 3

Jeff Woodward

SYBEX ®

San Francisco ✦ Paris ✦ Düsseldorf ✦ Soest

Acquisitions Editor: Dianne King
Developmental Editor: Christian T.S. Crumlish
Copy Editor: Alex Miloradovich
Project Editor: Janna Hecker Clark
Technical Editor: Daniel A. Tauber
Word Processors: Scott Campbell, Ann Dunn, and Susan Trybull
Book Designer: Ingrid Owen
Chapter Art and Layout: Charlotte Carter
Screen Graphics: Delia Brown, Cuong Le, and Thomas Goudie
Desktop Publishing Specialists: M.D. Barrera and Dina F. Quan
Proofreaders: Dina F. Quan, Lisa Haden, and David Avilla Silva
Indexer: Nancy Guenther
Cover Designer: Kelly Archer
Cover Photographer: David Bishop

Library of Congress Card Number: 91-75004
ISBN: 0-89588-801-7

Manufactured in the United States of America

10 9 8 7 6 5 4 3 2 1

Acknowledgments

Teach Yourself Harvard Graphics 3 is a unique concept in computer book tutorials, and many fine individuals have contributed to its creation. I would like to express my gratitude to everyone for their hard work, and especially thank the SYBEX proofreading and typesetting teams as well as the following individuals.

Christian Crumlish, my developmental editor, for his expert guidance in getting me started in the right direction.

Janna Hecker Clark, my project editor, whose pleasant, understanding manner reassured me when I needed it most.

Alex Miloradovich, my copy editor, for his incisive eye for detail, economy, and organization.

Dan Tauber, my technical editor, for insuring the accuracy of each step in this tutorial. His technical contributions are an integral part of this book.

Delia Brown for her patient assistance in producing the screen graphics.

Charlotte Carter for her creative efforts in design and layout.

I would also like to express my appreciation to Dianne King and Dave Clark, Acquisitions Editors; Barbara Gordon, Managing Editor; and Dr. Rudolph Langer, Editor-in-Chief, for their continued support.

And I congratulate and thank Software Publishing Corporation for continuing to make Harvard Graphics one of the finest presentation programs on the market.

Jeff Woodward
November 1991
Santa Clarita, California

Contents at a Glance

Table of Contents

Introduction

Teach Yourself Harvard Graphics 3 is a visual, step-by-step users' guide to Harvard Graphics 3.0. If you are new to computerized presentation graphics, upgrading from an earlier version of the program, or making the transition from another presentation graphics software, this book can put you on the fast track to excellence.

As a reference manual, your Harvard Graphics documentation does an excellent job of providing detailed technical information. However, it does not always show you what to do with that information. A tutorial format would compromise its primary role. *Teach Yourself Harvard Graphics 3* is the perfect companion volume for your documentation. Its sole purpose is to teach you, with the ease and convenience of a tutorial, to use the program's wide array of powerful presentation tools.

Every aspect of this book has been carefully designed to build upon and increase your level of skill and confidence in a logical, sequential manner. The visual format allows you to learn through a series of computer screen illustrations accompanied by clear, concisely written instructions. Notes and cross-references provide special tips and shortcuts, and point the way to sources of further information.

✦ An Overview of Harvard Graphics

Harvard Graphics is a full-featured graphics presentation program that allows you to create a variety of powerful charts and organize them into presentations.

There are several versions of Harvard Graphics. This book covers version 3.0 for IBM or 100%-compatible 286, 386, or 486 computers with at least 640K of RAM, a hard disk, one floppy-disk drive, and a graphics display card.

With Harvard Graphics you can build masterful text, pie and column, XY, and organization charts.

- Text charts include title, bullet, and table charts.
- Pie and column charts allow you to graphically illustrate percentages of a total value.
- XY charts let you display the relationship of more than one data series charted along x and y axes.

+ Organization charts allow you to show the hierarchical relationships be-tween people, functions, or objects with a network of interconnected boxes.

The Harvard Graphics Draw feature lets you enhance your charts with a stock library of symbols, or create new chart objects with a variety of draw tools. The Gallery, a Harvard Graphics feature that includes specially designed and for-matted charts, is not covered in this book.

✦ What's New in Release 3.0

Harvard Graphics 3.0 includes many powerful new features, yet it remains com-patible with earlier versions of the program. Files created in Harvard Graphics versions 2.0, 2.1, and 2.3 can be used in Harvard Graphics 3.0, and files created in Harvard Graphics 3.0 can be used in Harvard Graphics 2.3. Symbols created in any 2.x version can also be converted for use in 3.0 by retrieving them into the Harvard Graphics Draw screen.

Release 3.0 has been enhanced in the following areas.

+ New chart regions for greater flexibility in chart arrangement.

+ More enhancement options for text, pie, and XY charts.

+ A new icon-based drawing interface with more than 35 powerful drawing tools for creating and editing charts and symbols.

+ Enhanced drawing features for adding bitmap files in .PCX and .PCC and black-and-white or gray-scale TIFF formats.

+ Additional Bitstream scalable typefaces.

+ A variety of color palettes, and the ability to create custom palettes.

+ Improved presentation options for making global formatting modifications.

+ The ability to automatically include newly created charts in existing presentations.

+ A variety of new import and output devices and drivers.

+ A new screen preview function for displaying charts exactly as they look when printed or outputted.

- The ability to choose nine different paper sizes.
- Context-sensitive help.
- Unlimited file size.
- A built-in macro program.
- A built-in memory manager.
- A DOS shell.
- Pull-down menus.
- An on-line tutorial.

✦ How to Use This Book

Unlike most computer books, *Teach Yourself Harvard Graphics 3* uses a balanced mix of text and screen illustrations in a series of practical exercises designed to let you teach yourself to use the program. Each numbered step consists of written instructions with three-dimensional graphics of keyboard commands, followed by an illustration of the resulting display on your screen.

.1   Click on **Create chart** or press ⌊**1**⌋ to display the Chart menu.

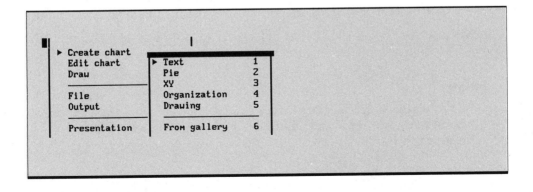

♦ **2**   Click on **Text** or press ⌊**1**⌋ to display the Text chart menu.

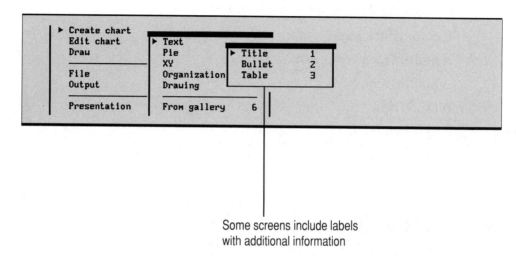

Some screens include labels
with additional information

Step 1 of this exercise tells you to place the mouse pointer on the **Create chart** menu item and click the left mouse button, or to press the number 1 key to display the Chart menu. Step 2 shows you how to display the Text chart menu.

You will also see the following special features throughout the book.

Note

Notes Provide Supplementary Information   This special feature supplies helpful hints, warnings, and additional information to assist you in the learning process.

When you see two connected keys such as ⌊CTRL⌋⌊**S**⌋ you should press and hold the first key, press the second key, and then release both keys.

Cross-references direct you to further or related information in this book, your Harvard Graphics documentation, or other available sources.

✦ A Quick Tour through the Chapters

The best way to use *Teach Yourself Harvard Graphics 3* is to complete the chapters in sequence, and work the tutorial exercises from beginning to end.

Chapter 1 *Getting Started with Harvard Graphics* introduces you to the program, and provides some helpful hints for creating masterful presentations. This chapter also teaches you to start the program; use the function keys, speed keys, and Main Menu; get help; set up your output devices; and exit the program.

Chapter 2 *Building Effective Text Charts* teaches you to build and save title, bullet, and table charts; to view the current status of your chart on screen; and to create chart legends.

Chapter 3 *Advancing Your Editing and Output Skills* introduces the editing options; teaches you to retrieve and clear charts; edit chart notes; spell-check charts; select special and international characters; change text attributes; and produce output on printers, plotters, and film recorders.

Chapter 4 *Creating Persuasive Pie and Column Charts* teaches you to construct pie charts, convert pie charts to column charts, and to modify and work with pie slices and column sections.

Chapter 5 *Illustrating Your Ideas with XY Charts* shows you how to build, convert, and enhance bar, line, area, high/low/close, and point charts.

Chapter 6 *Establishing a Framework with Organization Charts* guides you through the process of building organization charts and working with chart boxes, display, and enhancement options.

Chapter 7 *Customizing the Program to Suit Your Style* shows you how to create templates, record and run macros, modify program and chart defaults, work with various fonts, and configure Harvard Graphics to run outside applications.

Chapter 8 *Building Masterful Presentations* teaches you to edit and enhance a group of charts, and use them to build a presentation. This chapter also introduces the ScreenShow feature.

Chapter 9 *Enhancing Your Presentations with Draw* introduces you to the new Draw feature, which lets you create original charts and chart objects, enhance existing charts, and work with a variety of Harvard Graphics symbols.

Appendix A shows you how to install Harvard Graphics on your hard disk. If you're a beginner, there's also some helpful general information on how to install your mouse, make backup copies of your program disks, and use your keyboard and computer with Harvard Graphics.

Appendix B teaches you how to import Lotus, Excel, ASCII, and dBASE data into Harvard Graphics. It also shows you how to export Harvard Graphics files to Professional Write, EPS, HPBL files, CGM metafiles, and PCX bitmap files.

✦ Before You Begin

Before you begin with Chapter 1, there are a few definitions and conventions you should be aware of.

- ✦ When you create a chart, you enter data in a worksheet. Harvard Graphics calls this worksheet a *data form*. In this book we consistently use the term "worksheet."

- ✦ Many of the charts this book teaches you to produce are more commonly referred to as graphs. Harvard Graphics uses the word "chart" to describe all presentation graphics.

- ✦ Column charts are constructed and display data in the same way as pie charts. Column charts and XY bar charts are similar in appearance. Do not confuse these two chart types. Column charts do not have x and y axes.

When you work through the exercises in this book, be sure to create and save your charts as instructed. Most of these charts are retrieved and reused in later exercises.

Note

Gaining Maximum Benefit from This Book   Many people are intimidated by instructions of any sort. I want to offer some excellent advice on this problem before we get started. Forget it! This book is designed to make the process of teaching yourself Harvard Graphics as easy and painless as possible. If you relax, begin at the beginning, and follow the simple step-by-step instructions, you'll be creating masterful charts in no time.

You must install Harvard Graphics on your hard disk before you get started.

Refer to Appendix A for complete installation instructions and information on how to use your computer with Harvard Graphics.

1

Getting Started with Harvard Graphics

◆   If you are new to Harvard Graphics, this is a must read chapter. It relates many helpful hints for preparing effective presentations, and gets you started in the step-by-step process of teaching yourself to use the program. If you have experience producing presentation graphics, especially with previous versions of Harvard Graphics, this chapter is a reminder of some important concepts.

Before you begin, be sure to read the Introduction. It contains an overview of the many kinds of charts Harvard Graphics enables you to prepare, an update on the new features in Release 3.0, and important information on how you can gain the maximum benefit from using this book. You should also have made backup copies of your Harvard Graphics program disks, installed your mouse, and installed Harvard Graphics on your hard disk.

See Appendix A for an explanation of these procedures and an overview of basic hardware and software operating methods.

◆ Welcome to Harvard Graphics
◆ Getting Started

✦ Welcome to Harvard Graphics

Harvard Graphics is relatively easy to use. It allows you to create a full range of text, pie, column, XY axis, and organization charts with little or no training. Your most important goal, however, should be to communicate your ideas in the most effective and efficient way possible. This section is designed to help you accomplish that goal.

The Benefits of Harvard Graphics

Let's take a look at some of the many ways Harvard Graphics can help you prepare more effective presentations.

- Organizes and streamlines your ideas and concepts.
- Highlights and clarifies your key presentation points.
- Increases your persuasive power.
- Enhances your credibility.
- Enlivens your presentation with printed charts, overhead transparencies, and slides.
- Allows you to depict trends and strategic concepts.
- Maximizes audience retention by visually supporting your message.

Building Masterful Presentations

Harvard Graphics is such an option rich environment, it's easy to lose sight of your primary purpose. To help you communicate your ideas in the most effective and efficient way possible, observe these helpful hints for building masterful presentations.

Arrows Arrows can be used to emphasize specific points. Too many arrows can confuse and lessen the impact of your presentation.

Pie Charts Pie charts are an effective way to make a point. More than eight pie slices can make your charts difficult to interpret.

Chart Legends Chart legends can be used to label the components of a chart. They can also divide the viewer's attention. Place figures and labels directly on columns or pie slices if possible.

Spell Checking The spell checking function can correct embarrassing errors. Attention to detail is one of the main building blocks for masterful presentations.

Fonts A variety of font designs, sizes and styles can enhance your presentation. Choose fonts which are simple enough and large enough for easy reading, or your audience may lose sight of your message.

Special Effects Special effects can add spice to your presentation. Use these effects sparingly, or your audience may become more interested in your special effects than your message.

Patterns and Solid Colors Patterns and solid colors can be used to differentiate the components of a chart. Since patterns can be difficult to decipher, your charts may be more effective if you use solid colors.

Visual Presentation Aids You can output your finished charts as printed handouts, slides and overhead transparencies. Use these aids in a supporting role only. A picture can be worth a thousand words, but it's better to speak most of them than to try putting them all on a single chart.

Here are some important general guidelines to always bear in mind.

- ✦ Restraint, consistency and attention to detail build masterful presentations.
- ✦ Simple chart designs create instant recognition.

- A separate chart for each key idea focusses viewer attention.
- The fewer charts grouped on a single slide, overhead transparency or printed handout, the greater the impact.

Components of a Chart

Like building a house, you first need to understand the basic components of a chart and how it is put together. Let's take a look at a typical chart.

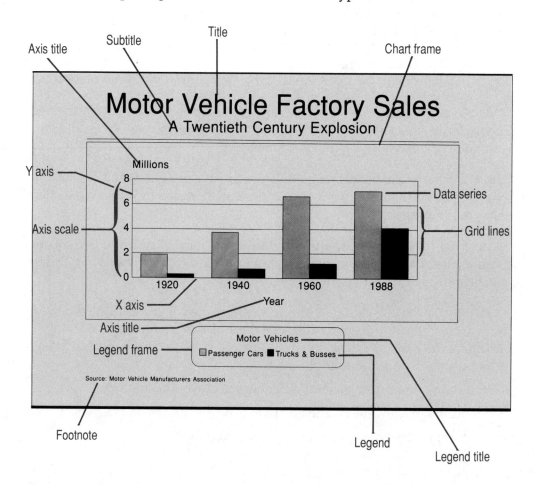

Title	Descriptive heading which identifies the chart.
Subtitle	Secondary heading for additional information.
Axis title	Descriptive heading which labels the data on an axis.
Axis scale	System of marks placed at fixed intervals to measure chart data.
Y axis	Vertical reference line for measuring data.
X axis	Horizontal reference line for measuring data.
Footnote	Source information for chart data.
Legend	Group of symbols with descriptive text to identify columns, pie slices, and other chart data.
Legend title	Descriptive heading which identifies the legend.
Legend frame	Graphic border which frames the legend elements.
Grid lines	Series of intersecting lines to help measure chart data against axis scale values.
Data series	Set of numbers represented by a pie slice, column, bar or other chart element.
Chart frame	Graphic border which frames entire chart.

✦ Getting Started

This section teaches you how to start the program, display and select menu options, use the major function keys, get help, set up your printer, plotter, or film recorder, and exit the program.

Starting the Program

The following steps show you how easy it is to start your computer, change to the HG3 directory, and start Harvard Graphics.

If you haven't installed Harvard Graphics on your hard disk, please refer to Appendix A.

✦ **1**   Turn on your monitor and computer. You may be prompted to enter the current date. If not, you will probably see the DOS prompt shown in step 3.

```
Current date is Wed  4-01-1992
Enter new date (mm-dd-yy): _
```

✦ **2**   Type in the current date if it isn't already displayed, and press ⏎.

```
Current date is Wed  4-01-1992
Enter new date (mm-dd-yy):
Current time is 12:00:00.00
Enter new time: _
```

✦ **3**   Type in the current time if you need to, and press ⏎. The DOS C prompt appears.

```
Current date is Wed  4-01-1992
Enter new date (mm-dd-yy):
Current time is 12:00:00.00
Enter new time:

C>_
```

Some computers bypass the date and time prompts and immediately display the DOS prompt. Some DOS prompts also include directory names like C>123 or C>WP51.

When the DOS C prompt appears, the operating system is ready to use. From here you can start Harvard Graphics.

Note

Incorrect Entries and Error Messages   If you make an incorrect entry and get an error message, don't worry. The screen will display another DOS C prompt below an incorrect entry. Enter the correct information at the new prompt.

✦ **4**   Type **CD HG3** at the C prompt and press ⏎.

```
C>CD HG3

C>
```

✦ **5**   Type **HG3** and press ⏎. Harvard Graphics starts and the Main Menu is displayed.

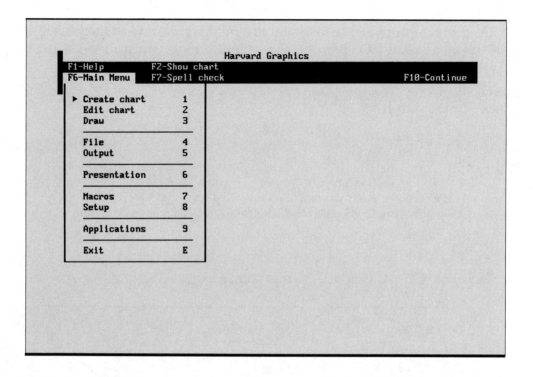

Keep the Main Menu on your screen while you explore the Function Keys, Speed Keys, and Main Menu features.

Function Keys

Several function key options are displayed above the Main Menu. When you press the appropriate key, the following function is activated.

F1-Help   Displays helpful information about the menu option or chart item you are currently working with.

F2-Show chart   Shows the current status of the chart you are working on.

F6-Main Menu   Displays the Main Menu on the current screen.

F7-Spell check Locates and suggests word corrections for misspelled text.

F10-Continue Saves charts and program configurations, and also selects menu options.

Speed Keys

Speed keys provide convenient shortcuts to a variety of functions. The speed key sequence is usually shown next to its menu option.

The following sequences are useful on a regular basis.

CTRL F1	Displays a complete speed key list.
CTRL G	Displays the Get chart menu.
CTRL S	Displays the Save chart menu.

For a quick speed key reference see the inside covers of this book.

Main Menu Features

The Main Menu provides direct access to certain features, or displays pull-down or pop-up menus from which you can access other features.

The following list describes these features.

Create chart	Create a new chart.
Edit chart	Edit an existing chart.
Draw	Start the Draw program to create draw charts, or add symbols, bitmap images, and drawings to existing charts.
File	Retrieve and save charts and templates, or import and export data.
Output	Output a chart to a printer, film recorder, or plotter.

Presentation	Create, retrieve, edit and save presentations.
Macros	Create and load and run macros.
Setup	Setup and edit default values, select output devices and fonts, establish international settings, and work with palettes.
Applications	Return to DOS and run other programs without exiting Harvard Graphics.

Let's put what you've learned into practice by selecting some menu items with your keyboard or mouse.

Note

Selecting Menu Items with a Mouse   To click on an item means to place the mouse pointer on the item and click the left button. To double-click on an item means to press the left mouse button twice in rapid succession. The right mouse button usually cancels an action and returns the screen to its previous display. These commands are described in the text.

◆ **1**   To display the File menu using a mouse, move the pointer to **File** and click the left mouse button. From the keyboard, press ▣ or press ▣ or ▣ until the menu arrow is aligned with **File** and then press ▣ or ▣.

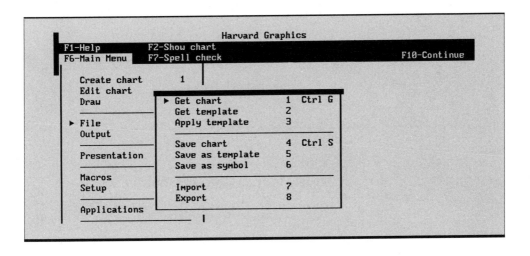

♦**2**   Click the right mouse button or press ⌈ESC⌉ to cancel the File menu.
The Main Menu remains on your screen.

Note

Returning to the Main Menu   Some options display up to three levels of
menus. Pressing ⌈ESC⌉ or clicking the right mouse button will return you to the
previously displayed menu. You may have to press ⌈ESC⌉ or click the right
mouse button more than once to return to the Main Menu.

Getting Help

When you need help with a particular feature it's nice to have the information a
keystroke or mouse click away. Harvard Graphics has context sensitive help so
you can get specific information while you work. A complete Help Menu can
also be displayed.

Let's look at how the help function works.

♦**1**   With the arrow keys, move the menu arrow to **Create chart** on the
Main Menu.

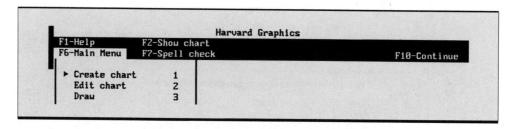

◆ **2**   Place the mouse pointer on **F1-Help** and click the left button, or just press [F1]. The Help window is displayed with information on the Create chart option.

Scroll arrow reveals more information. ──────

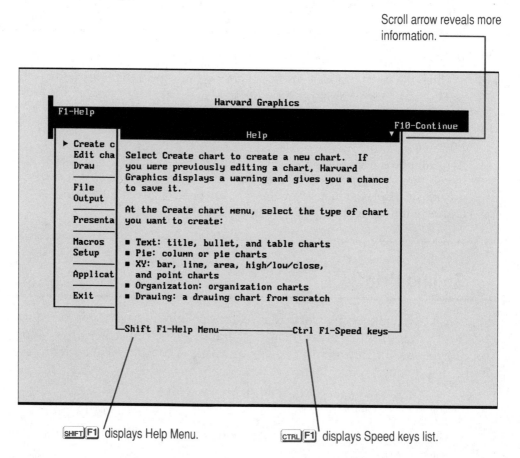

[SHIFT][F1] displays Help Menu.   [CTRL][F1] displays Speed keys list.

◆ **3**   Place the mouse pointer and click on the down scroll arrow or press
[PG DN] to move down a screen.

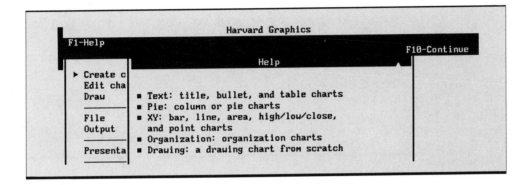

◆ **4**   Press [↑] or [↓] to move up or down one line at a time. If you press [↑]
three times your screen should look like the following one.

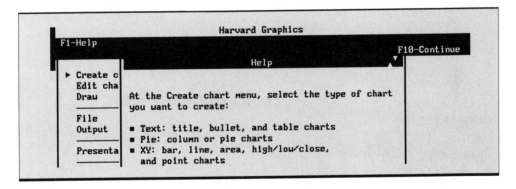

✦ **5**   Click on the up scroll arrow or press ⟨PG UP⟩ to move up one screen.

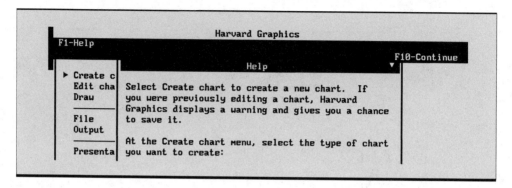

✦ **6**   Click the right mouse button or press ⟨ESC⟩ to return to the Main Menu.

Output Device Setup

Harvard Graphics lets you produce charts and graphs on output devices such as printers, film recorders, or plotters.

Refer to your output device manual for the following information before you begin the setup procedure.

- ✦ Brand name and model number.
- ✦ Parallel port LPT1, LPT2, or LPT3.
- ✦ Serial port COM1 or COM2.
- ✦ Serial port baud rate 9600, 4800, 2400, 1200, or 300.
- ✦ Serial port parity odd, even, or none.
- ✦ Serial port data bits 7 or 8.
- ✦ Serial port stop bits 1 or 2.

The following instructions guide you through the printer setup procedure, but they can also be used for plotter or film recorder setup. The Main Menu should be displayed on your screen.

◆ **1**   Click on **Setup** or press ⟦8⟧.

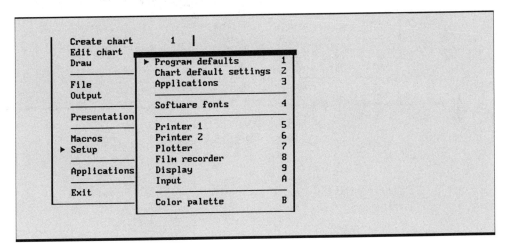

◆ **2**   Click on **Printer 1** or press ⟦5⟧. The Printer 1 Setup Menu appears with the HP LaserJet II selected by default.

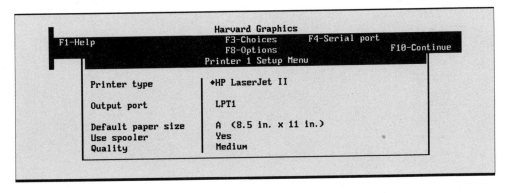

✦ **3** Click on **F3-Choices** or press ⊞ to display a list of printer models.

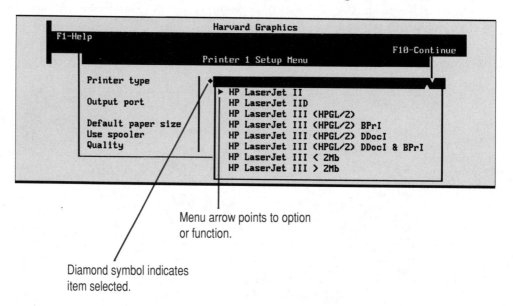

Menu arrow points to option
or function.

Diamond symbol indicates
item selected.

✦ **4** Click on the up or down scroll arrows or press ⬆ or ⬇ to scroll through the list of printer models until the menu arrow is next to your model.

✦ **5** Click on your device name or press ↵. On the following screen HP LaserJet III <2Mb is selected.

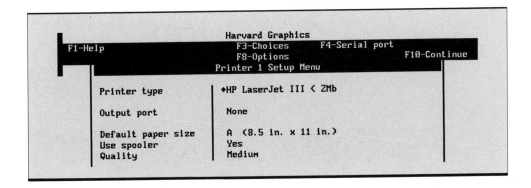

✦ **6** To display a list of output ports, double-click on **Output port** or press ⬇ once to align the diamond symbol with **Output port** and press F3.

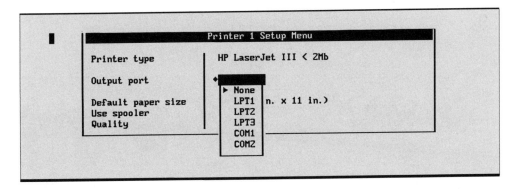

✦ **7**   Click on your type of output port or press ⬇ until the menu arrow points to it and then press ⏎. Skip to step 11 if you selected a parallel port such as LPT1. If you selected a serial port, continue with steps 8, 9, and 10.

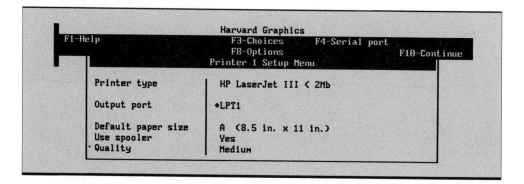

✦ **8**   Click on **F4-Serial port** or press **F4** to display the serial port default settings.

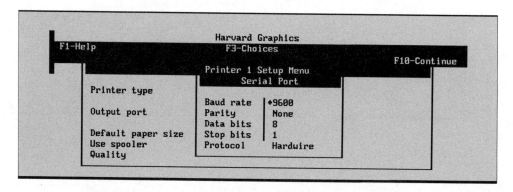

✦ **9**   Click on **F3-Choices** or press **F3** to display the options for each item on the list, and make your selection using the mouse or keyboard method described in step 7.

✦ **10** When you have changed all the settings to match your printer specifications, click on **F10-Continue** or press 🔟 to complete the configuration.

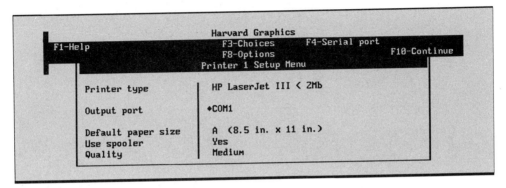

✦ **11** Double-click on **Default paper size** or press ⬇ to move the diamond symbol to the Default paper size item and press 🖲 to display a size list. Select the size you plan to use in your printer. On the following screen 8½ × 11 paper is selected.

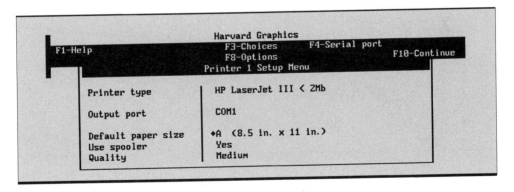

Note

Film Recorder Setup   To set up a film recorder, select your recorder's film type and size rather than paper size.

◆ **12**   Double-click on **Use spooler** or press ⎵ to move the diamond symbol to the Use spooler item and press F3. **Yes** turns the output spooler on, and **No** turns it off.

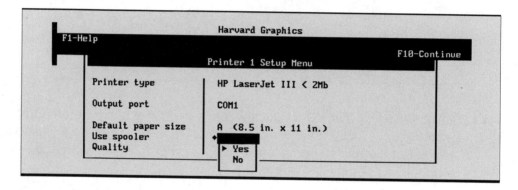

Note

Output Spooler Functions and Benefits   An output spooler temporarily stores the data being sent to the printer, plotter, or film recorder. This process frees up Random Access Memory (RAM) by storing this data in a special file on your hard disk, which allows you to perform other tasks in Harvard Graphics while your output device is working.

See Chapter 7 for more information on the output spooler.

✦ **13**   Click on **Yes** or select this option with the menu arrow and press ⏎.

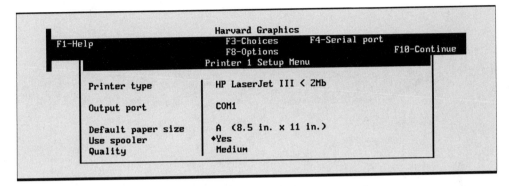

✦ **14**   Double-click on **Quality** or press ⏎ to move the diamond symbol to the Quality item and press F3 to display a list of output qualities. Some output devices offer only two levels of quality.

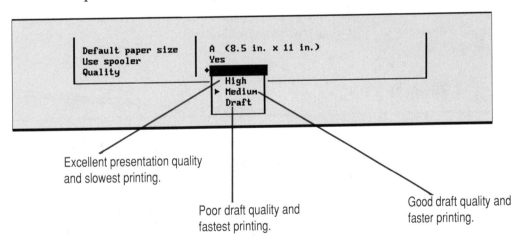

Excellent presentation quality and slowest printing.

Poor draft quality and fastest printing.

Good draft quality and faster printing.

◆ **15** Click on the output quality you want or select your choice with the menu arrow and press ⏎. On the following screen the High option is selected.

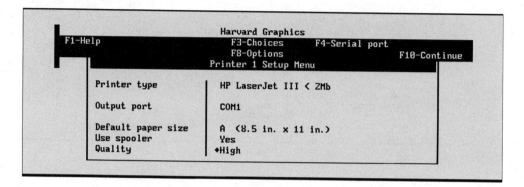

◆ **16** Click on **F10-Continue** or press 🔳 to save your selections.

To set up a second printer, a plotter, or a film recorder, select the appropriate device names and options in the Setup menus as you retrace the steps for printer setup.

Exiting the Program

So far you have taught yourself to start Harvard Graphics, use the function and speed keys, work with the menu system, get help, and set up your output devices. Your final task is to teach yourself to exit the program.

✦ **1**   Click the right mouse button or press ⓔsꞔ until the Main Menu appears.

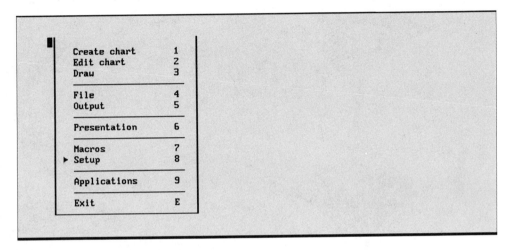

```
    ▌    Create chart      1
         Edit chart        2
         Draw              3

         File              4
         Output            5

         Presentation      6

         Macros            7
       ▶ Setup             8

         Applications      9

         Exit              E
```

✦ **2**   Click on **Exit** or press Ⓔ to return to the DOS prompt.

```
c>_
```

✦ Summary

If you've read the Introduction and worked with the step-by-step procedures in this chapter, you've established an excellent foundation for teaching yourself to create your own presentations.

Chapter 2 starts you on the road to building masterful text charts.

2

Building Effective
Text Charts

◆ Text charts are the basic building blocks of business presentations. With the Harvard Graphics text chart function you can create title charts, bullet charts, and table charts. Title charts allow you to introduce major topics and subject areas. Bullet charts make it possible for you to emphasize lists of facts and ideas. Table charts let you organize data into columns.

Many of the skills you teach yourself as you work with text charts are essential to all the other charts you create with Harvard Graphics. If you are a beginner, you should read the Introduction and complete Chapter 1 and this chapter before you skip ahead.

Remember to keep your charts clear and simple. Text which is too densely concentrated, too small, or set in too many font styles and sizes, can make your charts confusing and difficult to read.

- ◆ Creating Title Charts
- ◆ Working with Show, Save and Redisplay
- ◆ Creating Bullet Charts
- ◆ Creating Table Charts
- ◆ Creating Chart Legends

✦ Creating Title Charts

Let's begin by creating a title chart to introduce the main topic of your first presentation.

Note

Correcting Typing Errors   To correct a typo, press ⌫. This deletes the character to the left of the cursor. When you've erased your mistake, retype the text.

For additional editing techniques, refer to Chapter 3.

✦ **1**   Start Harvard Graphics. The Main Menu should be displayed.

✦ **2**   Click on **Create chart** or press ① to display the Chart menu.

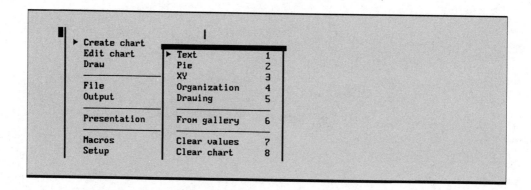

✦ **3**   Click on **Text** or press ①̲ to display the Text chart pop-up menu.

```
  ■
    ▶ Create chart           |
      Edit chart       ▶ Text
      Draw               Pie         ▶ Title       1
                         XY            Bullet      2
      File               Organization  Table       3
      Output             Drawing
```

✦ **4**   Click on **Title** or press ①̲ to display a Title Chart worksheet.

```
                          Title Chart
   F1-Help        F2-Show chart            F4-Draw        F5-Mark
   F6-Main Menu   F7-Spell/Text  F8-Options              F10-Continue
   ───────────────────────────── Top ─────────────────────────────




   ──────────────────────────── Middle ───────────────────────────




   ──────────────────────────── Bottom ───────────────────────────


```

The title chart worksheet is divided into top, middle, and bottom regions. The amount of text you can enter in each region is limited.

Top Region	Four lines of text.
Middle Region	Eight lines of text.
Bottom Region	Four lines of text.

Note

Characters Per Line and Text Size   Text charts are limited to 100 characters per line. Harvard Graphics automatically adjusts the size of the text based on the number of characters you enter. The more characters you enter, the smaller the text size.

♦ 5   The cursor should be in the upper left corner of the Top region. Type **MEGAPRODUCTS UNLIMITED** in all capital letters.

```
                              Title Chart
   F1-Help          F2-Show chart                F4-Draw        F5-Mark
   F6-Main Menu     F7-Spell/Text   F8-Options                  F10-Continue
   ────────────────────────────────── Top ──────────────────────────────
   MEGAPRODUCTS UNLIMITED_
```

♦ 6   Press [TAB] to move the cursor to the beginning of the second line. Type **Regional Sales Conference** in upper and lowercase letters.

```
                              Title Chart
   F1-Help          F2-Show chart                F4-Draw        F5-Mark
   F6-Main Menu     F7-Spell/Text   F8-Options                  F10-Continue
   ────────────────────────────────── Top ──────────────────────────────
   MEGAPRODUCTS UNLIMITED
   Regional Sales Conference_
```

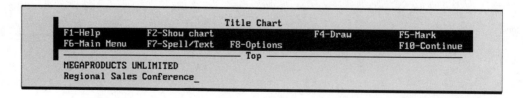

Note

Moving the Cursor   ⌨TAB moves the cursor down to the next line. SHIFT TAB moves the cursor up to the previous line. To move the cursor to another region, press TAB or SHIFT TAB as many times as needed.

✦**7**   Press TAB and type **A Banner Year For Sales**.

✦**8**   Press TAB twice to reach the first line in the middle region. Type the text on the following screen, pressing TAB twice between each line.

```
————————————————————— Middle —————————————————————
Overall Five-Year Synopsis

MegaProducts Best Sellers

Regional Sales Comparison_
```

✦**9**   Press TAB four times to reach the first line in the bottom region. Type **Conference to be followed by a reception in the Egyptian Paradise Room**.

```
————————————————————— Bottom —————————————————————
Conference to be followed by a reception in the Egyptian Paradise Room_
```

✦ Working with Show, Save, and Redisplay

Your title chart worksheet is complete, but it doesn't look like the finished version you would present to your clients or associates. This section shows you how to display the current status of your chart on screen, save your chart in permanent memory, and redisplay your current worksheet.

Viewing the current status of your chart on screen lets you see how it's going to look before you generate a printout, overhead transparency or slide.

✦ **1**   Display the worksheet version of your chart, and then click on **F2-Show chart** or press F2 to show the current status of your chart.

MEGAPRODUCTS UNLIMITED
Regional Sales Conference
A Banner Year for Sales

Overall Five-Year Synopsis

MegaProducts Best Sellers

Regional Sales Comparison

Conference to be followed by a reception in the Egyptian Paradise Room

---

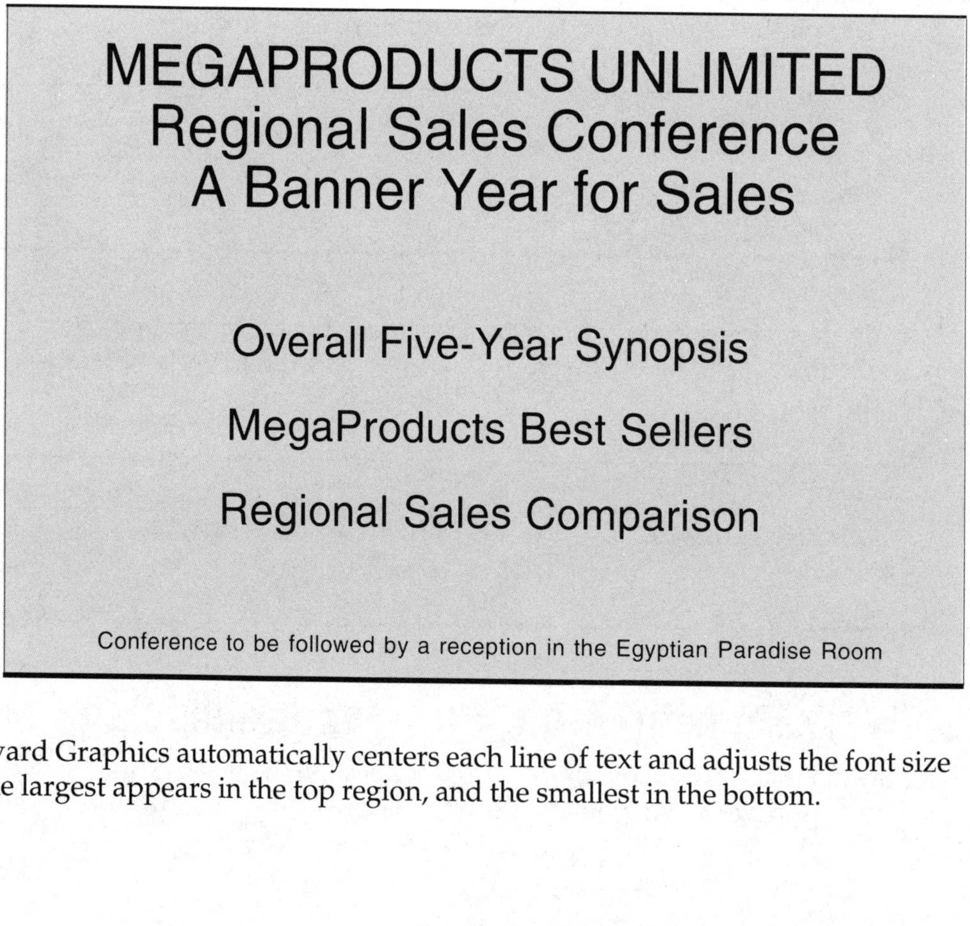

Harvard Graphics automatically centers each line of text and adjusts the font size so the largest appears in the top region, and the smallest in the bottom.

Note

Using the Show Chart Function   Show chart can display your chart at any time in the creative or editing process. When appearance and format options are selected or changed, click on **F2-Show chart** or press F2 to view the current status of your chart.

At this point your text chart exists in your computer's temporary or Random Access Memory (RAM). To store your chart in permanent memory, you must save the data on a disk.

◆ **2**   Click the right mouse button twice or press ESC twice to return to the Main Menu.

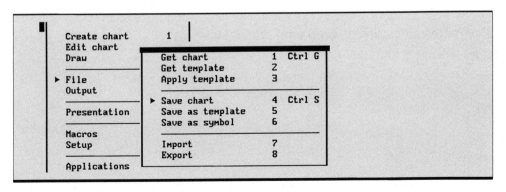

◆ **3**   Click on **File** or press 4 to display the File menu.

◆ **4**   Click on **Save chart** or press ④ to display the Save Chart menu.

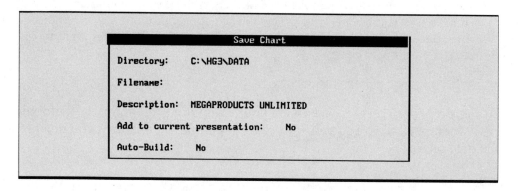

The list below explains the main features of each item on the Save Chart menu.

Directory	Files are automatically saved to the default directory unless you select this item and type a new drive letter or directory path.
Filename	Enter eight characters or less, but do not type an extension since .CH3 will automatically be assigned.
Description	The current title appears by default, but you can type up to 40 characters to help you identify the file.
Add to current presentation	If no specific group of charts is being prepared for presentation, one will be created.
Auto-Build	An advanced feature not covered in this book.

For more information on preparing presentation files, see Chapter 8.

٠ **5**   The cursor is automatically positioned to enter the file name. Type
BESTSALE and press ⏎ to move to the description line.

```
Directory:    C:\HG3\DATA

Filename:     BESTSALE

Description:  MEGAPRODUCTS UNLIMITED
```

٠ **6**   Type **Regional Sales Conference**. MEGAPRODUCTS UNLIMITED
is overwritten.

```
Directory:    C:\HG3\DATA

Filename:     BESTSALE

Description:  Regional Sales Conference_
```

٠ **7**   Click on **F10-Continue** or press F10 to save the chart with the name
BESTSALE.CH3 and return to the Main Menu.

Note

Save Chart Speed Keys   The speed keys CTRL S display the Save Chart
pop-up menu from anywhere in the Harvard Graphics program. Save your
work as often as possible using the method described in step 7. If you accidentally delete your work or the power fails you can only retrieve the most recently
saved version.

To redisplay your worksheet for editing, let's use the Edit chart function on the
Main Menu.

✦ **8** Click on **Edit chart** or press ②️ to redisplay your current worksheet.

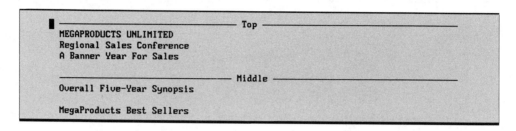

✦ **9.** Click the right mouse button or press ⎋ to return to the Main Menu.

✦ Creating Bullet Charts

A bullet chart uses symbols or numbers to emphasize listed items in a presentation or report. Harvard Graphics lets you create bulleted lists, change bullet styles, and change the order of the items on the chart.

Let's create a simple bullet chart. Begin by displaying the Main Menu.

✦ **1** Click on **Create Chart** and then **Text** or press ①️ and ①️ to display the Text chart pop-up menu.

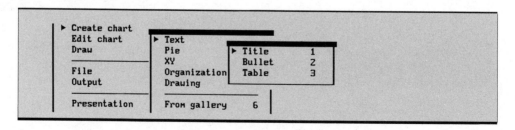

✦ **2**   Click on **Bullet** or press ⧴2⧵ to display the Bullet Chart worksheet.
The cursor should be located on the chart title line.

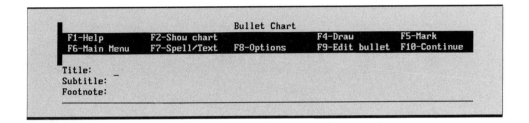

The bullet chart worksheet has the following special features.

Footnote	Allows you to enter chart source information in addition to a title and subtitle.
Bullet Region	Can contain up to 24 bulleted items with a limit of 48 lines of text.
F9-Edit Bullet	Lets you change individual bullet styles, sizes and colors.

Note

Automatic Placement of Bullets   You do not have to type the bullet symbol for each item. Harvard Graphics automatically places a bullet on the first line of text entered on the worksheet and on each line entered after a blank line space. This feature lets you create bulleted items with two or more single spaced lines of text.

✦ **3** Make sure the cursor is at the chart title line and type **Maximizing the Use of Your Money**. If you make a typing error, remember to delete it by pressing [BKSP ⬅] and retyping the correct text.

```
                                  Bullet Chart
        F1-Help         F2-Show chart                F4-Draw        F5-Mark
        F6-Main Menu    F7-Spell/Text   F8-Options   F9-Edit bullet F10-Continue

        Title:      Maximizing the Use of Your Money_
        Subtitle:
        Footnote:
```

✦ **4** Press [TAB] to move the cursor to the subtitle line and type **Use It or Lose It**.

```
                                  Bullet Chart
        F1-Help         F2-Show chart                F4-Draw        F5-Mark
        F6-Main Menu    F7-Spell/Text   F8-Options   F9-Edit bullet F10-Continue

        Title:      Maximizing the Use of Your Money
        Subtitle: Use It or Lose It_
        Footnote:
```

✦ **5** Press [TAB] and type **Source: Customer Protection Guide**.

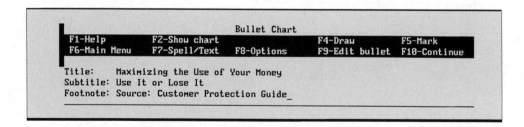

```
                                  Bullet Chart
        F1-Help         F2-Show chart                F4-Draw        F5-Mark
        F6-Main Menu    F7-Spell/Text   F8-Options   F9-Edit bullet F10-Continue

        Title:      Maximizing the Use of Your Money
        Subtitle: Use It or Lose It
        Footnote: Source: Customer Protection Guide_
```

♦ **6**   Press ⟨TAB⟩ to move into the bullet region. Type the list on the following screen. Remember to press ⟨TAB⟩ twice after each line to automatically create a bullet for each line of bulleted text.

```
Title:    Maximizing the Use of Your Money
Subtitle: Use It or Lose It
Footnote: Source: Customer Protection Guide
_____

       · Before You Buy

       · After You Buy

       · Managing Your Product Complaint

       · Writing an Effective Complaint Letter

       · Letter-writing Hints_
```

♦ **7**   Click on **F2-Show chart** or press ⟨F2⟩ to view the current status of your chart.

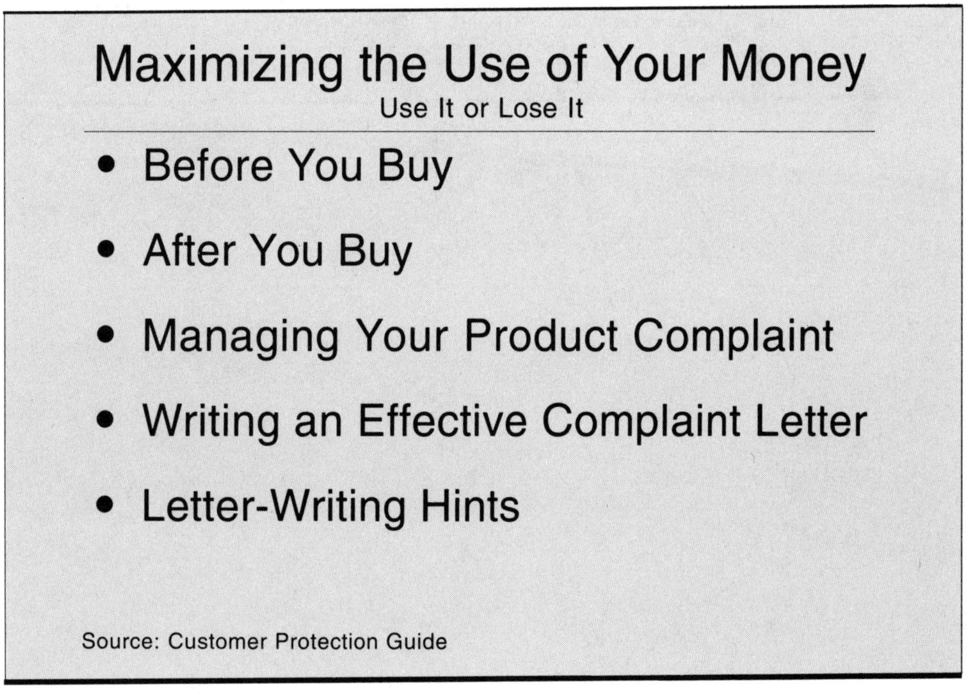

Maximizing the Use of Your Money
Use It or Lose It

- Before You Buy

- After You Buy

- Managing Your Product Complaint

- Writing an Effective Complaint Letter

- Letter-Writing Hints

Source: Customer Protection Guide

⬩ **8**   Click the right mouse button or press ⌷ESC⌷ to return to your worksheet.

Modifying Bullets

You can add variety to your charts with different bullet styles, sizes, and colors. You can also select Arabic or Roman numerals instead of bullets.

Let's change the style of one of the bullets on your chart. Your bullet chart worksheet should be displayed.

⬩ **1**   Using the arrow keys, move the cursor to the **A** in **After You Buy** and click on **F9-Edit bullet** or press ⌷F9⌷ to display the Edit Current Bullet menu. The diamond symbol should indicate the current bullet type.

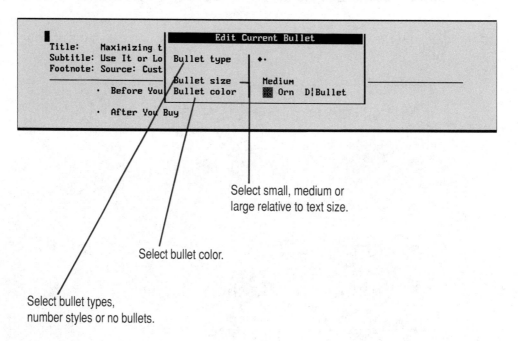

Select small, medium or large relative to text size.

Select bullet color.

Select bullet types, number styles or no bullets.

✦ **2**   Click on **F3-Choices** or press F3 to display the Bullet styles menu.

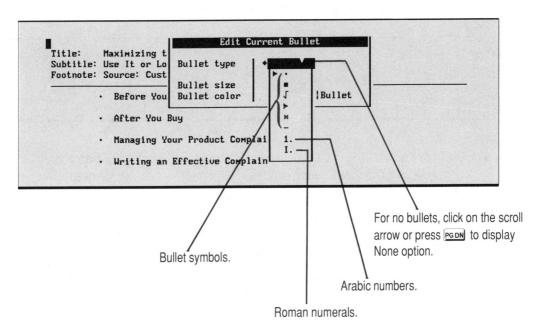

Bullet symbols.

For no bullets, click on the scroll
arrow or press PGDN to display
None option.

Arabic numbers.

Roman numerals.

✦ **3**   Click on ✓ or press ⬇ to move the menu arrow to ✓ and press ↵.
The diamond symbol should now indicate ✓ as the current bullet
type.

◆ **4** Click the right mouse button or press ⟨ESC⟩ to return to your worksheet. The ✓ bullet has replaced the • bullet.

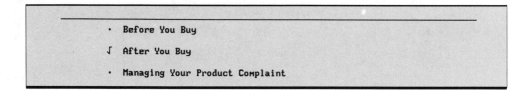

◆ **5** Click on **F2-Show chart** or press ⟨F2⟩ to view the current status of your chart, and then click the right mouse button or press ⟨ESC⟩ to return to your worksheet.

You can experiment with various bullet styles, sizes, and colors by selecting the appropriate menu options and retracing the previous steps. Be sure to return your selections to their original settings before continuing with this exercise.

Harvard Graphics also lets you change all the bullets at the same time. Let's change the bullets on your chart into triangles. Your worksheet should be displayed.

◆ **6** Click on **F8-Options** or press ⟨F8⟩ to display the Chart options menu.

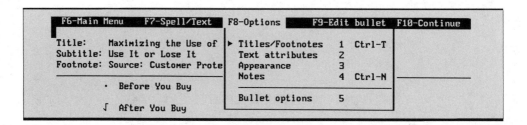

♦ **7** Click on **Bullet options** or press ⑤ to display the Bullet Options menu.

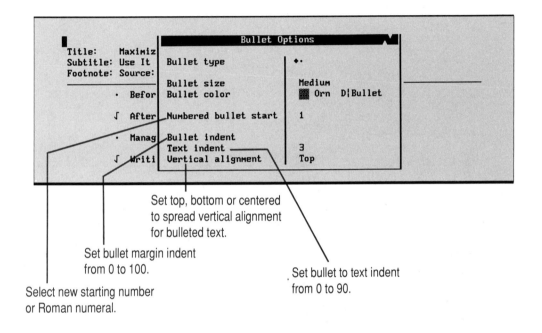

Select new starting number or Roman numeral.

Set bullet margin indent from 0 to 100.

Set top, bottom or centered to spread vertical alignment for bulleted text.

Set bullet to text indent from 0 to 90.

Note

Continuing Numbered Lists on Other Charts   When you select Arabic or Roman numerals instead of a bullet symbol, and your listed items continue onto another chart, select **Numbered bullet start** from the Bullet Options menu. Assign the appropriate starting number or numeral to the first item on the second chart. All the numbered items on the second chart automatically follow your new starting number.

✦ **8**   Click on **F3-Choices** or press F3 to display the Bullet styles menu.

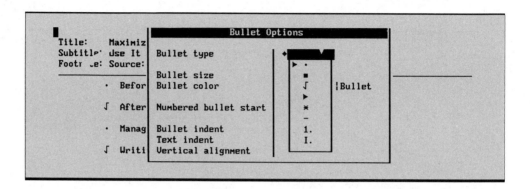

✦ **9**   Click on ➤ or move the menu arrow to ➤ and press ⏎. Click the
right mouse button or press ESC to return to your worksheet.

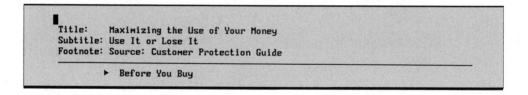

✦ **10**   Click on **F2-Show chart** or press F2 to view the current status of your
chart. All the bullets on your chart should be changed to the ➤ symbol.

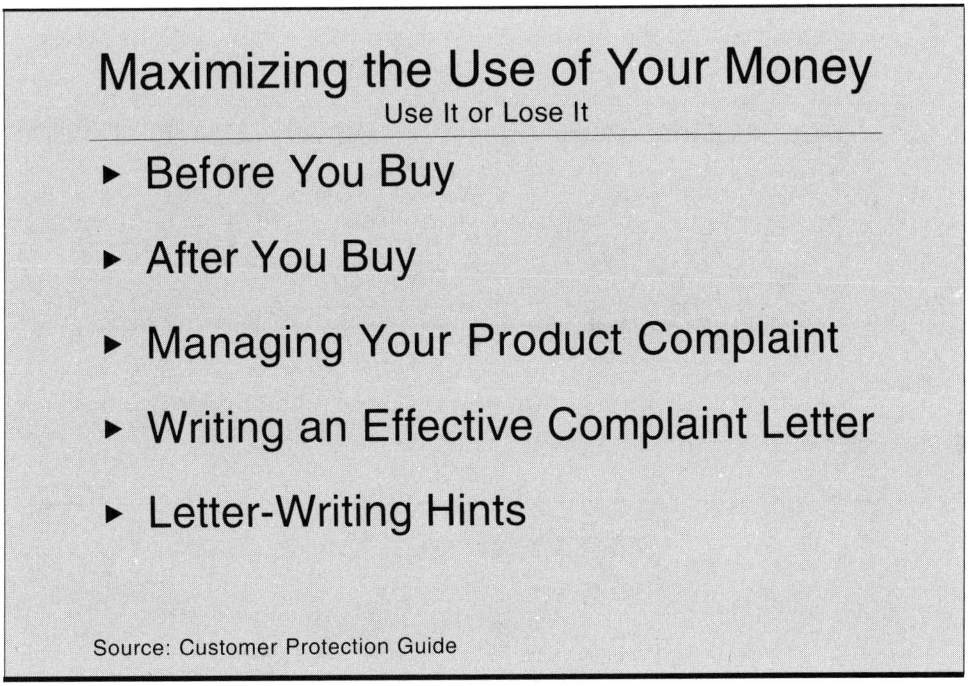

Maximizing the Use of Your Money
Use It or Lose It

▸ Before You Buy

▸ After You Buy

▸ Managing Your Product Complaint

▸ Writing an Effective Complaint Letter

▸ Letter-Writing Hints

Source: Customer Protection Guide

✦ **11**   Click the right mouse button or press ⎋ESC to return to your worksheet.

Text Alignment

All the text on your bullet chart is aligned with the left margin directly below the titles. Let's focus attention on the bulleted items by modifying the bullet and text indentation and changing the vertical alignment. Your bullet chart worksheet should be displayed.

✦ **1** Click on **F8-Options** or press F8 to display the Chart options menu.

```
┌──────────────────────────────────────────────────────────────────────────┐
│ F6-Main Menu   F7-Spell/Text  █F8-Options█   F9-Edit bullet  F10-Continue  │
│                                                                            │
│ Title:   Maximizing the Use of ▶ Titles/Footnotes  1  Ctrl-T              │
│ Subtitle: Use It or Lose It      Text attributes   2                      │
│ Footnote: Source: Customer Prote Appearance        3                      │
│                                  Notes             4  Ctrl-N ─────────    │
│          ▶ Before You Buy                                                 │
│                                  Bullet options    5                      │
│          ▶ After You Buy                                                  │
└──────────────────────────────────────────────────────────────────────────┘
```

✦ **2** Click on **Bullet options** or press 5 to display the Bullet Options menu.

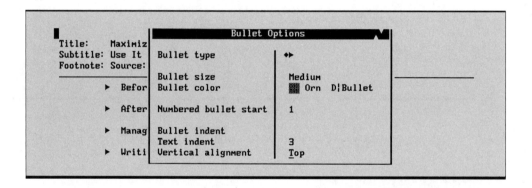

✦ **3** Click on **Bullet indent** or move the diamond symbol to **Bullet indent** and type **10**.

```
┌──────────────────────────────────────────────────────────────────────────┐
│        ▶ After  Numbered bullet start │ 1                                 │
│                                                                            │
│        ▶ Manag  Bullet indent         │ 10_                               │
│                 Text indent           │ 3                                 │
│        ▶ Writi  Vertical alignment    │ Top                              │
└──────────────────────────────────────────────────────────────────────────┘
```

✦ **4**   Click on **Text indent** or move the diamond symbol to **Text indent** and type **5**.

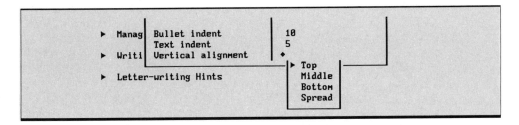

✦ **5**   Double-click on **Vertical alignment** or move the diamond symbol to **Vertical alignment** and then click on **F3-Choices** or press F3 to display the vertical alignment options.

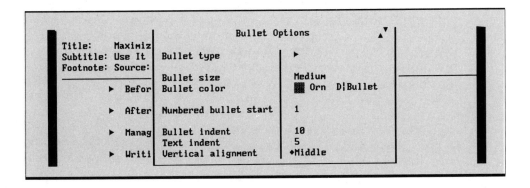

✦ **6**   Click on **Middle** or move the menu arrow to **Middle** and press ↵ to return to the Bullet Options menu.

✦ **7**   Click on **F2-Show chart** or press F2 to view your chart with the bulleted items indented and centered between the titles and footnote.

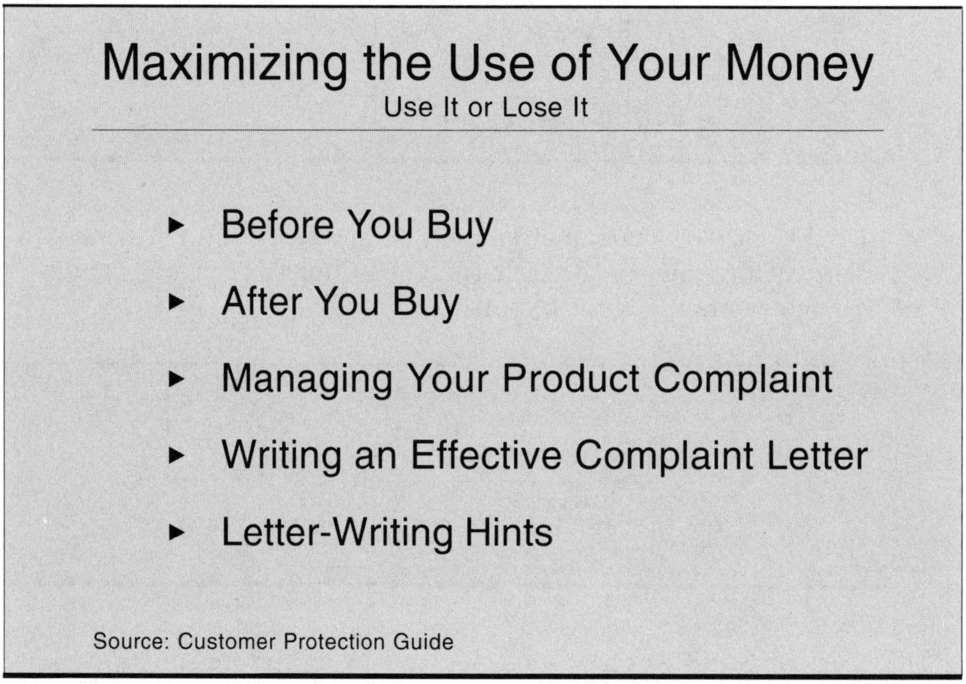

Maximizing the Use of Your Money
Use It or Lose It

▸ Before You Buy

▸ After You Buy

▸ Managing Your Product Complaint

▸ Writing an Effective Complaint Letter

▸ Letter-Writing Hints

Source: Customer Protection Guide

✦ **8**   Click the right mouse button three times or press ESC three times to return to the Main Menu.

✦ **9**   Click on **File** to display the File menu and click on **Save chart** or press 4 and 4 to display the Save Chart menu. Type **Consumer** at the Filename prompt.

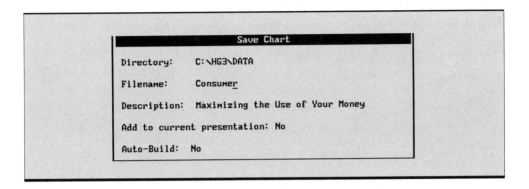

✦ **10**   Click on **F10-Continue** or press F10 to save the file with the name
CONSUMER.CH3 and return to the Main Menu.

✦ Creating Table Charts

Table charts organize words and numbers into columns and rows. Let's construct
a simple table chart. Begin with the Main Menu displayed on your screen.

✦ **1**   To display the Table Chart worksheet, click on **Create chart** and **Text
Chart** and then **Table** or press 1 and 1 and 3.

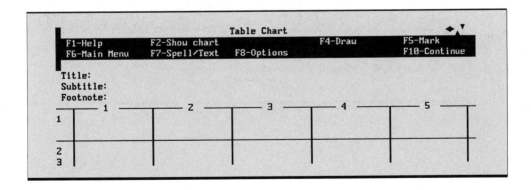

The table chart worksheet has the following special features.

Top Region	To enter your title, subtitle and footnote.
Columns	24 vertical columns numbered left to right.
Rows	24 horizontal rows numbered top to bottom.
Cell	Data entry area at intersection of column and row.
Scroll arrows	Allow you to scroll through columns and rows.

Note

How Table Charts Handle Text   Row 1 has two lines for entering column titles. You can type up to 50 characters per line in each cell. Lines of text longer than 11 characters will scroll off the left side of the worksheet column, but appear in full on your finished chart. Harvard Graphics automatically adjusts text size to fit in a single cell. The more text you enter, the smaller the text size.

◆ **2**   Type the title, subtitle, and footnote information displayed on the following screen.

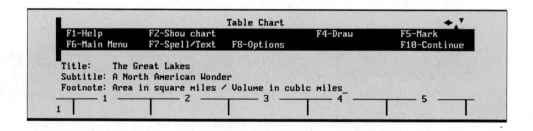

✦ **3** Press ⎄TAB to place the cursor in the first cell in column 1 and type
Name for the column 1 title.

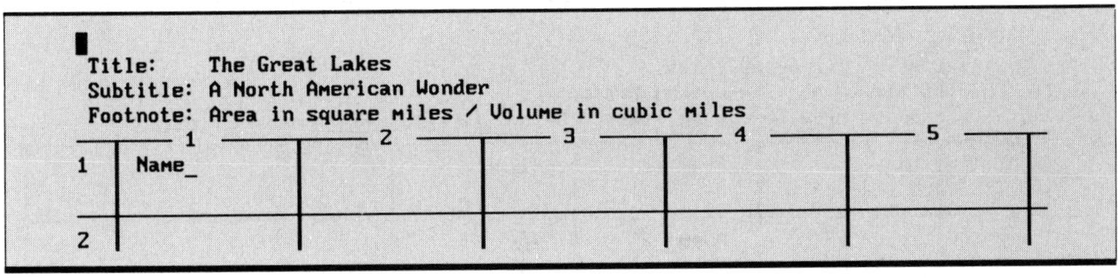

```
■
 Title:    The Great Lakes
 Subtitle: A North American Wonder
 Footnote: Area in square miles / Volume in cubic miles
 ─────── 1 ─────── 2 ─────── 3 ─────── 4 ─────── 5 ───
 1 │ Name_
 2 │
```

Note

Moving the Cursor   To move the cursor with a mouse, place the mouse
pointer in the cell and click the left button. ⎄TAB moves the cursor forward one
cell. ⇧SHIFT ⎄TAB moves the cursor back one cell. ⬇ and ⬆ move the cursor down
or up.

✦ **4** Use ⎄TAB or the mouse to move the cursor to the first cells in columns 2
and 3. Type the titles shown on the following screen.

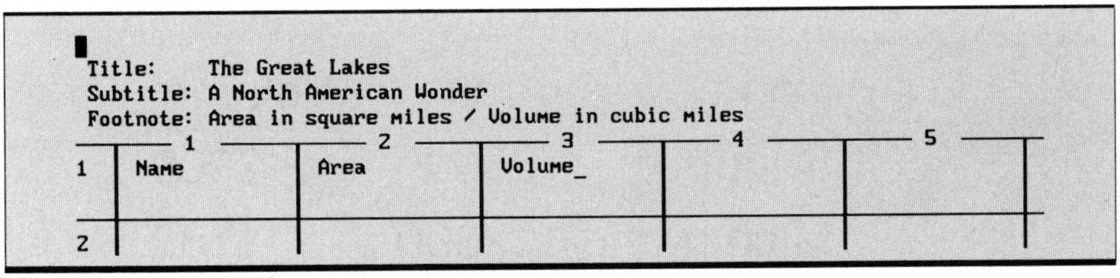

```
■
 Title:    The Great Lakes
 Subtitle: A North American Wonder
 Footnote: Area in square miles / Volume in cubic miles
 ─────── 1 ─────── 2 ─────── 3 ─────── 4 ─────── 5 ───
 1 │ Name      Area      Volume_
 2 │
```

♦ **5.** Press SHIFT TAB twice and ↵ twice to place the cursor in the first cell in row 2 and type the names and numbers shown on the following screen.

```
■
 Title:     The Great Lakes
 Subtitle: A North American Wonder
 Footnote: Area in square miles / Volume in cubic miles
 ———— 1 ———— 2 ———— 3 ———— 4 ———— 5 ————
 1 │ Name        Area         Volume
   │
 2 │ Superior    20600        2900
 3 │ Michigan    22300        1180
 4 │ Huron        9100         850
 5 │ Erie         4980         116
 6 │ Ontario      3560         393_
```

♦ **6** Click on **F2-Show chart** or press F2 to view your table chart. Notice how Harvard Graphics automatically aligns your numerical entries along the right edge of each cell.

The Great Lakes
A North American Wonder

Name	Area	Volume
Superior	20600	2900
Michigan	22300	1180
Huron	9100	850
Erie	4980	116
Ontario	3560	393

Area in square miles / Volume in cubic miles

٠ **7.** Click the right mouse button or press ⌜ESC⌟ to return to your worksheet.

Table Chart Options

You can modify the appearance of your table chart by placing grid lines between the rows and columns, changing the grid line width, adjusting the positions of your columns and rows, changing text alignment, and displaying numbers in scientific notation or with thousands separators.

Note

Menu Handling Tip   Here's a shortcut for displaying all the F8-Options menus for the chart you are working on. When one of the F8-Options menus such as Table Options is displayed and scroll arrows are available, simply click on the down or up arrows, or press ⌜PG DN⌟ and ⌜PG UP⌟ to move to the next F8-Options menu. This allows you to select options from various menus without having to reaccess them through F8-Options.

Let's begin by creating grid lines between your columns and rows. Your table chart worksheet should be displayed.

◆ 1   Click on **F8-Options** or press F8.

Adds grid lines, changes line colors, and alters table size.

Manually sets column and row size, text and numeric alignment, and number displays.

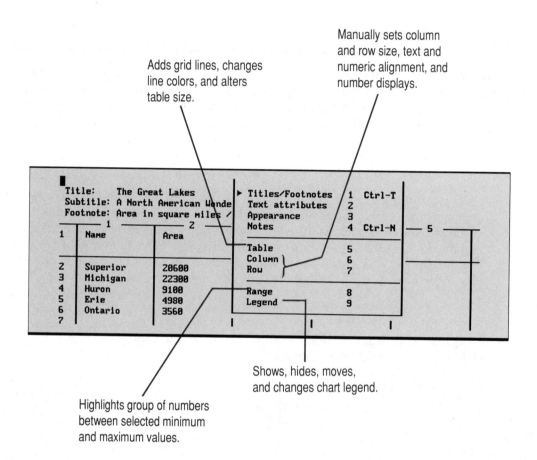

Highlights group of numbers between selected minimum and maximum values.

Shows, hides, moves, and changes chart legend.

◆ **2** Click on **Table** or press ⑤ to display the Table Options menu.

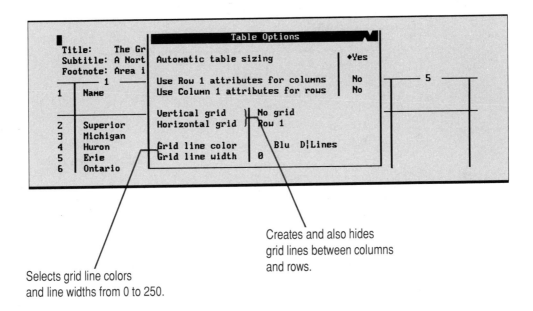

Selects grid line colors
and line widths from 0 to 250.

Creates and also hides
grid lines between columns
and rows.

◆ **3** Double-click on **Vertical grid** or move the diamond symbol to
Vertical grid and then click on **F3-Choices** or press F3.

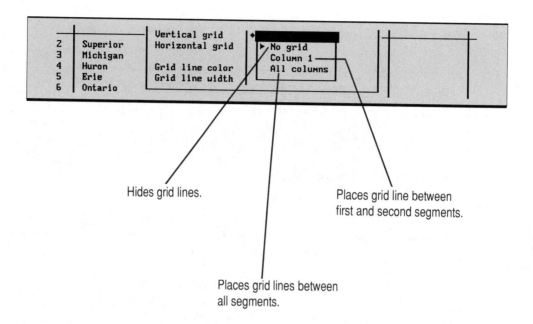

Hides grid lines.

Places grid line between
first and second segments.

Places grid lines between
all segments.

✦ **4**   Click on **All columns** or move the menu arrow to **All columns**
and press ↵.Double-click on **Horizontal grid** or move the diamond
symbol to **Horizontal grid** and then click on **F3-Choices** or press F3.
Select **All rows**.

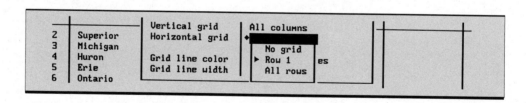

Now let's change the width of the grid lines you created.

◆ **5**   Click on **Grid line width** or move the diamond symbol to **Grid line width**. Type **6** and press F10 to return to your worksheet. You can choose any width measurement between 0 and 250.

```
                            Table Chart                              ◆ ▾
   F1-Help        F2-Show chart              F4-Draw        F5-Mark
   F6-Main Menu   F7-Spell/Text   F8-Options                F10-Continue

 Title:    The Great Lakes
 Subtitle: A North American Wonder
 Footnote: Area in square miles / Volume in cubic miles
        ┌────── 1 ──────┬────── 2 ──────┬────── 3 ──────┬────── 4 ──────┬────── 5 ──────
      1 │ Name          │ Area          │ Volume        │               │
        │               │               │               │               │
        │               │               │               │               │
      2 │ Superior      │ 20600         │ 2900          │               │
      3 │ Michigan      │ 22300         │ 1180          │               │
```

◆ **6**   Click on **F2-Show chart** or press F2 to view the current status of your chart.

The Great Lakes
A North American Wonder

Name	Area	Volume
Superior	20600	2900
Michigan	22300	1180
Huron	9100	850
Erie	4980	116
Ontario	3560	393

Area in square miles / Volume in cubic miles

◆ **7**   Click the right mouse button or press ⏎ESC to return to your worksheet.

Take some time to experiment with each of the options on the Table Options menu. Use the Show chart feature to view the result of your changes. Remember to return the options to their original settings before you continue.

Let's learn how to create narrower or wider columns and create more space between columns.

Note

Automatic Table Sizing   With this option set to **Yes**, Harvard Graphics automatically sets the column and row positions according to text size. Choosing **No** allows you to manually set the column and row positions.

◆ **8**   Click on **F8-Options** and then **Table** or press ⏎F8 and ⏎5 to display the Table Options menu. Click on **Automatic table sizing** or press ⏎F3 and select **No**.

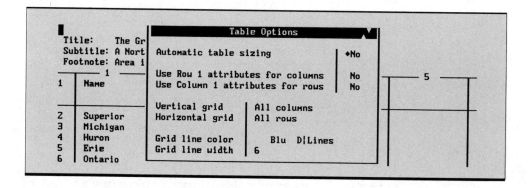

◆ **9**   Click on the down scroll arrow or press [PG DN] to move to the Column
Options menu.

Aligns text and numbers
with left or right margins,
cell center, or decimal point.

Sets left and right column
positions from 0 to 100.

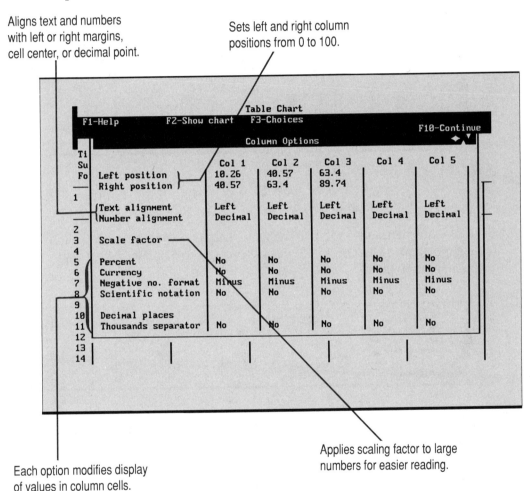

Each option modifies display
of values in column cells.

Applies scaling factor to large
numbers for easier reading.

◆ **10** Change the entries in columns 1 and 3 to match the following screen. These changes maintain the current width of each column, but add space with a value of 5 between them.

```
                                    Column Options                    F10-Continue
                                                                         ◆▲▼
 Ti
 Su
 Fo                        Col 1     Col 2     Col 3     Col 4     Col 5
     Left position        ▐5.26▌    40.57     ▐68.4▌
     Right position       ▐35.57▌   63.4      ▐94.74▌
 1

     Text alignment       Left      Left      Left      Left      Left
     Number alignment     Decimal   Decimal   Decimal   Decimal   Decimal
```

◆ **11** Click on **F2-Show chart** or press F2 to view the current status of your table chart. Press ESC to return to your worksheet.

◆ **12** Move the diamond symbol to the word **Left** in the first cell in the Text alignment row. Click on **F3-Choices** or press F3 to display the Text alignment pop-up menu.

```
     ▲
          Text alignment     ◆▐        ▌eft      Left      Left      Left
          Number alignment    ▶ Left    ecimal   Decimal   Decimal   Decimal
     2                          Center
     3    Scale factor          Right
     4                          Spread
     5    Percent                        o        No        No        No
```

◆ **13** Click on **Center** or move the menu arrow to **Center** and press ⏎.

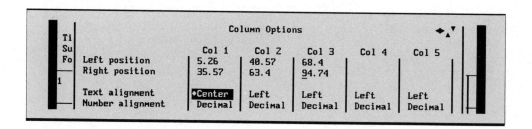

```
                                    Column Options                        ◆▲▼
 Ti
 Su
 Fo                        Col 1     Col 2     Col 3     Col 4     Col 5
     Left position         5.26      40.57     68.4
     Right position        35.57     63.4      94.74
 1

     Text alignment       ◆Center    Left      Left      Left      Left
     Number alignment      Decimal   Decimal   Decimal   Decimal   Decimal
```

✦ **14** Follow procedures similar to those in steps 12 and 13 and change the Number alignment and Thousands separator entries in columns 2 and 3 to match the following screen.

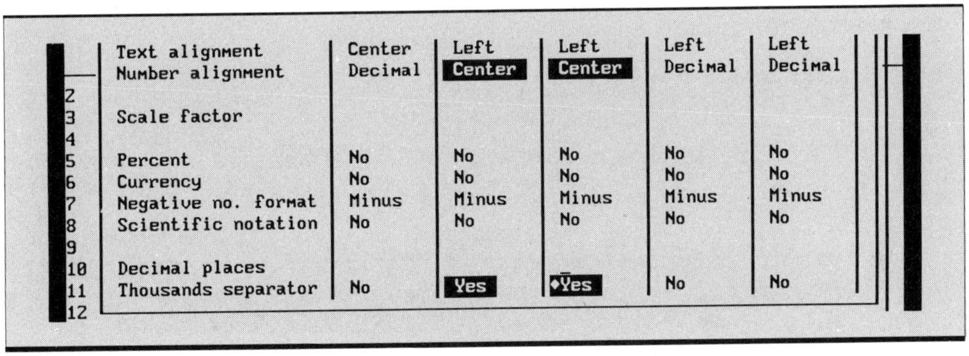

```
         Text alignment      Center   Left     Left     Left     Left
         Number alignment    Decimal  Center   Center   Decimal  Decimal
 2
 3       Scale factor
 4
 5       Percent             No       No       No       No       No
 6       Currency            No       No       No       No       No
 7       Negative no. format Minus    Minus    Minus    Minus    Minus
 8       Scientific notation No       No       No       No       No
 9
10       Decimal places
11       Thousands separator No       Yes      Yes      No       No
12
```

✦ **15** Select **F2-Show chart** to view the current status of your chart.

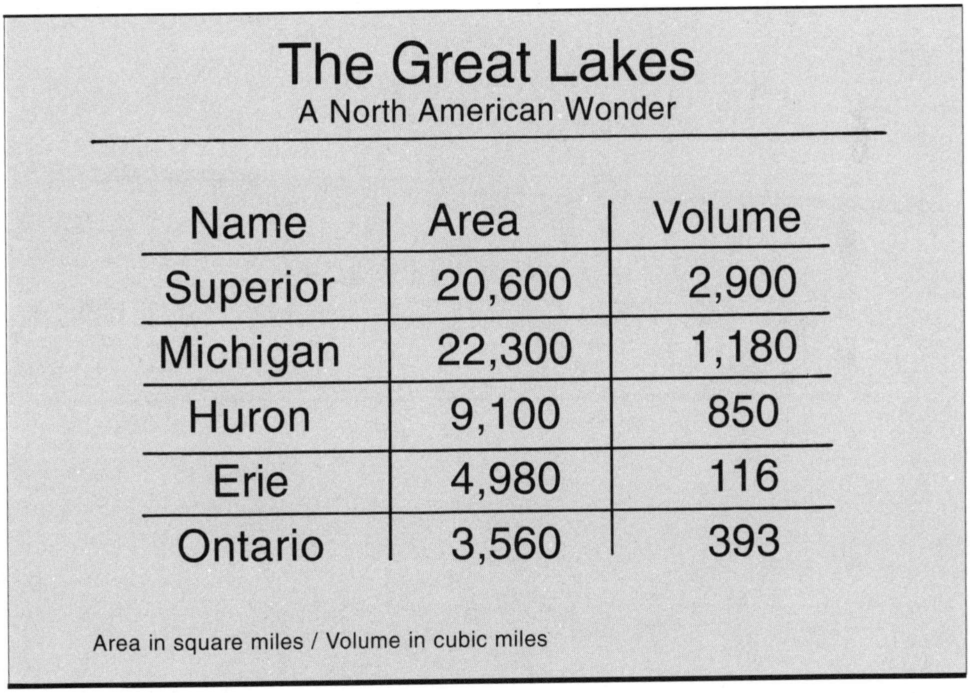

The Great Lakes
A North American Wonder

Name	Area	Volume
Superior	20,600	2,900
Michigan	22,300	1,180
Huron	9,100	850
Erie	4,980	116
Ontario	3,560	393

Area in square miles / Volume in cubic miles

✦ **16** When you've finished viewing your chart, click the right mouse button or press ᴇsc to return to the Column Options menu.

Take some time to change other items on the Column Options menu and display the results with the F2-Show chart function. Return your chart to its original settings before continuing.

Now let's change the row position.

✦ **17** Click on the down scroll arrow or press ᴘɢᴅɴ to move to the Row Options menu.

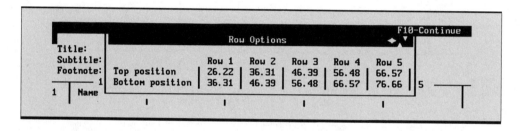

✦ **18** Check your cursor position and type **21.31** as shown. This changes Row 1 width from 10 to 15.

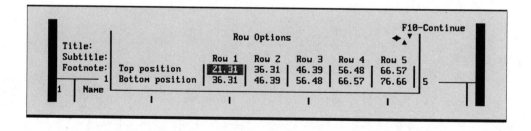

✦ **19** Select **F2-Show chart** to view the change. The column labels now occupy a larger vertical space than the rows below them.

The Great Lakes
A North American Wonder

Name	Area	Volume
Superior	20,600	2,900
Michigan	22,300	1,180
Huron	9,100	850
Erie	4,980	116
Ontario	3,560	393

Area in square miles / Volume in cubic miles

✦ **20** Click the right mouse button twice or press ESC twice to return to your worksheet.

Table Ranges

A table range is a group of numbers which fall between designated values. This allows you to highlight a particular group of numbers to focus attention on important data.

Display your current worksheet to begin the following exercise.

◆ **1**   Select **F8-Options** and then click on **Range** or press 8 to display the Range Options menu.

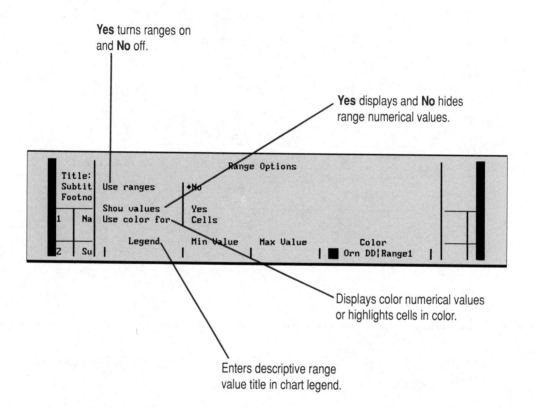

Yes turns ranges on and **No** off.

Yes displays and **No** hides range numerical values.

Displays color numerical values or highlights cells in color.

Enters descriptive range value title in chart legend.

◆ **2**   Select **Use ranges** with the mouse or keyboard. Select **Yes** and press TAB to move the cursor to the first line under Legend.

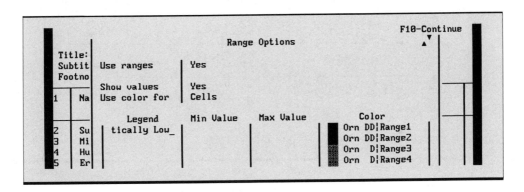

✦ **3**   Type **Critically Low** to enter the range title for the chart legend in our next exercise. Your range title entry scrolls beyond the Legend column boundaries, but the complete title is entered on your chart legend.

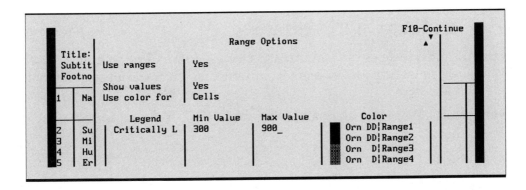

✦ **4**   Press ⊡ to move the cursor and type a minimum value of **300** and a maximum value of **900**.

✦ **5** Select **F2-Show chart** to view your chart with highlighted numbers.

The Great Lakes
A North American Wonder

Name	Area	Volume
Superior	20,600	2,900
Michigan	22,300	1,180
Huron	9,100	850
Erie	4,980	116
Ontario	3,560	393

Area in square miles / Volume in cubic miles

✦ **6** Click the right mouse button twice or press ⌷ESC⌷ twice to return to the Table Chart worksheet.

✦ Creating Chart Legends

Legends provide descriptive information for the data and symbols in a chart. With the step-by-step methods in this section, you can create legends for table, pie, and XY charts.

Let's create a legend for your table chart. Your worksheet should be displayed.

◆ **1**   Click on **F8-Options** or press ⌊F8⌋ to display the Options menu. Select **Titles/Footnotes** to display the Titles/Footnotes menu.

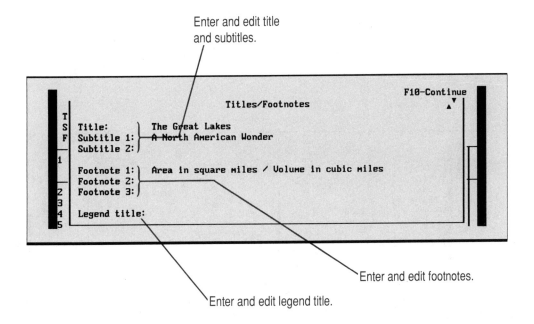

Enter and edit title and subtitles.

Enter and edit footnotes.

Enter and edit legend title.

◆ **2**   Move the cursor to **Legend title:** and type **Drought Affected Lakes**.

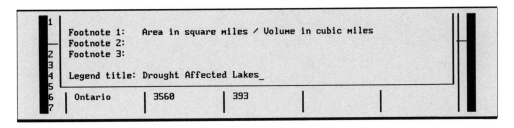

✦ **3**   Return to the Options menu and select **Legend** to display the
Legend Options menu. You can also use the scroll arrows or PGUP or
PGDN to access this menu directly from the Titles/Footnotes menu.

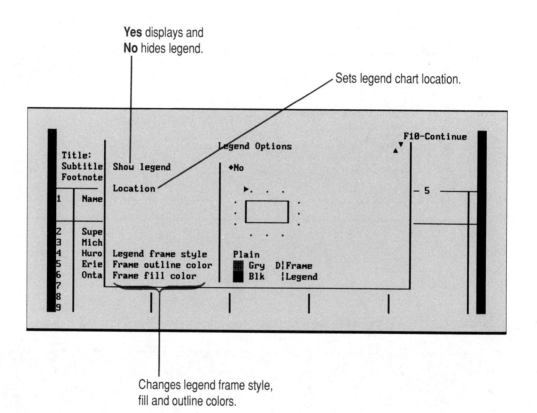

Yes displays and
No hides legend.

Sets legend chart location.

Changes legend frame style,
fill and outline colors.

◆ 4   Click on **Show legend** or press ⒡⒊ and select **Yes**.

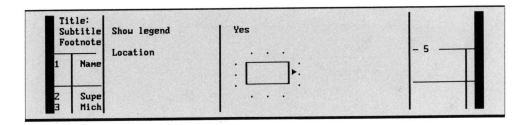

◆ 5   Click on the center dot on the right side of the legend box or press ⒯ⒶⒷ
to move the menu arrow to **Location** and press the spacebar to move
the arrow to the correct dot. This centers the legend on the right side
of your chart.

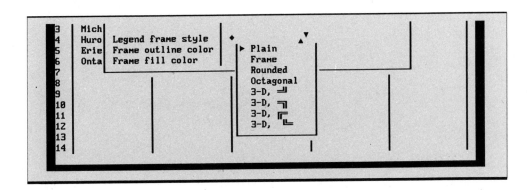

◆ 6   Press ⒯ⒶⒷ to move the diamond symbol to **Legend frame style** and
select **F3-Choices** to display the Frame style menu.

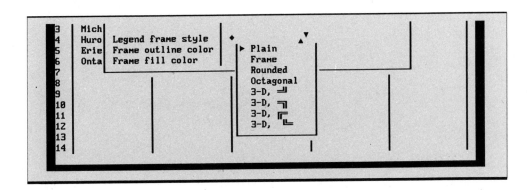

⋆ **7**   Select **Octagonal** and then **F2-Show chart** to view your table chart with a legend. The legend overlaps the chart data because Automatic table sizing is set to **No**.

The Great Lakes
A North American Wonder

Name	Area	Volume
Superior	20,600	2,900
Michigan	22,300	
Huron	9,100	
Erie	4,980	116
Ontario	3,560	393

Drought Affected Lakes
☐ Critically Low

Area in square miles / Volume in cubic miles

⋆ **8**   Click the right mouse button or press ⒺⓈⒸ to return to the Legend Options menu, and press ⓅⒼⓊⓅ four times to display the Table Options menu.

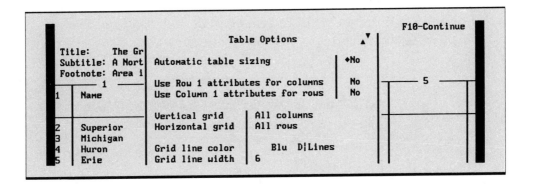

◆**9** Change Automatic table sizing to **Yes** and select **F2-Show chart**.
Your chart data has been resized to accommodate the legend.

The Great Lakes
A North American Wonder

Name	Area	Volume
Superior	20,600	2,900
Michigan	22,300	1,180
Huron	9,100	**850**
Erie	4,980	116
Ontario	3,560	**393**

Drought Affected Lakes
☐ Critically Low

Area in square miles / Volume in cubic miles

✦ **10** Return to the Main Menu and click on **File** and then **Save chart** or press ⟨4⟩ and ⟨4⟩ to display the Save Chart menu.

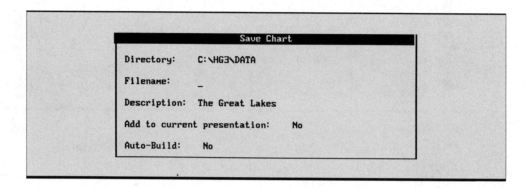

✦ **11** Type **LAKES** at the Filename prompt. Notice the description, **The Great Lakes**, has been automatically entered from the chart title. Press ⟨F10⟩ to save your table chart with the name LAKES.CH3.

✦ **12** Click on **Exit** or press ⟨E⟩ to exit Harvard Graphics.

✦ Summary

In this chapter you taught yourself to create title, bullet, and table charts as well as chart legends. You also learned to show, save and redisplay your charts.

Chapter 3 teaches you some advanced techniques which are essential to your performance in later chapters.

3

Advancing Your Editing and Output Skills

✦ This chapter teaches you a variety of chart management skills from retrieving, clearing, editing and enhancing charts, to producing output on printers, plotters, and film recorders. Chapter 3 applies to all the charts you create with Harvard Graphics, and paves the way to building more masterful presentations in future chapters.

- ✦ Retrieving Charts
- ✦ Clearing Charts
- ✦ Editing Chart Text
- ✦ Creating Chart Notes
- ✦ Spell Checking
- ✦ Working with Text Attributes
- ✦ Enhancing Your Charts
- ✦ Producing Output

✦ Retrieving Charts

Once you have saved a chart in permanent memory, you must retrieve it before you can work on it again. Let's retrieve your BESTSALE.CH3 file.

✦ **1**   Start Harvard Graphics and display the Main Menu.

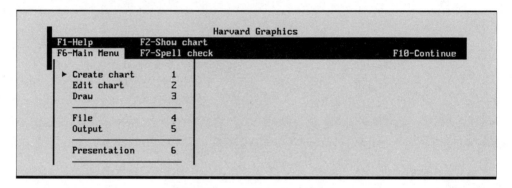

✦ **2**   Click on **File** or press **4** to display the File menu.

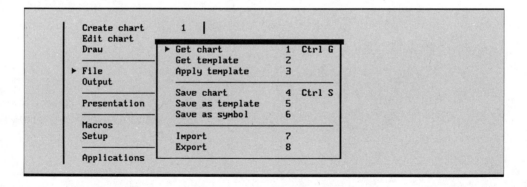

◆ **3**   Click on **Get chart** or press ① to display the Get Chart listing of
your directories and files. The speed keys [CTRL] [G] display the Get
chart directory from anywhere in the program.

Sorts files alphabetically.

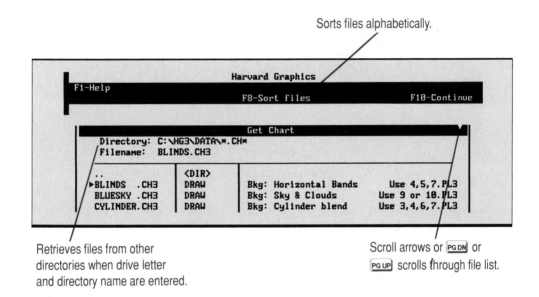

Retrieves files from other
directories when drive letter
and directory name are entered.

Scroll arrows or [PG DN] or
[PG UP] scrolls through file list.

◆ **4**   Click on **F8-Sort files** or press [F8] to alphabetize your file list.

Shows currently selected file.

◆ **5**   To retrieve and show the current version of your chart, press ⬇ or ⬆ to move the menu arrow to BESTSALE.CH3 and then press ⏎ or F10. You can also perform this operation in a single step by clicking the mouse on the file name.

MEGAPRODUCTS UNLIMITED
Regional Sales Conference
A Banner Year for Sales

Overall Five-Year Synopsis

MegaProducts Best Sellers

Regional Sales Comparison

Conference to be followed by a reception in the Egyptian Paradise Room

◆ **6**   Click the right mouse button or press ESC to return to the chart worksheet.

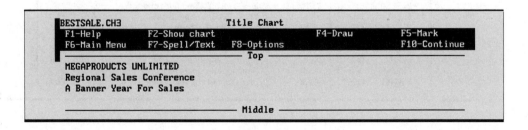

✦ Clearing Charts

The chart you just retrieved is the current chart in Random Access Memory (RAM). It will remain in RAM until you save it or clear it from memory. The original version remains on the storage disk in permanent memory. If you make a mistake while working on the current chart you can revert to the original by clearing the current version of all its titles and data, and retrieving the original from memory. You can also clear the chart entirely, including any options you selected.

Let's clear the BESTSALE.CH3 worksheet of all titles and data. The options you've chosen will not be affected.

✦ **1**   Select **F6-Main Menu** and **Create chart** or press F6 and ① to display the Chart menu.

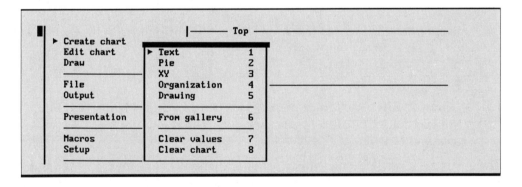

✦ **2**   Click on **Clear values** or press ⑦ to clear the chart of titles and data. Any previously selected options remain active.

✦ **3**   To clear your chart of all titles, data, and options, return to the Main Menu, click on **Create chart** and **Clear chart** or press ⟨1⟩ and ⟨8⟩.

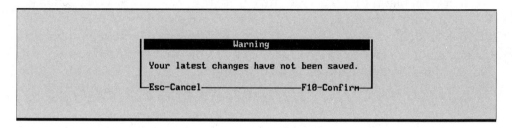

Note

Working With the Save Chart Warning Message   When you clear all the values from a chart, clear the chart values and options, or edit a chart and attempt to exit the program without saving, Harvard Graphics displays a warning message so you won't lose valuable data. Select **Esc-Cancel** to cancel the operation and then save the chart, or select **F10-Confirm** to clear the chart without saving the current version.

✦ **4**   Click on **F10-Confirm** or press ⟨F10⟩ to clear the chart of all titles, data, and options. The current worksheet is cleared and the Main Menu is displayed.

The current chart has been cleared from RAM. You can retrieve another chart from permanent memory or create a new one. The original BESTSALE.CH3 is alive and well on your storage disk.

✦ Editing Chart Text

This section covers some simple text editing techniques to speed up and enhance your chart-making abilities.

Inserting and Deleting

Inserting or deleting lines in existing text can help you edit your chart for maximum impact.

✦ **1**   Select **File** from the Main Menu and then **Get chart** from the File menu or use the speed keys `CTRL` `G`. Retrieve your BESTSALE.CH3 chart.

✦ **2**   Press `ESC` to display the worksheet and move the cursor to the **R** in **Regional** on the second line in the top region.

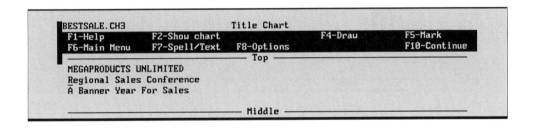

Note

Moving the Cursor With the Mouse   Place the mouse pointer on the desired space and click the left mouse button.

✦ **3**   Press `CTRL` `INS` to insert a blank line and move the following text down one line.

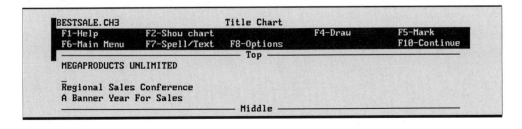

◆ **4** Move the cursor to the blank line above the footnote in the bottom region.

```
─────────────────────────── Bottom ───────────────────────────
Conference to be followed by a reception in the Egyptian Paradise Room

─────────────────────────────────────────────────────────────
```

◆ **5** Press CTRL DEL to delete the blank line and move the text below up one line.

```
─────────────────────────── Bottom ───────────────────────────
Conference to be followed by a reception in the Egyptian Paradise Room


─────────────────────────────────────────────────────────────
```

Note

Deleting Single Characters   To delete single characters, press DEL. Text to the right of the cursor will be pulled to the left. Pressing BKSP deletes characters to the left of the cursor.

Typeover and Insert

You can use the typeover or insert modes to enter new text at the cursor location. Typeover replaces existing characters as you type in new ones. Typeover is automatically operating when you start Harvard Graphics. Entering new text in the insert mode pushes existing characters to the right.

✦ **1**   In the middle region of your chart, move the cursor to the **S** in
Synopsis.

```
                        ─── Middle ───────────────────

   Overall Five-Year S̲ynopsis

   MegaProducts Best Sellers

   Regional Sales Comparison
```

✦ **2**   Press [INS] to activate the insert mode. When the cursor changes to a
flashing rectangle, the insert mode is active.

```
                        ─── Middle ───────────────────

   Overall Five-Year ▮ynopsis

   MegaProducts Best Sellers
```

✦ **3**   Type **Sales** and press the spacebar. As the new word is inserted, the
existing characters move to the right.

```
                        ─── Middle ───────────────────

   Overall Five-Year Sales ▮ynopsis

   MegaProducts Best Sellers
```

✦ **4**   Move the cursor to the **B** in **Best Sellers** on the second line in the
middle region.

```
                        ─── Middle ───────────────────

   Overall Five-Year Sales Synopsis

   MegaProducts ▮est Sellers
```

✦ **5**   Press [INS] to return to the typeover mode and type **Best Selling Product Lines** to overwrite the existing text.

```
┌──────────────────────────── Middle ────────────────────────────┐
│                                                                 │
│    Overall Five-Year Sales Synopsis                             │
│                                                                 │
│    MegaProducts Best Selling Product Lines_                     │
│                                                                 │
└─────────────────────────────────────────────────────────────────┘
```

Special Characters and Formats

Special characters and formats are symbols, international characters, and foreign time and date styles which are not found on your keyboard. If your presentation has a technical aspect or an international audience, you may want your charts to contain the proper formats and symbols.

Let's place a special character in your BESTSALE.CH3 chart.

✦ **1**   Place the cursor at the second blank space after the word **Synopsis** in the middle region.

```
┌──────────────────────────── Middle ────────────────────────────┐
│                                                                 │
│    Overall Five-Year Sales Synopsis _                           │
│                                                                 │
│    MegaProducts Best Selling Product Lines                      │
│                                                                 │
└─────────────────────────────────────────────────────────────────┘
```

✦ **2**   Click on **F7-Spell/Text** or press [F7] to display the Spell/Text menu.

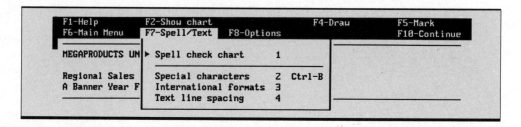

✦ **3**   Click on **Special characters** or use the speed keys CTRL B to display a list of special characters. Press ⬇ to scroll through the list and place the menu arrow on the » symbol.

```
                                                              F10-Continue
┌─────────────────────────── Top ───────────────────────────┐
 MEGAPRODUCTS UNLIMITED    ┌─── Special Characters ───┐
 Regional Sales Conferen   │ Character    Decimal Value │
 A Banner Year For Sales   │                            │
                           │      ₨         158         │
 Overall Five-Year Sales   │      ×         207         │
                           │      ƒ         159         │
 MegaProducts Best Selli   │      £         156         │
                           │      ¿         168         │
 Regional Sales Comparis   │      ¡         173         │
                           │      "         202         │
                           │      "         203         │
                           │      «         174         │
 Conference to be follow   │ ►   »         175         │  ian Paradise Room
                           └────────────────────────────┘
```

✦ **4**   Click on the » symbol or press ⏎ The symbol appears on your worksheet.

```
─────────────────────────── Middle ───────────────────────────

 Overall Five-Year Sales Synopsis »_

 MegaProducts Best Selling Product Lines

 Regional Sales Comparison
```

Note

Shortcut for Entering Special Characters   Each special character has a
decimal value which is listed in the Special Characters menu. To instantly
place special characters in your worksheet, move the cursor to where you
want the symbol, then press and hold ⟨ALT⟩ while you type the three digit number on the numerical keypad. The symbol will appear at the cursor location.

♦ **5**   For practice, place the » symbol two spaces after the end of each of
the two remaining lines in the middle region.

```
───────────────────────── Middle ─────────────────────────

Overall Five-Year Sales Synopsis »

MegaProducts Best Selling Product Lines »

Regional Sales Comparison »_
```

Now let's explore some of the international formats you can select with Harvard
Graphics.

♦ **6**   Click on **F7-Spell/Text** or press ⟨F7⟩ to display the Spell/Text menu.

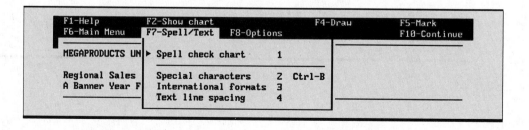

```
F1-Help          F2-Show chart                  F4-Draw          F5-Mark
F6-Main Menu     F7-Spell/Text   F8-Options                      F10-Continue

MEGAPRODUCTS UN ▶ Spell check chart      1

Regional Sales   Special characters      2  Ctrl-B
A Banner Year F  International formats    3
                 Text line spacing        4
```

◆**7** Click on **International formats** or press ③. The International Formats menu appears.

```
┌───────────────────────────────────────────────────────────────┐
│                                                                 │
│  ┌─────────────────┌──────International Formats──────┐──────┐   │
│  MEGAPRODUCTS UNLIMI                                              │
│                     Date format              ◆M/D/Y              │
│  Regional Sales Conf Date separator          /                  │
│  A Banner Year For S                                            │
│  ─────────────────── Time format             am/pm  ─────────── │
│                      Time separator          :                  │
│  Overall Five-Year S                                            │
│                      Thousands/Decimal                          │
│  MegaProducts Best S   separator             ,/.                │
│                                                                 │
│  Regional Sales Comp Currency symbol         $                  │
│                      Currency position       0100               │
│  └──────────────────└──────────────────────────────┘───────┘   │
│                                                                 │
└───────────────────────────────────────────────────────────────┘
```

To select an option from the International Formats menu, click on the option and
then **F3-Choices** or move the diamond symbol to the option item and press ⒡₃ to
display a list of choices. The option and choice you select only applies to your
current chart.

The following list shows the available options and choices with examples of how
each selection will look in your chart.

Option	Formats	Example
Date format	M/D/Y	11/3/92
	D/M/Y	3/11/92
	Y/M/D	92/11/3
Date separator	/	11/3/92
	.	11.3.92
	-	11-3-92

Option	Formats	Example
Time format	am/pm	8:30pm
	24-hour	20:30
Time separator	:	5:45am
	.	5.45am
	,	5,45am
Thousands/ Decimal separator	,/.	15,000.00
	./,	3.000,00
	space/,	42 000,00
Currency symbol	$	$100
	¢	52¢
	£	£100
Currency position	@100	$100
	100@	100$
	@ 100	£ 100
	100 @	100 £

Note

Selecting Currency Symbols   Currency symbols are selected from the Special Characters menu. Review the previous section for information on entering these symbols in your worksheet.

◆ **8**   Click the right mouse button or press [ESC] to return to the chart worksheet.

Any international format options you selected are now active in your current worksheet.

Line Spacing

Line spacing with Harvard Graphics is based on a percentage of text size. Single-line spacing is 85%. Double-line spacing is 170%. Let's change BESTSALE.CH3 to double-space, or 170%.

The BESTSALE.CH3 worksheet should be displayed on your screen.

♦ **1**   Click on **F7-Spell/Text** or press ⒡⒠.

```
  F1-Help           F2-Show chart                  F4-Draw          F5-Mark
  F6-Main Menu      F7-Spell/Text   F8-Options                      F10-Continue

  MEGAPRODUCTS UN ► Spell check chart        1

  Regional Sales    Special characters       2  Ctrl-B
  A Banner Year F   International formats     3
                    Text line spacing        4
```

♦ **2**   Click on **Text line spacing** or press ⒣ to display the menu. The default is 85%, or single-space.

```
  BESTSALE.CH3                  Title Chart
    F1-Help
                                                        F10-Continue

                                Text Line Spacing
  MEGAPRODUCTS UNLIMITED
                                Line spacing: 85
  Regional Sales Conference
  A Banner Year For Sales
                              ——— Middle ———
```

♦ **3**   Type **170** and click on **F10-Continue** or press ⒡⒠.

✦ **4**   Click on **F2-Show chart** or press ⌨F2⌨ to show the current status of your chart. It should now be double-spaced.

MEGAPRODUCTS UNLIMITED

Regional Sales Conference

A Banner Year for Sales

Overall Five-Year Sales Synopsis »

MegaProducts Best Selling Product Lines »

Regional Sales Comparison »

Conference to be followed by a reception in the Egyptian Paradise Room

---

✦ **5**   Click the right mouse button or press ⌨ESC⌨ to return to the worksheet. Repeat steps 1 through 3 to return line spacing to 85%.

✦ Creating Chart Notes

Chart notes allow you to create references and clarifying documents for each of your charts. This section teaches you how to enter text into a chart note.

Display the BESTSALE.CH3 worksheet on your screen.

✦ **1**   Select **F8-Options** to display the Options menu.

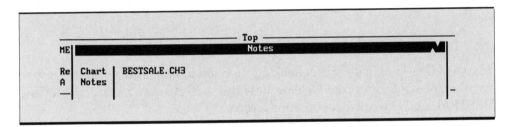

✦ **2**   Click on **Notes** or press ③. The speed keys ⸢CTRL⸥⸢N⸥ also display the
Chart Notes screen for the current chart.

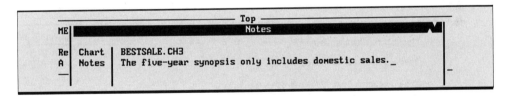

✦ **3**   Type the text shown on the following screen.

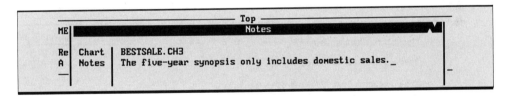

✦ **4**   Click the right mouse button or press ⸢ESC⸥ to return to the worksheet.

Note

Working With Chart Notes   A chart note is saved as part of the data linked to a particular chart. Your worksheet filename appears on the note pad. Your notes can have 11 lines of text with a limit of 60 characters per line. Lines will not wordwrap. You must press ⏎ or ⟨TAB⟩ at the end of each line.

For information on chart note printing and creating presentations, see the section on producing output in this chapter and Chapter 8.

✦ Spell Checking

Harvard Graphics has a spell checking function to help you avoid the embarrassment of misspelled words. To learn how the spell checker works, display the BESTSALE.CH3 worksheet on your screen.

✦ **1**   Move the cursor to the final **s** in **Synopsis** and press ⟨DEL⟩ to misspell the word.

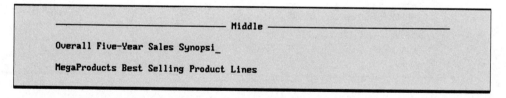

✦ **2**   Select **F7-Spell/Text** to display the menu.

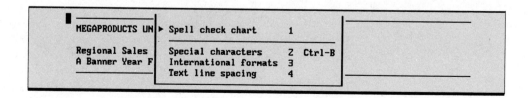

٭ **3** Click on **Spell check chart** or press ⬛1 and the spell checker begins searching your chart. When the menu on the following screen appears, you are asked to make certain choices.

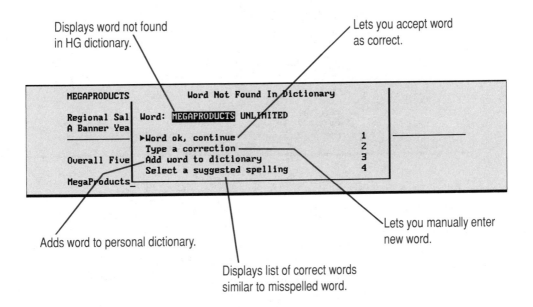

Displays word not found in HG dictionary.

Lets you accept word as correct.

Adds word to personal dictionary.

Lets you manually enter new word.

Displays list of correct words similar to misspelled word.

٭ **4** Click on **Word ok, continue** or press ⬛1 to accept MEGAPRODUCTS as correct. **Synopsi** is identified next.

◆ **5**   Click on **Select a suggested spelling** or press ④ to display a list of
similar words.

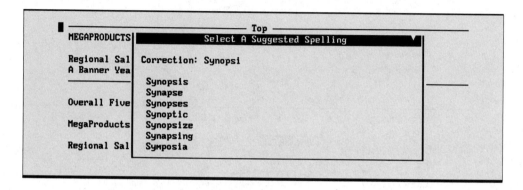

```
■                              ──────── Top ────────
MEGAPRODUCTS│              Select A Suggested Spelling          ▼
            │
Regional Sal│ Correction: Synopsi
A Banner Yea│
            │      Synopsis
            │      Synapse
Overall Five│      Synopses
            │      Synoptic
MegaProducts│      Synopsize
            │      Synapsing
Regional Sal│      Symposia
```

◆ **6**   Click on **Synopsis** or use ⬇ to choose **Synopsis** and press ↵ to
accept this word as correct.

```
MEGAPRODUCTS           Improper Capitalization

Regional Sal   Word: MegaProducts Best Selling Product Li
A Banner Yea
               ▶Word ok, continue                        1
                Type a correction                        2
Overall Five    Add word to dictionary                   3
                Select a suggested spelling              4
MegaProducts_
```

◆ **7**   Select **Word ok, continue** when the next word is displayed to end
the spell checking procedure.

```
Regional Sales Conference
A Banner Year For Sales
                          ┃ Spell Check Status ┃
Overall Five-Year Sales Sy      Complete
```

✦ 8   Click the right mouse button or press ⎋ to return to the worksheet. Synopsis should now be correctly spelled.

Note

Master and Personal Dictionaries   The main dictionary is named MASTER.DCT. Your personal dictionary is named PERSONAL.DCT.

Your Harvard Graphics documentation contains information on which personal dictionaries are compatible with this version of Harvard Graphics.

✦ Working with Text Attributes

Harvard Graphics lets you enhance and emphasize text in a variety of ways. You can select different fonts, font styles, font sizes, colors, and alignments. This process is often called character formatting.

In this section you can teach yourself to change the text attributes of a title chart. The Text Attributes menus vary slightly for other chart types, but the basic skills you learn in the following exercises apply to all the charts in this book.

Changing an Entire Chart

Let's change the text attributes of your entire chart. This section does not provide an example of every available text attribute, but you can easily experiment with each of the available options without harming your documents.

The BESTSALE.CH3 worksheet should be displayed on your screen.

◆ **1**   Select **F8-Options** to display the Options menu and select
Text attributes to display the Text Attributes menu.

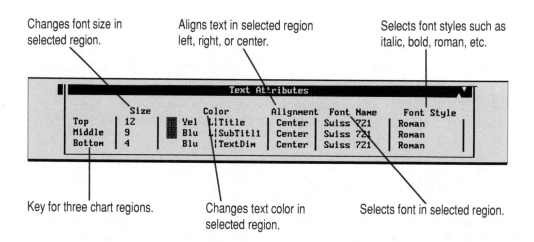

Changes font size in selected region.

Aligns text in selected region left, right, or center.

Selects font styles such as italic, bold, roman, etc.

Key for three chart regions.

Changes text color in selected region.

Selects font in selected region.

◆ **2**   To display the Font menu and select a font for the top region of your
chart, double-click on the top listing for **Swiss 721** in the Font Name
column. You can also move the diamond symbol to **Swiss 721** and
press F3.

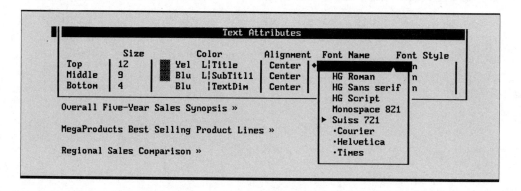

✦ **3**   Click on **Courier** or move the menu arrow to **Courier** and press F10 to change the font name in the top region.

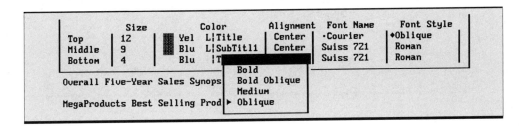

✦ **4**   To change the style of the Courier font for the top region, double-click on **Oblique** in the Font Style column or move the diamond symbol to **Oblique** and press F3. The Courier font styles list appears.

✦ **5**   Select **Bold** and then click on **F2-Show chart** or press F2 to view the text changes in the top region.

MEGAPRODUCTS UNLIMITED

Regional Sales Conference
A Banner Year for Sales

Overall Five-Year Sales Synopsis »

MegaProducts Best Selling Product Lines »

Regional Sales Comparison »

Conference to be followed by a reception in the Egyptian Paradise Room

---

✦ **6**   Click the right mouse button twice or press ⌷ESC⌷ twice to return to the worksheet.

Changing Blocks of Text

This feature lets you mark a block of text, from single characters to large groups of text, and selectively change its attributes.

Use the BESTSALE.CH3 worksheet for the following exercise.

✦ **1** Move the cursor to the **M** in **MEGAPRODUCTS UNLIMITED**.

```
BESTSALE.CH3                    Title Chart
F1-Help         F2-Show chart              F4-Draw        F5-Mark
F6-Main Menu    F7-Spell/Text   F8-Options                F10-Continue
─────────────────────────────── Top ───────────────────────────────
MEGAPRODUCTS UNLIMITED

Regional Sales Conference
A Banner Year For Sales
────────────────────────────── Middle ─────────────────────────────
```

✦ **2** Click on **F5-Mark** or press [F5] to mark the beginning of your block.

✦ **3** Move the cursor to the **D** in **UNLIMITED** and **MEGAPRODUCTS UNLIMITED** is highlighted.

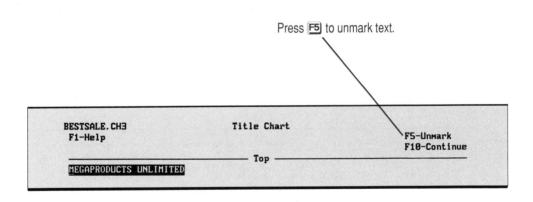

Press [F5] to unmark text.

```
BESTSALE.CH3                    Title Chart
F1-Help                                          F5-Unmark
                                                 F10-Continue
─────────────────────────────── Top ───────────────────────────────
MEGAPRODUCTS UNLIMITED
```

✦ **4** Click on **F10-Continue** or press F10 to display the Marked Text Options menu.

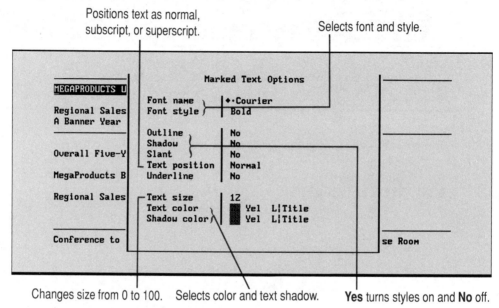

Positions text as normal, subscript, or superscript.

Selects font and style.

Changes size from 0 to 100. Selects color and text shadow. **Yes** turns styles on and **No** off.

✦ **5** Click on **Font name** or press F3 to display the font menu. Select **Helvetica**.

✦ **6** Double-click on **Outline** or move the diamond symbol to **Outline** and press F3. Select **Yes**.

```
                              Marked Text Options
 ┌──────────────┐
 │MEGAPRODUCTS U│    Font name       ·Helvetica
 │              │    Font style      Bold
 │Regional Sales│
 │A Banner Year │    Outline         ◆Yes
 │              │    Shadow          No
 └──────────────┘
```

✦ **7**   Return to the worksheet and select **F2-Show chart** to view your chart
with the title in outline Helvetica.

✦ **8**   Click the right mouse button or press ⎋ to return to the worksheet.

✦ **9**   Click on **F6-Main Menu** and **File** and then **Save chart** to display the
Save Chart menu. You can also press F6 and 4 and then 4 or the
speed keys CTRL S.

✦ **10**   Click on **F10-Continue** or press F10 to save the BESTSALE.CH3 chart.

✦ Enhancing Your Charts

Appearance options let you change the text sizing, orientation, proportions, and palettes of individual regions of your chart, and enhance them with background drawings and frames.

Note

Select Appearance Options Before You Create a Chart   Appearance options should be selected before you create a chart. Changing the options on existing charts can radically alter the chart's appearance.

Let's select a few appearance options and then create a new chart to observe their effect. You can experiment with the other appearance options not covered in this exercise.

The Main Menu should be displayed on your screen.

✦ **1**   Click on **Create chart** and **Text chart** and then **Bullet**. You can also press ⬚1⬚ and ⬚1⬚ and then ⬚2⬚ to display a new worksheet.

✦ **2**   Click on **F8-Options** or press ⬚F8⬚ to display the Options menu.

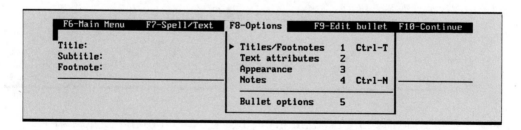

✦ **3** Select **Appearance** to display the Appearance Options menu.

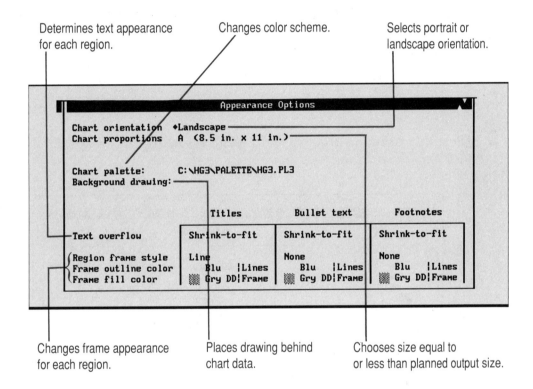

Determines text appearance for each region.

Changes color scheme.

Selects portrait or landscape orientation.

Changes frame appearance for each region.

Places drawing behind chart data.

Chooses size equal to or less than planned output size.

✦ **4** Click on **Chart orientation** or press F3 to display the pop-up menu.

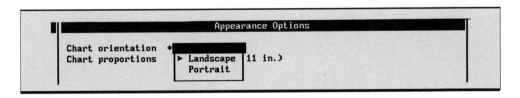

◆ **5**   Click on **Portrait** or move the menu arrow to **Portrait** and press ⏎.

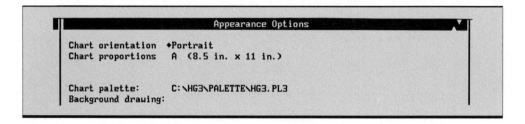

◆ **6**   Select **Background drawing** and **F3-Choices** to display a list of stock background drawings and frames.

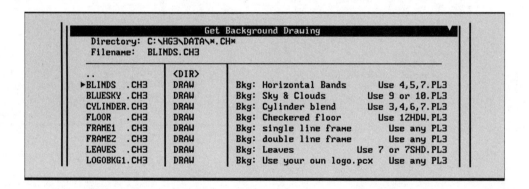

◆ **7**   Click on **FRAME2.CH3** or place the menu arrow and press ⏎ to automatically return to the Appearance Options menu.

```
┌─────────────────────────────────────────────────────────────┐
│ ▌      ══════════════ Appearance Options ══════════════    ◥ │
│                                                               │
│   Chart orientation    Portrait                               │
│   Chart proportions    A  (8.5 in. x 11 in.)                  │
│                                                               │
│                                                               │
│   Chart palette:       C:\HG3\PALETTE\HG3.PL3                 │
│   Background drawing:◆C:\HG3\DATA\FRAME2.CH3                  │
└─────────────────────────────────────────────────────────────┘
```

✦ **8**   In the Footnotes menu box opposite the Region frame style, click on
None or move the diamond symbol to **None**.

```
┌─────────────────────────────────────────────────────────────────┐
│                    Titles        Bullet text       Footnotes      │
│                                                                   │
│  Text overflow     Shrink-to-fit   Shrink-to-fit   Shrink-to-fit  │
│                                                                   │
│  Region frame style Line          None           ◆None            │
│  Frame outline color    Blu D│Lines    Blu D│Lines    Blu D│Lines │
│  Frame fill color   ▓ Gry DD│Frame ▓ Gry DD│Frame ▓ Gry DD│Frame  │
└─────────────────────────────────────────────────────────────────┘
```

✦ **9**   Click on **F3-Choices** or press ⬚F3⬚ to display a pop-up menu with a
variety of frame styles.

```
┌─────────────────────────────────────────────────────────────────┐
│   Chart palette:      C:\HG3\PA ┌► None    ┐                       │
│   Background drawing: C:\HG3\DA │  Plain   │                       │
│                                 │  Frame   │                       │
│                                 │  Rounded │                       │
│                                 │  Octagonal│                      │
│                            Tit  │  3-D, ⌐┘ │ let text    Footnotes │
│                                 │  3-D, ⌐┐ │                       │
│   Text overflow     Shrink-     │  3-D, ┌─ │ k-to-fit  Shrink-to-fit│
│                                 └──────────┘                       │
│   Region frame style Line                           ◆None          │
└─────────────────────────────────────────────────────────────────┘
```

✦ **10** Click on **Octagonal** or place the menu arrow and press ⏎.

	Titles	Bullet text	Footnotes
Text overflow	Shrink-to-fit	Shrink-to-fit	Shrink-to-fit
Region frame style	Line	None	✦Octagonal
Frame outline color	Blu D¦Lines	Blu D¦Lines	Blu D¦Lines
Frame fill color	▓ Gry DD¦Frame	▓ Gry DD¦Frame	▓ Gry DD¦Frame

✦ **11** Return to your chart worksheet and enter the text on the following screen.

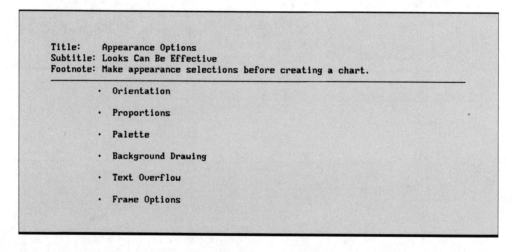

```
Title:    Appearance Options
Subtitle: Looks Can Be Effective
Footnote: Make appearance selections before creating a chart.

        ·  Orientation

        ·  Proportions

        ·  Palette

        ·  Background Drawing

        ·  Text Overflow

        ·  Frame Options
```

✦ **12** Click on **F2-Show chart** or press F2 to view your enhanced chart.

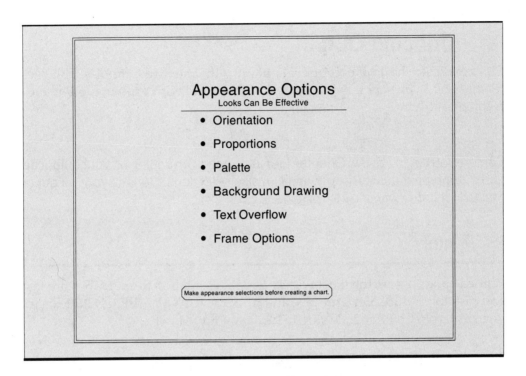

✦ **13** Click the right mouse button or press ⎋ until you return to the Main Menu.

✦ **14** Select **Create chart** and **Clear chart**. You are warned that the latest changes have not been saved.

✦ **15** Click on **F10-Confirm** or press ⎊ to clear your bullet chart from memory and return to the Main Menu.

✦ Producing Output

You can create charts of exceptional quality with Harvard Graphics. This section teaches you to present them to the rest of the world with printer, plotter, and film recorder output.

Before you begin, review Chapter 1 for information on setting up your output device, and making print quality, paper and film size selections. Consult your output device manual for individual use instructions.

Printers

Printed handouts are the most widely used presentation format. They are fast and easy to produce. Let's retrieve and print the CONSUMER.CH3 title chart you created in Chapter 2. Be sure to turn on your printer.

✦ **1** From the Main Menu, click on **File** and **Get chart** or press ④ and ① to select and retrieve the CONSUMER.CH3 chart. Remember to press F8 to sort your files alphabetically.

✦ **2** Click the right mouse button or press ESC to display your worksheet.

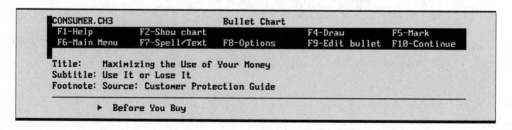

```
CONSUMER.CH3                    Bullet Chart
  F1-Help        F2-Show chart               F4-Draw        F5-Mark
  F6-Main Menu   F7-Spell/Text   F8-Options  F9-Edit bullet F10-Continue

Title:    Maximizing the Use of Your Money
Subtitle: Use It or Lose It
Footnote: Source: Customer Protection Guide

        ▶  Before You Buy
```

✦ 3   Select **F6-Main Menu** to display the Main Menu and click on
       Output or press ⑤ to display the Output pop-up menu.

Produces chart
presentation list.

Selects output device.

Produces three charts to a page,
chart notes, or presentations on disk.

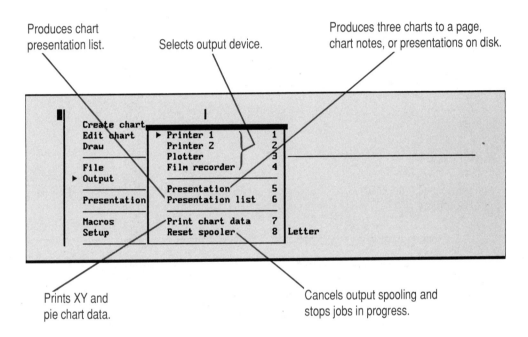

```
  ■               |
       Create chart
       Edit chart    ▶ Printer 1         1
       Draw            Printer 2         2
                       Plotter           3
       File            Film recorder     4
     ▶ Output
                       Presentation      5
       Presentation    Presentation list 6

       Macros          Print chart data  7
       Setup           Reset spooler     8  Letter
```

Prints XY and
pie chart data.

Cancels output spooling and
stops jobs in progress.

Note

Printing and Previewing the Current Chart You must create or retrieve a chart before you can print it. If you try to print without a current chart, Harvard Graphics will ask you to create or retrieve one first. It's also an excellent idea to preview your chart by selecting **F2-Preview** before you commit yourself to printer, plotter, or film recorder output.

✦**4** Click on **Printer 1** or **Printer 2** or press ⬜1 or ⬜2 to display the Output to Printer menu.

Selects 1 to 99 copies for continuous feed. Set single sheet pause option with **F8-Options**.

Shows current printer and port type.

Selects print quality and (speed) for Draft (fastest), Medium (faster), High (slow).

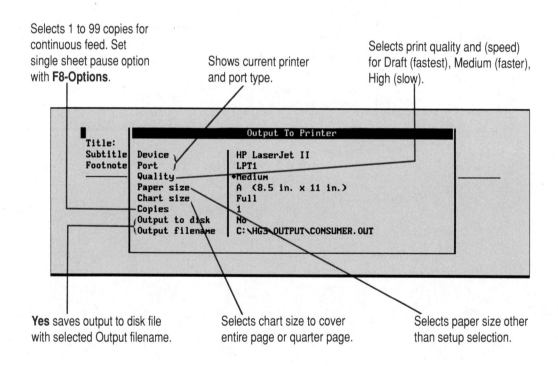

Yes saves output to disk file with selected Output filename.

Selects chart size to cover entire page or quarter page.

Selects paper size other than setup selection.

✦ **5**   Click on **F2-Preview** or press ⎡F2⎤ to get a preview of your printed chart.

Maximizing the Use of Your Money
Use It or Lose It

- ▶ Before You Buy

- ▶ After You Buy

- ▶ Managing Your Product Complaint

- ▶ Writing an Effective Complaint Letter

- ▶ Letter-Writing Hints

Source: Customer Protection Guide

✦ **6**   Click the right mouse button or press ⎡ESC⎤ to display the Output to printer menu. Select **F10-Continue** to start printing.

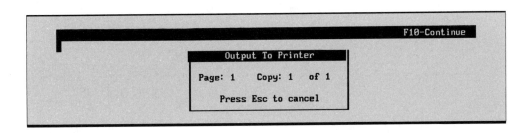

```
                                                    F10-Continue

        ┌──────────────────────────────┐
        │       Output To Printer      │
        │ Page: 1    Copy: 1   of 1    │
        │    Press Esc to cancel       │
        └──────────────────────────────┘
```

Note

Output Status Box Functions   The status box shows the progress of your printer, plotter, or film recorder output. Click on **Esc** or press Esc to cancel the process. When the status box disappears, the job is completed.

Plotters

Although the process is much slower, plotters usually generate higher quality output than printers. A plotter can also produce high resolution overhead transparencies which are ideal for presentations to large audiences.

Plotter output procedures are similar to those used for printing. Make sure your plotter is turned on and properly set up before you begin the following exercise. Retrieve the CONSUMER.CH3 chart to the screen and display the Main Menu.

✦ **1**   Select **F6-Main Menu** and **Output** to display the Output pop-up menu and then select **Plotter** or press 3 to display the Output to Plotter menu.

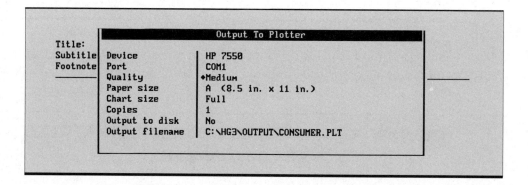

✦ **2**   Click on **F8-Options** or press ⟨F8⟩ to display the Plotter Options menu.

Selects narrow or wide pen.

Selects pen change pause and color process options.

Yes prints in black and **No** in selected colors or gray scales.

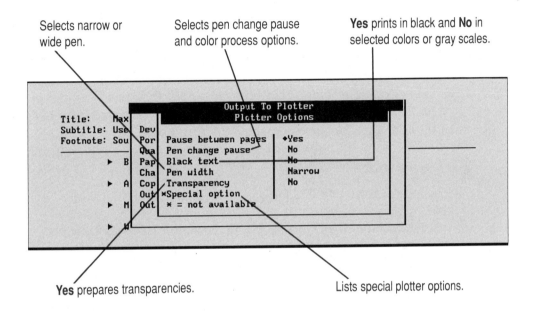

Yes prepares transparencies.

Lists special plotter options.

Note

Selecting Output to Plotter Options   The plotter options you select depend on the plotter type designated at the initial setup. Some plotters do not allow you to send output to disk files, nor do they always support the same paper sizes.

Refer to Chapter 1 for more information on plotter setup. Consult your plotter manual for details on output handling and individual use characteristics.

✦ **3**   Make your selections and click the right mouse button or press ⟨ESC⟩ to return to the Output to Plotter menu.

✦ **4**   Click on **F10-Continue** or press F10 to begin plotting. The status box monitors the progress of your plotter output.

Film Recorders

Presenting your charts on slides can increase the impact of your message. Slides often provide higher quality output than paper printouts or overhead transparencies. Your initial investment can yield excellent returns, especially if you make numerous presentations to large audiences. Some specialty computer companies provide complete film recording services from your chart data on disk.

Retrieve the CONSUMER.CH3 chart and display the Main Menu.

✦ **1**   Select **Output** and then click on **Film recorder** or press 4 to display the Output to Film Recorder menu.

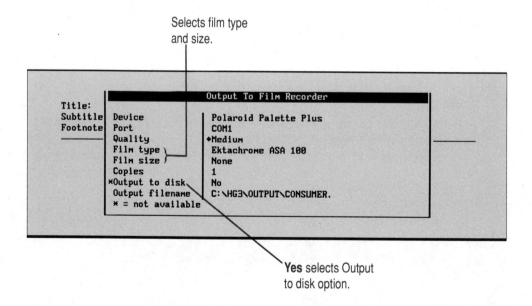

Selects film type and size.

```
                        Output To Film Recorder
Title:
Subtitle   Device           Polaroid Palette Plus
Footnote   Port             COM1
           Quality          ✦Medium
           Film type ⟩      Ektachrome ASA 100
           Film size ⟩      None
           Copies           1
          *Output to disk   No
           Output filename  C:\HG3\OUTPUT\CONSUMER.
           * = not available
```

Yes selects Output to disk option.

✦ **2** Click on **F8-Options** or press F8 to display the Film Recorder
Options menu.

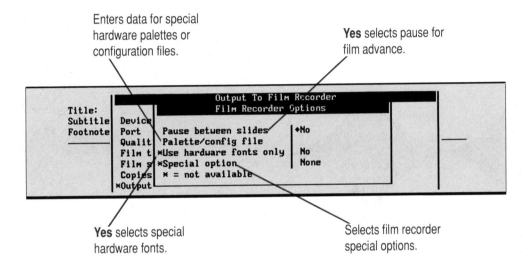

Enters data for special
hardware palettes or
configuration files.

Yes selects pause for
film advance.

Yes selects special
hardware fonts.

Selects film recorder
special options.

✦ **3** Make your selections and return to the Output to Film Recorder
menu.

✦ **4** Click on **F10-Continue** or press F10 to record your chart on film. The
status box monitors your film recorder output.

✦ Summary

In this chapter you taught yourself many useful chart management techniques
for handling and outputting effective and persuasive presentations. Chapter 4
teaches you to build masterful pie and column charts, one of the more sophisti-
cated presentation formats you can create with Harvard Graphics.

4

Creating Persuasive Pie and Column Charts

✦ Pie and column charts are an excellent way to illustrate selected parts of a whole. Each pie slice or column section represents a numerical value or percentage of the total value. Column charts, which are similar to certain types of bar charts covered in the next chapter, display their data in vertical columns divided into sections.

This chapter teaches you to construct and enhance pie charts, and to convert pie charts to column charts.

- ✦ Creating Pie Charts
- ✦ Converting Pies to Columns
- ✦ Creating Multiple Pie or Column Charts
- ✦ Working with Slices and Sections
- ✦ Enhancing Your Charts

✦ Creating Pie Charts

Many of the methods for creating pie and column charts are similar to those you learned for text charts.

Before you begin, review the first 3 chapters of this book. Many of the procedures covered in those chapters apply to all the charts you can create with Harvard Graphics.

Let's enter the data for your pie chart. Start Harvard Graphics and display the Main Menu.

✦1 Click on **Create chart** or press **1** to display the Chart menu.

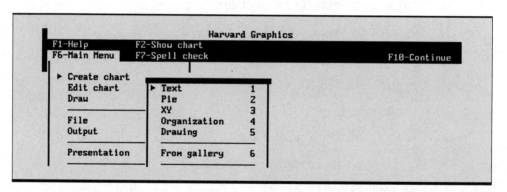

✦2 Click on **Pie** or press **2** to display the Pie Chart 1 worksheet.

```
                                    Pie Chart 1                              ▼
  ▌  F1-Help          F2-Show chart  F3-Choices      F4-Draw      F5-Mark    ▲
     F6-Main Menu     F7-Spell/Text  F8-Options      F9-Pie data  F10-Continue

  Title:          _
  Subtitle:
  Footnote:
  Pie title:


  Slice        Label              Value    Cut      Color      Pattern

    1  |                       |           No  | ▓ Cyn  D┊S |    0
```

⬥ **3** Type the title, subtitle, footnote, pie title, labels, and value data
shown on the following screen. You can type up to 100 characters
per line in the title region.

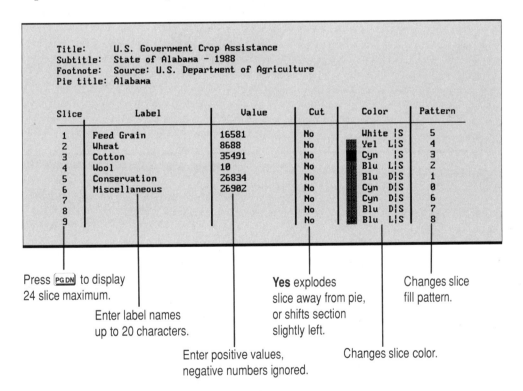

```
  Title:      U.S. Government Crop Assistance
  Subtitle:   State of Alabama - 1988
  Footnote:   Source: U.S. Department of Agriculture
  Pie title: Alabama


  Slice        Label              Value    Cut      Color      Pattern

    1   Feed Grain             16581       No       White ┊S     5
    2   Wheat                   8688       No       Yel  L┊S     4
    3   Cotton                 35491       No       Cyn  ┊S      3
    4   Wool                      10       No       Blu  L┊S     2
    5   Conservation           26834       No       Blu  D┊S     1
    6   Miscellaneous          26902       No       Cyn  D┊S     0
    7                                      No       Cyn  D┊S     6
    8                                      No       Blu  D┊S     7
    9                                      No       Blu  L┊S     8
```

Press PG DN to display
24 slice maximum.

Enter label names
up to 20 characters.

Enter positive values,
negative numbers ignored.

Yes explodes
slice away from pie,
or shifts section
slightly left.

Changes slice color.

Changes slice
fill pattern.

✦ **4**   Click on **F2-Show chart** or press ⊞ to view the current status of your pie chart.

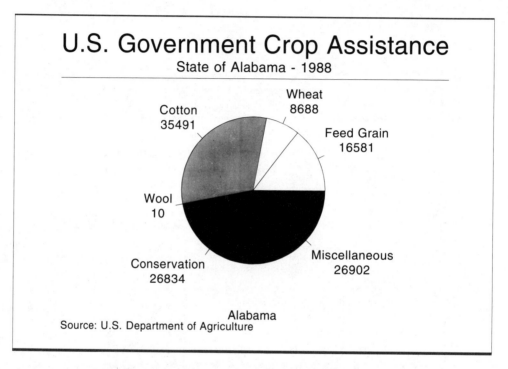

✦ **5**   Click the right mouse button or press ⎋ to return to your worksheet.

✦ Converting Pies to Columns

Let's convert your pie chart into a column chart. Display your current Pie Chart 1 worksheet.

♦ **1**   Click on **F8-Options** or press [F8] to display the Options menu.

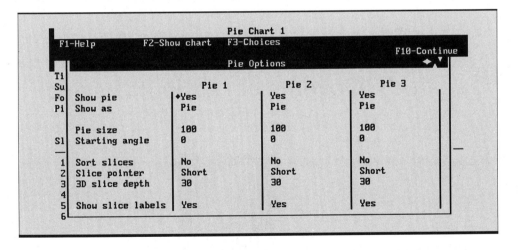

♦ **2**   Click on **Pie options** or press [6] to display the Pie Options menu.

♦ **3**   In the Pie 1 column opposite the Show as option, double-click on **Pie** or move the diamond symbol to **Pie** and press [F3]. A pop-up menu is displayed.

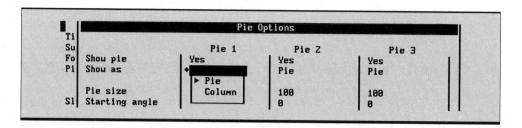

✦ **4**   Click on **Column** or move the menu arrow to **Column** and press ⏎.

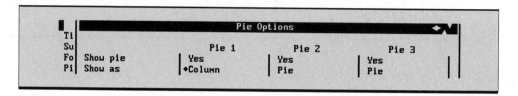

✦ **5**   Select **F2-Show chart** to view the current status of your chart.

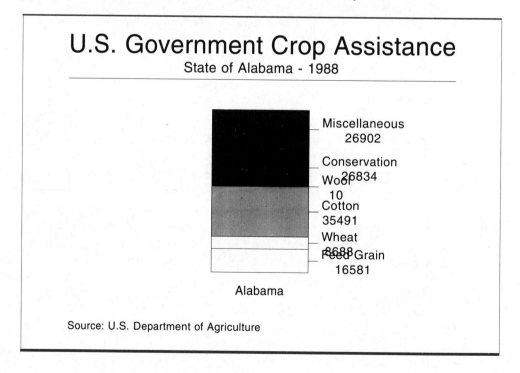

Note

Readjusting Chart Labels With Text Attributes   Labels often overlap when pie slices and column sections are small. Changing the label text size corrects this problem.

Refer to the text attributes section in Chapter 3 for information on resizing your chart text.

✦ **6**   Click the right mouse button or press ⟨ESC⟩ to return to your worksheet and repeat steps 1 through 5 to convert your column back to a pie.

✦ Creating Multiple Pie or Column Charts

You can place up to six pies or columns on a single chart. Harvard Garphics automatically resizes all the pies or columns to fit.

Let's add a second pie to your chart. Display the Pie Chart 1 worksheet on your screen.

Note

Cluttered Charts Can Be Confusing   Too many slices or sections on a single chart, and too many pies or columns on a multiple item chart can confuse your audience and degrade the impact of your presentation. Don't be dazzled by Harvard Graphic's features. Keep it simple and gain the benefits.

Refer to Chapter 1 for further hints on building masterful charts.

✦ **1** Click on **F9-Pie data** or press F9 to display the Pie Data menu.

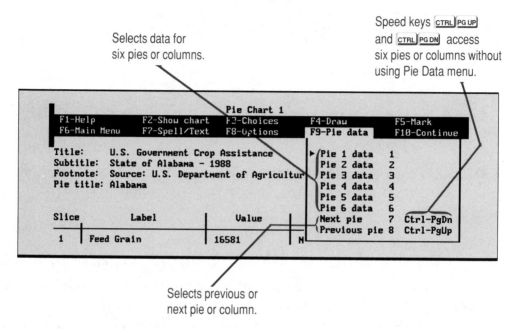

Selects data for
six pies or columns.

Speed keys CTRL PG UP
and CTRL PG DN access
six pies or columns without
using Pie Data menu.

Selects previous or
next pie or column.

✦ **2** Click on **Pie 2 data** or press 2 to display the Pie Chart 2 worksheet. Edit the chart subtitle, enter a new pie title, and type the slice labels and values on the following screen.

```
Title:     U.S Government Crop Assistance
Subtitle:  States of Alabama & Colorado - 1988
Footnote:  Source: U.S. Department of Agriculture
Pie title: Colorado
```

Slice	Label	Value	Cut	Color		Pattern
1	Feed Grain	94992	No	Cyn	D¦S	0
2	Wool	6023	No	Blu	D¦S	1
3	Wheat	67569	No	Blu	L¦S	2
4	Conservation	94927	No	Cyn	¦S	3
5	Miscellaneous	17019	No	Yel	L¦S	4

✦ **3**   Select **F2-Show chart** to view the current status of your chart.

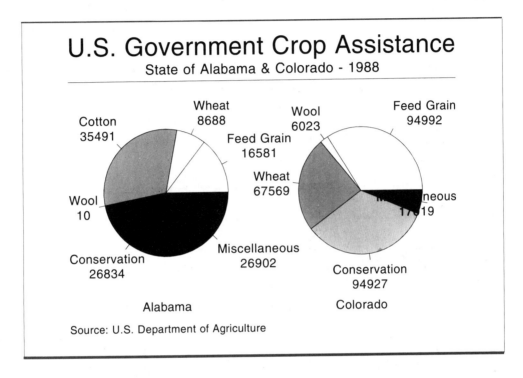

✦ **4**   Return to the Main Menu and click on **File** and **Save chart** or press
        4 and 4 . Save your chart with the Filename CROPS.

✦ Working with Slices and Sections

There are several options for manipulating pie slices and column sections. They
can be deleted, added and reordered. With the Cut option, they can be exploded
or shifted for added emphasis. They can also be filled with a variety of patterns
and colors.

Let's create a new pie chart and explore some of these options. The procedures you teach yourself in the following exercises also apply to column charts.

Deleting and Adding

When your charts need updating or editing, Harvard Graphics makes it easy to delete or add pie slices or column sections.

Display the Main Menu on your screen.

✦ **1**   Click on **Create chart** and **Pie** or press ⬜1 and ⬜2 to display the Pie Chart 1 worksheet. Enter the information on the following screen.

```
Title:     Retail Market Sales
Subtitle:  Projected for 1993
Footnote:  Values are in units of merchandise
Pie title:


Slice        Label            Value      Cut        Color       Pattern

  1    │ Computers          │ 2700     │ No    │ ▌ Cyn  D┊S │    0
  2    │ Printers           │ 1350     │ No    │ ▌ Blu  D┊S │    1
  3    │ Control Centers    │ 1100     │ No    │ ▌ Blu  L┊S │    2
  4    │ Monitors           │ 3500     │ No    │ ▌ Cyn   ┊S │    3
  5    │ FAX Machines       │  900     │ No    │ ▌ Yel  L┊S │    4
```

✦ **2**   View the current status of your new pie chart by selecting **F2-Show chart**.

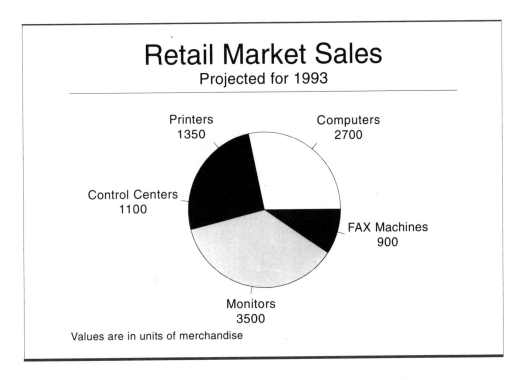

Retail Market Sales
Projected for 1993

✦ **3** To delete a slice of your pie, return to your worksheet and move the cursor to the **Control Centers** label.

Slice	Label	Value	Cut	Color	Pattern
1	Computers	2700	No	▨ Cyn D¦S	0
2	Printers	1350	No	▨ Blu D¦S	1
3	Control Centers	1100	No	▨ Blu L¦S	2
4	Monitors	3500	No	■ Cyn ¦S	3

✦ **4**　Press `CTRL`·`DEL` to delete the Control Centers entry and move the
remaining slices up one line.

Slice	Label	Value	Cut		Color	Pattern
1	Computers	2700	No		Cyn D¦S	0
2	Printers	1350	No		Blu D¦S	1
3	Monitors	3500	No		Cyn ¦S	3
4	FAX Machines	900	No		Yel L¦S	4

Note

Deleting an Entire Pie　To delete all the chart data, move the cursor to the
number one slice label and press `CTRL`·`DEL` until all the labels and values are
removed. To clear the chart titles as well as the data, return to the Main Menu
and select the Clear values function in the Create chart menu.

Refer to Chapter 3 for more information on clearing chart titles, data and options.

✦ **5**　Click on **F2-Show chart** or press `F2` to view your chart without the
Control Centers slice.

✦ **6**　To add a new slice to your pie, return to the worksheet and move the
cursor to the **Printers** label.

Slice	Label	Value	Cut		Color	Pattern
1	Computers	2700	No		Cyn D¦S	0
2	Printers	1350	No		Blu D¦S	1
3	Monitors	3500	No		Cyn ¦S	3
4	FAX Machines	900	No		Yel L¦S	4

✦ **7**　Press `CTRL`·`INS` to insert a blank line and type **Modems**. Press `TAB` and
type **800** in the values column.

Slice	Label	Value	Cut	Color	Pattern
1	Computers	2700	No	Cyn D¦S	0
2	Modems	800	No	Blu L¦S	2
3	Printers	1350	No	Blu D¦S	1
4	Monitors	3500	No	Cyn ¦S	3
5	FAX Machines	900	No	Yel L¦S	4
6			No	White ¦S	5

✦ **8**   Select **F2-Show chart** to view your modified chart. Click the right mouse button or press [ESC] to return to your worksheet.

Reordering

Let's reorder the slices in your pie chart. The following method also works for column sections, letting you reorder your sections in any way you desire.

Display the worksheet for the pie chart you created in the previous exercise.

✦ **1**   Move the cursor to **Monitors** and press [CTRL][↑] until the Monitors label and value moves to the top of the list.

Slice	Label	Value	Cut	Color	Pattern
1	Monitors	3500	No	Cyn ¦S	3
2	Computers	2700	No	Cyn D¦S	0
3	Modems	800	No	Blu L¦S	2
4	Printers	1350	No	Blu D¦S	1

✦ **2**   Move the cursor to **Modems** and press [CTRL][↓] until the Modems label and value moves down two lines.

Slice	Label	Value	Cut	Color	Pattern
1	Monitors	3500	No	Cyn ¦S	3
2	Computers	2700	No	Cyn D¦S	0
3	Printers	1350	No	Blu D¦S	1
4	FAX Machines	900	No	Yel L¦S	4
5	Modems	800	No	Blu L¦S	2
6			No	White ¦S	5

◆ **3**   Click on **F2-Show chart** or press ⟦F2⟧ to view the current status of your reordered chart.

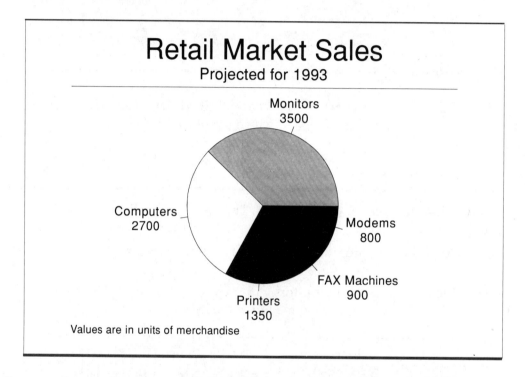

◆ **4**   Click the right mouse button or press ⟦ESC⟧ to return to your worksheet.

Cutting Slices and Sections

The Cut option lets you explode or shift a pie slice or column section to emphasize its importance. Exploded pie slices are moved outward a short distance. Shifted column sections are moved slightly to the left.

Let's cut a slice of the pie you created in the previous exercise. Your worksheet should be displayed on screen.

◆ **1**   Move the cursor to the **Computers** entry.

Slice	Label	Value	Cut	Color	Pattern
1	Monitors	3500	No	▮ Cyn ┊S	3
2	Computers	2700	No	▮ Cyn D┊S	0
3	Printers	1350	No	▮ Blu D┊S	1
4	FAX Machines	900	No	▮ Yel L┊S	4

✦ **2** Press ⎇TAB twice to move the diamond symbol to **No** in the Cut column. Click on **No** or press F3 and select **Yes**.

Slice	Label	Value	Cut	Color	Pattern
1	Monitors	3500	No	▮ Cyn ┊S	3
2	Computers	2700	◆Yes	▮ Cyn D┊S	0
3	Printers	1350	No	▮ Blu D┊S	1
4	FAX Machines	900	No	▮ Yel L┊S	4

✦ **3** Select **F2-Show chart** to see how the Cut option has exploded your pie.

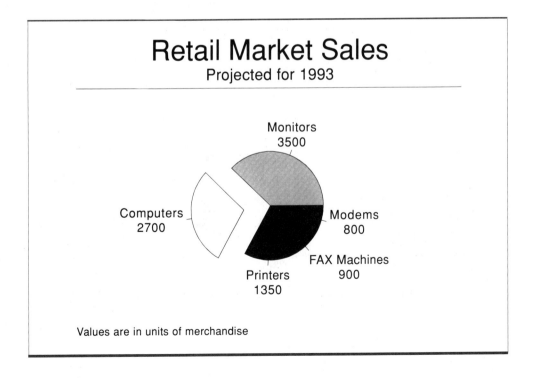

✦ **4**   Click the right mouse button or press [ESC] to return to your worksheet.

Colors and Fill Patterns

The colors and fill patterns you select for pie slices or column sections add impact and emphasis to your charts. Harvard Graphics allows you to output your charts in color or various shades of gray. You can also fill your slices and sections with a variety of patterns for non-color output. The default fill style is set for colors.

Let's change the color and fill pattern in a slice of the pie chart you created in the last exercise. Your worksheet should be displayed.

✦ **1**   Move the cursor to **Printers** and press [TAB] until the diamond symbol moves to the Colors column.

Slice	Label	Value	Cut	Color	Pattern
1	Monitors	3500	No	Cyn ¦S	3
2	Computers	2700	Yes	Cyn D¦S	0
3	Printers	1350	No	Blu D¦S	1
4	FAX Machines	900	No	Yel L¦S	4

✦ **2**   Click on **F3-Choices** or press [F3] to display the Colors pop-up menu.

Slice	Label			Color	Pattern
		►	Blu D¦Series2		
			Blu L¦Series3		
			Cyn ¦Series4		
1	Monitors		Yel L¦Series5	Cyn ¦S	3
2	Computers		White ¦Series6	Cyn D¦S	0
3	Printers		Blu DD¦GoalY1	Blu D¦S	1
4	FAX Machines		Cyn DD¦GoalY2	Yel L¦S	4
5	Modems		Orn ¦Draw1	Blu L¦S	2

✦ **3**   Click on **Orn ¦ Draw1** or place the diamond symbol and press [↵].

Slice	Label	Value	Cut	Color		Pattern
1	Monitors	3500	No	Cyn	¦S	3
2	Computers	2700	Yes	Cyn	D¦S	0
3	Printers	1350	No	Orn	¦D	1
4	FAX Machines	900	No	Yel	L¦S	4
5	Modems	800	No	Blu	L¦S	2

✦ **4** Select **F2-Show chart**, and if you have a color monitor, your pie slice should be orange.

✦ **5** Click the right mouse button or press ⎋ to return to your worksheet.

Note

Hiding a Slice Without Trying   Slices and sections can mysteriously disappear if you change their color to match the background. The data remains on the worksheet.

✦ **6** To change colors to patterns, click on **F8-Options** or press ⒡⑧ to display the Options menu.

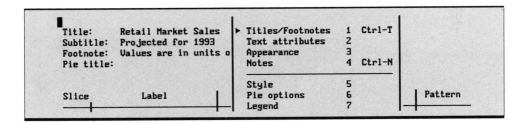

✦ **7** Click on **Style** or press ⑤ to display the Style Options menu.

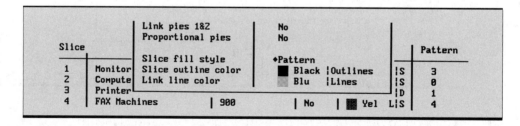

◆**8**   Double-click on **Slice fill style** or place the diamond symbol and
press F3.

◆**9**   Select **Pattern**.

◆**10**   Click the right mouse button or press ESC to exit the Style Options
menu. Click on **F2-Show chart** or press F2 to view your pie slice
patterns.

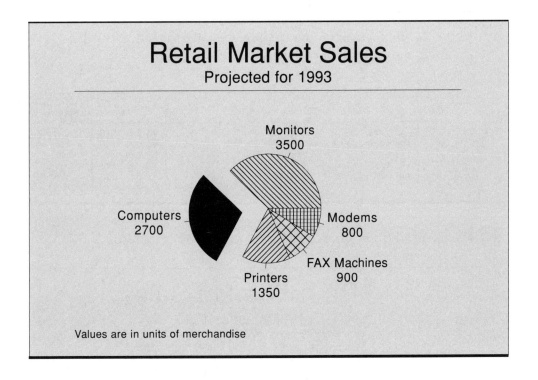

Note

Fill Pattern Choices   You can select from 12 different fill patterns. Fill patterns are numbered from 0 to 11.

✦ **11**   Return to your worksheet and move the cursor to **3** at the top of the Pattern column.

Slice	Label	Value	Cut	Color		Pattern
1	Monitors	3500	No	■ Cyn	:S	**3**
2	Computers	2700	Yes	▓ Cyn	D:S	0
3	Printers	1350	No	▒ Orn	:D	1
4	FAX Machines	900	No	▓ Yel	L:S	4
5	Modems	800	No	▒ Blu	L:S	2
6			No	■ White	:S	5

♦ **12** Type the numbers **6** through **10**. Press ⏎ after each number. This changes the pattern for each slice.

Slice	Label	Value	Cut	Color		Pattern
1	Monitors	3500	No	▇ Cyn	¦S	6
2	Computers	2700	Yes	▨ Cyn	D¦S	7
3	Printers	1350	No	▨ Orn	¦D	8
4	FAX Machines	900	No	▨ Yel	L¦S	9
5	Modems	800	No	▇ Blu	L¦S	10_
6			No	White	¦S	5

♦ **13** Click on **F2-Show chart** or press **F2** to view your patterns.

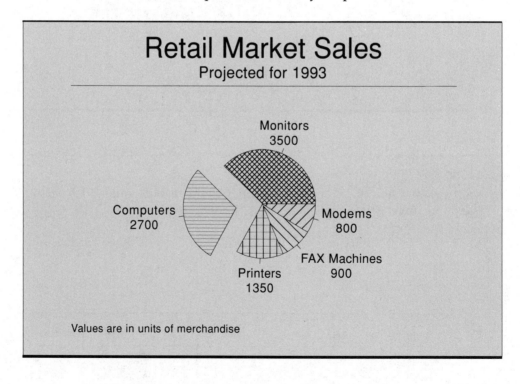

◆ **14** Click the right mouse button or press ᴇꜱᴄ to return to your worksheet.

◆ **15** Repeat steps 6 through 9 to change from **Pattern** to **Color**.

◆ **16** Save your chart with the Filename MARKET.

✦ Enhancing Your Charts

Harvard Graphics has many options which can enhance the appearance of your charts. In this section you can teach yourself how to build more creative and masterful charts with a variety of style and pie options, and by working with values and percents.

Refer to Chapters 2 and 3 for information on creating chart legends, editing chart text, selecting Special Characters and International Formats, and changing font types, styles and text sizes with the Text attributes function.

Style Options

Style options affect all the pies or columns in a chart. You can select enhancements such as 3D effects, text sizing, resizing pies or columns to proportional values, linking two pies or columns, label sharing, and color selection for fillings and borders.

Let's look at some of these options using the CROPS.CH3 chart you created earlier.

◆ **1**   Retrieve the CROPS.CH3 chart and press ⎋ to display the
         worksheet.

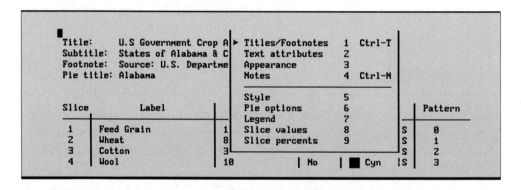

◆ **2**   Click on **F8-Options** or press [F8] to display the Options menu.

◆ **3**   Click on **Style** or press [5] to display the Style Options menu.

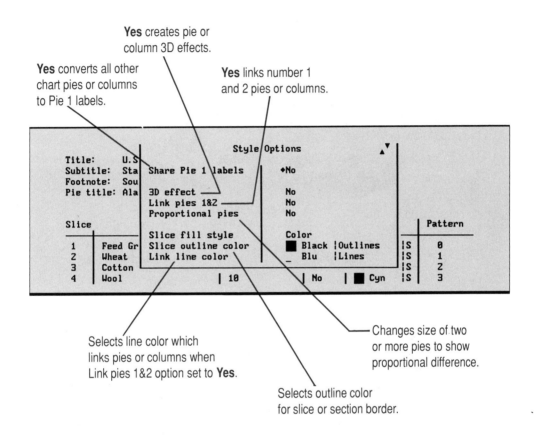

Yes creates pie or column 3D effects.

Yes converts all other chart pies or columns to Pie 1 labels.

Yes links number 1 and 2 pies or columns.

Selects line color which links pies or columns when Link pies 1&2 option set to **Yes**.

Selects outline color for slice or section border.

Changes size of two or more pies to show proportional difference.

✦ **4**   Double-click on **3D effect** or place the diamond symbol and press F3. Select **Yes**.

✦ **5**   Select **F2-Show chart** to view your 3D chart.

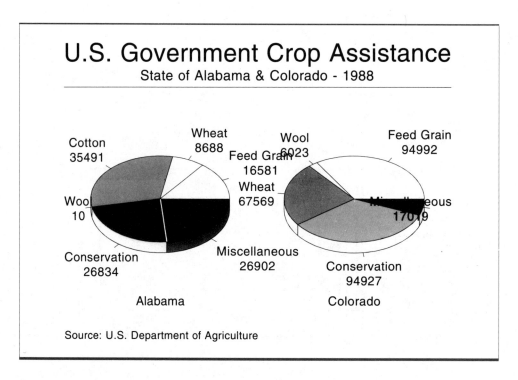

◆ **6** Click the right mouse button twice or press ⌜ESC⌝ twice to return to your worksheet.

Note

Special Considerations When Using 3D Effects The 3D effect can jumble chart labels and visually deceive your audience. Slices on the front edges of the pie may appear to be larger than their relative value.

The Feed Grain and Wool labels need readjustment. Let's correct this problem by changing the text size with the Text attributes option.

✦ **7**   Click on **F8-Options** and then **Text attributes** or press F8 and ② to display the Text attributes pop-up menu.

```
 ■
  Title:      U.S Government Crop A│ Titles/Footnot│           │
  Subtitle:   States of Alabama & C│▶ Text attribute│▶ For titles/footnotes  1
  Footnote:   Source: U.S. Departme│ Appearance     │  For labels            2
  Pie title:  Alabama              │ Notes          │
                                   │                └──────────
                                   │ Style          5          │
```

✦ **8**   Select **For labels** to display the Text Attributes Labels menu and change the Pie 1 and 2 label sizes to **3**.

```
                         Text Attributes Labels                ▼▲
                   Size      Color      Alignment  Font Name    Font Style
  Pie 1 labels    │ 3 │     Blu  L┊XL      –       Swiss 721    Roman
  Pie 2 labels    │ 3 │     Blu  L┊XL      –       Swiss 721    Roman
  Pie 3 labels      4       Blu  L┊XL      –       Swiss 721    Roman
  Pie 4 labels      4       Blu  L┊XL      –       Swiss 721    Roman
  Pie 5 labels      4       Blu  L┊XL      –       Swiss 721    Roman
  Pie 6 labels      4       Blu  L┊XL      –       Swiss 721    Roman
```

✦ **9**   Click on **F2-Show chart** or press   to view your chart with resized text.

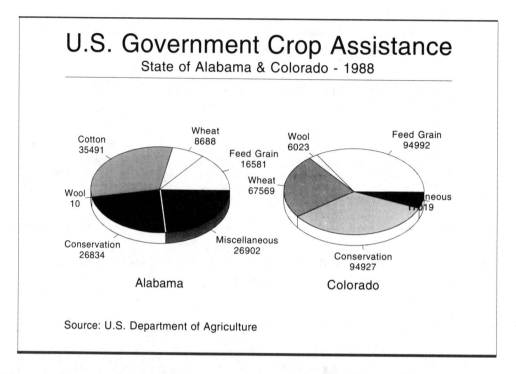

✦ **10** Press ᴇsᴄ to return to the Options menu and then press ᴘɢᴅɴ until the Style Options menu is displayed.

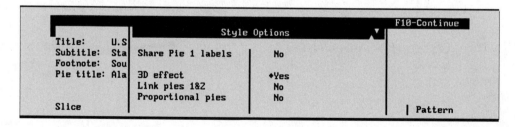

✦ **11** Select **3D effect** and change the option setting to **No**. This returns your chart to two dimensions.

✦ **12** To resize your pies in proportional values, double-click on **Proportional pies** or place the diamond symbol and press ⒡⒊. Select the **Yes** option.

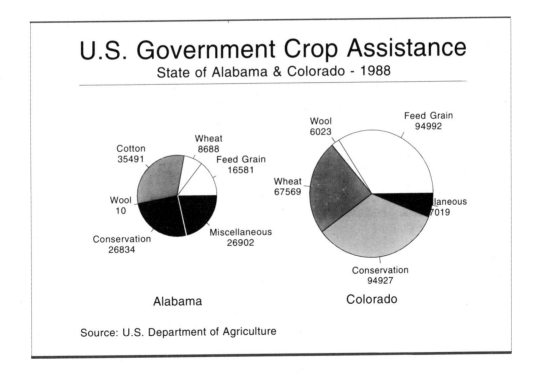

```
                                                                 F10-Continue
                                    Style Options              ▼
  Title:      U.S
  Subtitle:   Sta   Share Pie 1 labels         No
  Footnote:   Sou
  Pie title:  Ala   3D effect                  No
                    Link pies 1&2              No
                    Proportional pies          ◆Yes
  Slice                                                       | Pattern
```

✦ **13** Select **F2-Show chart** to view your proportional chart.

U.S. Government Crop Assistance
State of Alabama & Colorado - 1988

Cotton
35491

Wheat
8688

Feed Grain
16581

Wool
10

Conservation
26834

Miscellaneous
26902

Alabama

Wool
6023

Feed Grain
94992

Wheat
67569

laneous
7019

Conservation
94927

Colorado

Source: U.S. Department of Agriculture

◆ **14** Click the right mouse button or press [ESC] to return to the Style Options menu.

◆ **15** Select **Proportional pies** and then select **No** to return your pies to full size.

◆ **16** Click the right mouse button or press [ESC] to return to your worksheet.

Experiment with the other selections in the Style Options menu, and view the results with the Show chart function. When you are done, restore the options to their previous settings.

Pie Options

Pie options let you change individual pies or columns. You can alter the relative size of two of the pies or columns on your chart, rotate a pie, show or hide pies or columns, change between pies and columns, sort the order of the slices and sections, change the depth of 3D slices, and show or hide your labels.

Let's change the size of Pie 1 and 2 and rotate Pie 2 to improve the overall appearance and balance of your chart. Display the CROPS.CH3 worksheet on your screen.

◆ **1** Click on **F8-Options** or press [F8] and then select **Pie options** to display the Pie Options menu.

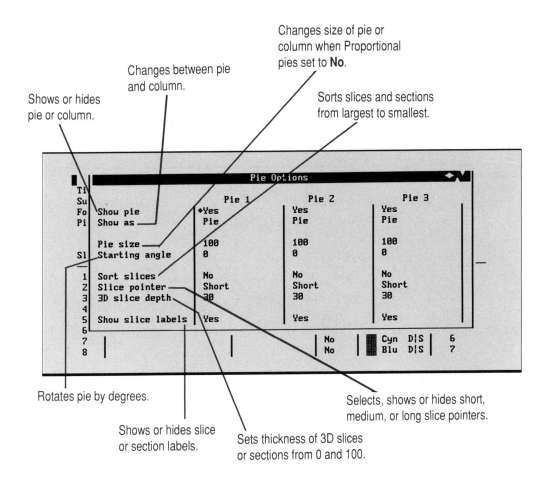

Changes size of pie or column when Proportional pies set to **No**.

Changes between pie and column.

Sorts slices and sections from largest to smallest.

Shows or hides pie or column.

Rotates pie by degrees.

Selects, shows or hides short, medium, or long slice pointers.

Shows or hides slice or section labels.

Sets thickness of 3D slices or sections from 0 and 100.

◆ **2**   In both the Pie 1 and Pie 2 columns across from the Pie size option, select **100** and type **50**. Press the spacebar to delete the extra 0.

✦ **3**   In the **Pie 2** column across from the Starting angle option, click on **0** or place the diamond symbol at **0** and type **35**.

		Pie 1	Pie 2	Pie 3	
Su					
Fo	Show pie	Yes	Yes	Yes	
Pi	Show as	Pie	Pie	Pie	
	Pie size	50	50	100	
Sl	Starting angle	0	35	0	

✦ **4**   Click on **F2-Show chart** or press F2 to view your resized and rotated charts. The Miscellaneous label, rotated 35 degrees, no longer overlaps the pie.

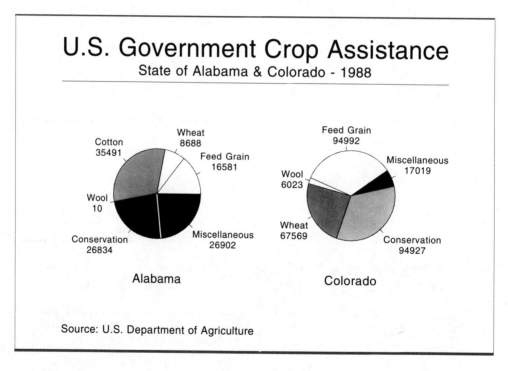

U.S. Government Crop Assistance
State of Alabama & Colorado - 1988

Alabama

Colorado

Source: U.S. Department of Agriculture

✦ **5**   Click the right mouse button twice or press ESC twice to return to your worksheet.

Take some time to explore the remaining options. Be sure to return the chart to its original settings before you continue.

Values and Percents

Harvard Graphics provides a variety of ways to format and display values as currency symbols, percentages and decimals, in scientific notation, combinations of numbers and text, and as straight numbers.

This section teaches you how to select some of these formats. Your CROPS.CH3 worksheet should be displayed.

. 1   Select **F8-Options** to display the Options menu and click on **Slice values** or press **8** to display the Slice Values menu.

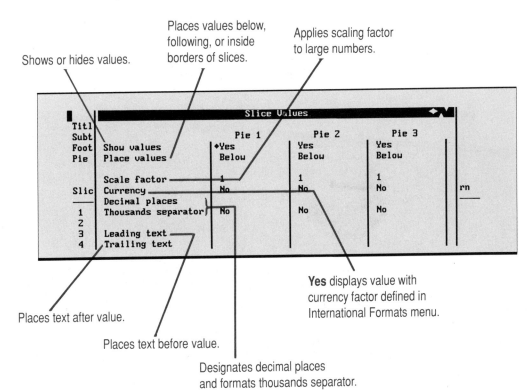

Shows or hides values.

Places values below, following, or inside borders of slices.

Applies scaling factor to large numbers.

Yes displays value with currency factor defined in International Formats menu.

Places text after value.

Places text before value.

Designates decimal places and formats thousands separator.

Refer to Chapter 3 for information on selecting special characters such as currency symbols, and using the International Formats menu.

✦ **2** Opposite the Currency and Thousands separator options, select **Yes** in both the Pie 1 and Pie 2 columns.

	Scale factor	1	1	1	
Slic	Currency	Yes	Yes	No	rn
	Decimal places				
1	Thousands separator	Yes	✦Yes	No	
2					
3	Leading text				

✦ **3** Select **F2-Show chart** to view your chart values displayed in dollar signs and thousands separated by commas.

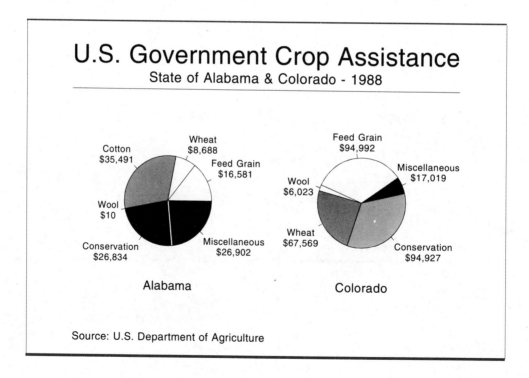

U.S. Government Crop Assistance
State of Alabama & Colorado - 1988

Source: U.S. Department of Agriculture

✦ **4**   To show percentages for each slice of Pie 1, return to the Slice Values
menu and press PGDN to move to the Slice Percents menu.

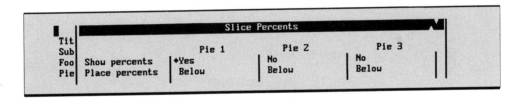

✦ **5**   In the Pie 1 column opposite the Show percents option, click on **No**
or press F3 and select the **Yes** option.

✦ **6**   Select **F2-Show chart** to view your chart with percentages added to
Pie 1.

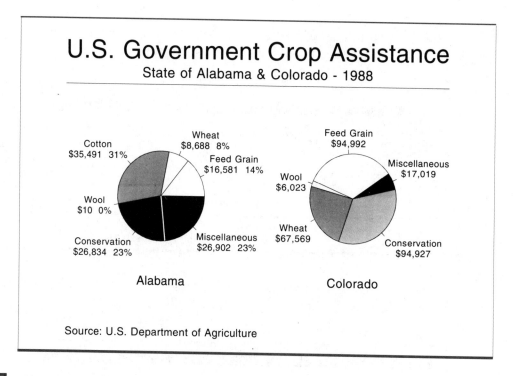

✦ **7**   Click the right mouse button twice or press ⎋ twice to return to your worksheet.

✦ **8**   Click on **F6-Main Menu**, **File**, and **Save chart** or press ⎘, ④, and ④ to save your worksheet with the Filename CROPS and then exit Harvard Graphics.

✦ Summary

In this chapter you taught yourself to create and enhance pie and column charts. Pie and column charts are created in the same manner, with the same options, and are easily converted from one to another. By now you should be feeling confident enough to experiment with the wide variety of powerful options for text, pie, and column charts.

Chapter 5 introduces you to XY charts which are another excellent way to convey your message with maximum impact and effectiveness.

5

Illustrating Your Ideas
with XY Charts

✦   XY charts are useful for showing changes over a period of time. An XY chart displaying quarterly profit and loss would have time measured in quarters plotted along the horizontal X axis, and profit or loss values along the vertical Y axis.

The types of XY charts this chapter teaches you to create, such as bar, line, area, and high/low/close charts, are all constructed in the same manner.

✦   Creating Bar Charts

✦   Converting Your Charts

✦   Creating High/Low/Close Charts

✦   Enhancing Your XY Charts

✦ Creating Bar Charts

XY charts have an X axis and a Y axis. The horizontal X axis defines one or more data series along the bottom edge of your chart. The vertical Y axis defines data series values on the left or right edges of your chart which are called Y1 and Y2 respectively.

Bar, Line, Area, and Point charts use the same XY Chart worksheet. The difference appears when Harvard Graphics shows, previews, or outputs your finished chart.

Bar charts display a data series in three types of rectangular shapes known as bars, stacked bars, or overlapped bars. Stacked bar charts, which are similar to the column charts you learned to create in Chapter 4, display one data series stacked upon another, and provide a total value for all the data. Overlapped bar charts display several data series one behind the other.

Line charts use symbols to represent the value of each data series, with the symbols connected by lines. Bar/line charts display data series in alternating patterns, with one series a bar and the next a line. Area charts display the cumulative total value of each data series stacked one on top of another similar to stacked bar charts. Point charts are line charts without lines, but with each data series value represented by a symbol.

This section teaches you to create a simple bar chart. What you learn enables you to create the other chart types just discussed. Examples of how bar, line, area, or point versions of your worksheet would look are shown in the next section on conversion. High/Low/Close charts are dealt with in a later section.

Refer to Chapters 1 through 4 for information on using the basic options available with Harvard Graphics.

Let's create a bar chart showing automobile industry growth in the twentieth century. Start Harvard Graphics and make sure the Main Menu is displayed.

✦ **1**   Click on **Create chart** or press ① to display the Chart menu.

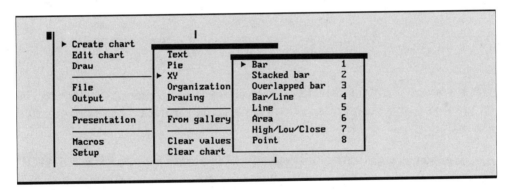

✦ **2**   Click on **XY** or press ③ to display the XY chart menu.

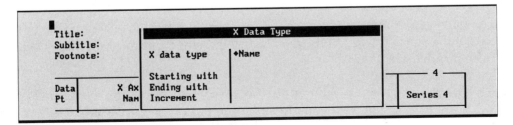

✦ **3**   Click on **Bar** or press ① to display the XY Chart worksheet and X Data Type menu.

✦ **4**   Click on **F3-Choices** or press **F3** to display a list of X axis data types.

Chooses X axis display
for names, dates, times,
or sequential numbers.

Selects starting point
for sequential or regular
interval data displays.

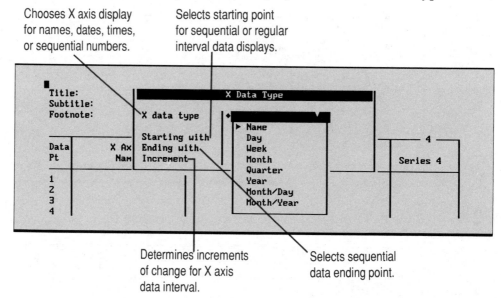

Determines increments
of change for X axis
data interval.

Selects sequential
data ending point.

When you select an X axis Data Type from the pop-up menu, the data you enter on your worksheet is manually or automatically formatted in one of the following ways.

Names   To manually specify label names for your X axis data points, enter any combination of letters, numbers, symbols, and spaces opposite each of the data points in the X axis column on your worksheet. Labels consisting of numbers only can include dates and times, and should not have any numerical value.

The following options automatically format your X axis labels when you enter data at the Starting with, Ending with, and Increment prompts on the X Data Type menu.

Day   Enter numbers from 1 to 365, or day names in any combination of upper or lowercase letters, either abbreviated of fully spelled.

Week	Enter numbers from 1 to 52.
Month	Enter numbers from 1 to 12, or month names in any combination of upper and lowercase letters, either abbreviated or fully spelled.
Quarter	Enter numbers from 1 to 4, placing an upper or lowercase Q before or after each entry.
Year	Enter all four or the last two digits of the year.
Month/Day	Enter numbers from 1 to 12 for the months and from 1 to 31 for days, or month and day names as previously described. A forward slash (/) or spaces can be used to separate text and numbers.
Month/Year	Enter numbers from 1 to 12 for the month, or month names, and either all four or the last two digits of the year.
Month/Day/Year	Enter numbers from 1 to 12 for months, and 1 to 31 for days, or month and day names, and either all four or the last two digits of the year.
Quarter/Year	Enter numbers from 1 to 4 for quarters, and either all four or the last two digits of the year, placing an upper or lowercase Q before or after each entry.
Numeric	Enter numeric values such as quantities, currencies and population figures. Harvard Graphics automatically sorts these values into the correct order.

Note

Manually Splitting Chart Labels   To split a chart name label into two lines, place the cursor where you want to split the line and then press and hold [ALT] while pressing [1][0] on the numeric key pad. A symbol appears, to show where the line splits.

Harvard Graphics automatically determines the Y axis scale based on the numeric values entered on your worksheet. Values over 1000 are automatically scaled. Scaled values, such as 200 to represent 200,000, are shown on the finished version of your chart as Y axis titles. Values over 10,000,000 are automatically displayed in scientific notation.

You can enter your numerical data in the following ways.

Numerical Data	Worksheet Entry	Chart Display
Negative numbers	−10 or (10)	−10
Positive numbers	+10 or 10	10
Scientific notation	10E2, 1E+002	1000
Decimal separators	. or ,	7.5 or 7,5

Let's automatically label the X axis starting with the year 1920, ending with 1980, and in twenty year increments.

♦ **5**   Click on **Year** or move the menu arrow to **Year** and press ⏎.

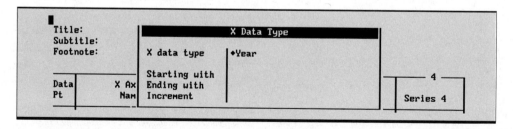

♦ **6**   Move the cursor to Starting with, type **1920** and press ⏎. Type **1980** at Ending with, press ⏎ and type **20** opposite Increment.

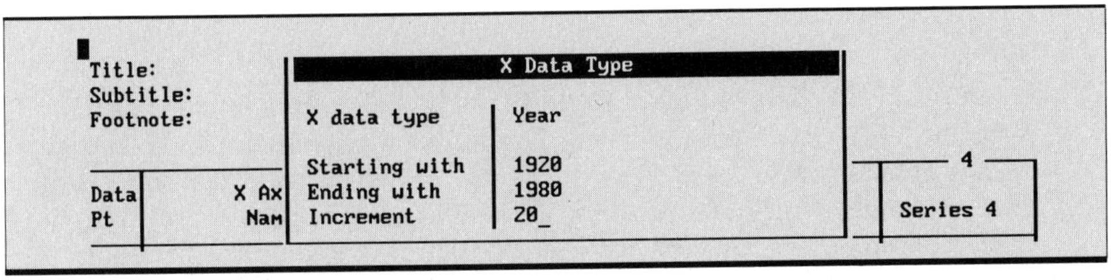

```
█
 Title:                              X Data Type
 Subtitle:
 Footnote:       X data type      Year

                 Starting with    1920                    ┌── 4 ──┐
 Data     X Ax  Ending with      1980
 Pt       Nam   Increment        20_                        Series 4
```

◆ **7** Click on **F10-Continue** or press F10 or ↵ to automatically place the labels on your worksheet.

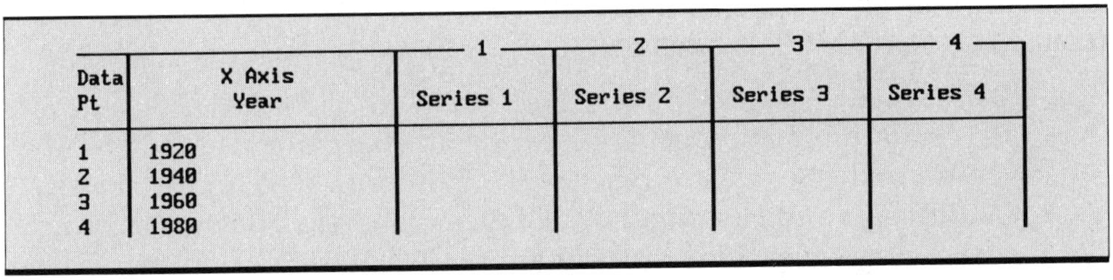

```
                              ┌── 1 ──┬── 2 ──┬── 3 ──┬── 4 ──┐
 Data     X Axis
 Pt       Year          Series 1  Series 2  Series 3  Series 4

  1       1920
  2       1940
  3       1960
  4       1980
```

◆ **8** Let's edit one of your labels by moving the cursor to the **0** in **1980** and typing **8**.

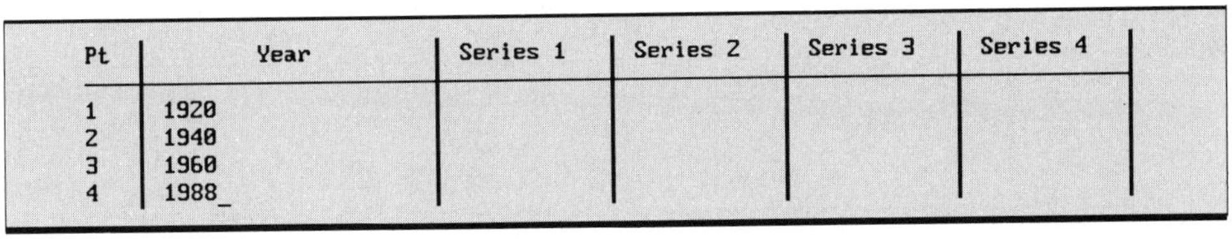

```
 Pt          Year          Series 1  Series 2  Series 3  Series 4

  1          1920
  2          1940
  3          1960
  4          1988_
```

◆ **9** Move the cursor to the title line and type the title, subtitle, and footnote shown on the following screen.

```
 F1-Help        F2-Show chart                F4-Draw      F5-Mark
 F6-Main Menu   F7-Spell/Text   F8-Options   F9-XY data   F10-Continue

 Title:     Motor Vehicle Factory Sales
 Subtitle:  A Twentieth Century Explosion
 Footnote:  Source: Motor Vehicle Manufacturers Association_
```

Note

Using the F9-XY Data Function To Edit Labels   Selecting **F9-XY data** displays the X Data Type pop-up menu. This lets you edit lengthy and complex strings of labels from the menu rather than the worksheet. The F9-XY data option also has built-in features for performing mathematical and statistical calculations, and for viewing series statistics. These options are not covered in this book.

Refer to your Harvard Graphics documentation for details on how to use the special features of the F9-XY data function.

◆ **10**   To create automatic legend titles for your chart, press [TAB] to move the cursor to the Series 1 and then Series 2 title boxes and type **Trucks and Busses** and **Passenger Cars**. Longer labels scroll beyond the borders of the series title boxes but appear in full on your finished chart legend.

Data Pt	X Axis Year	──── 1 ──── Trucks and	──── 2 ──── nger Cars_	──── 3 ──── Series 3	──── 4 ──── Series 4
1	1920				
2	1940				
3	1960				
4	1988				

◆ **11**   Type the numeric values for each series as shown on the following screen.

Data Pt	X Axis Year	──── 1 ──── Trucks and	──── 2 ──── Passenger	──── 3 ──── Series 3	──── 4 ──── Series 4
1	1920	321789	1905560		
2	1940	754901	3717385		
3	1960	1194475	6665863		
4	1988	4120574	7101617_		

✦ **12** Click on **F2-Show chart** or press F2 to view the current status of your chart. Harvard Graphics automatically creates a Y axis scale from the numeric values you entered in step 11, and a legend from the labels entered in step 10.

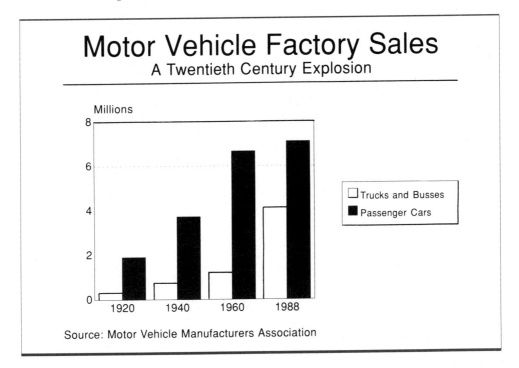

✦ **13** Click the right mouse button or press ESC to return to your worksheet.

✦ Converting Your Charts

With Harvard Graphics you can easily convert a simple bar chart to a stacked or overlapped bar chart, a line chart, bar/line chart, area chart, or point chart. The single exception is high/low/close charts which display data differently than other XY charts.

Let's convert your bar chart to a stacked bar chart. Display your bar chart worksheet.

◆ **1**   Click on **F6-Main Menu** or press [F6] to display the Main Menu. Select **Create chart** and **XY** to display the XY chart menu and then click on **Stacked bar** or press [2]. You are warned your previous edits have not been saved.

```
┌──────┬───────────┬──────────────────────────────────────────┬──────────┐
│ Data │  X Axis   │            │            │           │      │          │
│  Pt  │    Year   ├─────────────── Warning ──────────────────┤ Series 4 │
│      │           │                                          │          │
│  1   │   1920    │  Your latest changes have not been saved.│          │
│  2   │   1940    │                                          │          │
│  3   │   1960    └─Esc-Cancel────────────────F10-Confirm────┘          │
└──────┴───────────────────────────────────────────────────────────────┘
```

◆ **2**   There is no need to save this chart. Click on **F10-Confirm** or press [F10] and the Change Chart Type pop-up menu asks if you want to keep the current data from your chart.

```
┌────────────────────────────────────────────────────────────────────┐
│ F1-Help                      F3-Choices                              │
│                                                      F10-Continue    │
│                                                                      │
│  Title:     Motor Vehic┌──── Change Chart Type ────┐                 │
│  Subtitle:  A Twentieth│                           │                 │
│  Footnote:  Source: Mot│ Keep current data: ◆Yes   │ on              │
└────────────────────────────────────────────────────────────────────┘
```

Note

Saving Current Worksheets or Keeping Current Data   You would normally save your current worksheet before attempting to convert it to a different chart type. If you choose not to save, as in this exercise, you may elect to keep the current data as a basis for your converted chart. The default setting is **Yes**. Clicking on **Keep current data** or pressing [F3] and selecting **No**, means the converted chart has no current data or options.

.3   Since the Keep current data option is set to **Yes**, click on **F10-Continue** or press ⒇ to convert your chart with the same data.

.4   Click on **F2-Show chart** or press ⒇ to view your stacked bar chart.

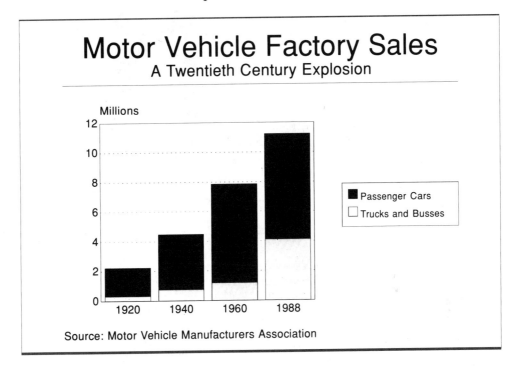

.5   Click the right mouse button or press ⒠ to return to the XY Chart worksheet.

.6   Click on **F6-Main Menu** and **File** and then **Save chart** or press ⒡ and ⒠ and then ⒠ again. Enter the Filename AUTOSALE and select **F10-Continue** to save your chart.

The following examples illustrate the other types of basic XY charts you can create with Harvard Graphics. Feel free to experiment with the chart conversion method you just learned. Be sure to retain the stacked bar chart named AUTOSALE in its original form for use in the next exercise.

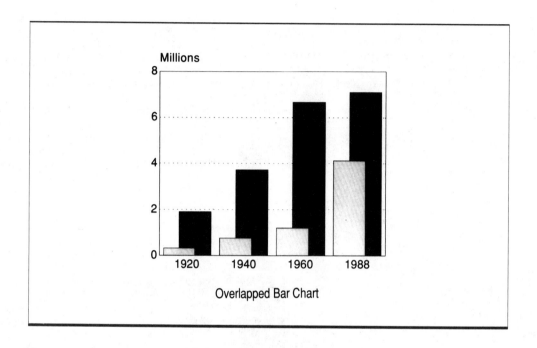

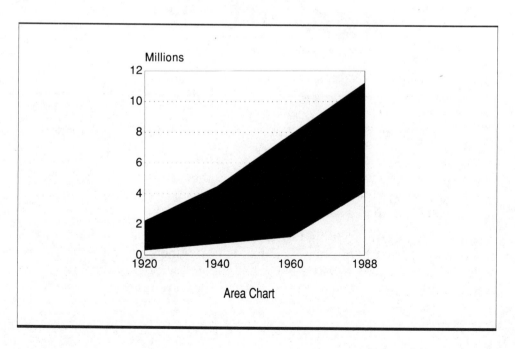

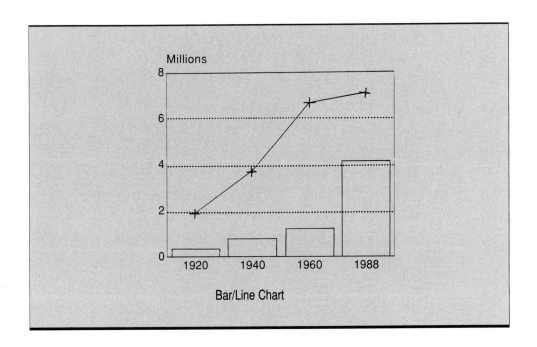

Bar/Line Chart

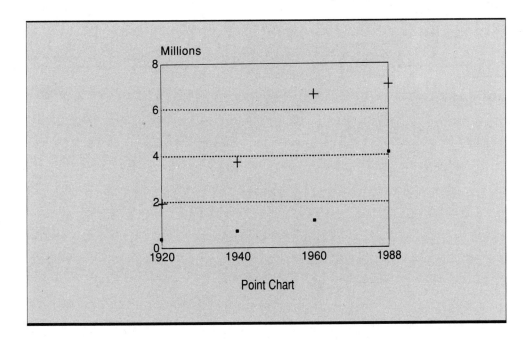

Point Chart

◆ Creating High/Low/Close Charts

High/low/close charts display data differently than other XY charts. They are excellent for showing data ranges, averages, profit and loss comparisons, stock market data, and for laying out work schedules.

Let's create a high/low/close chart to display average stock market fluctuation over a six month period.

◆ **1**   Select **F6-Main Menu** and **Create chart** and then **Clear chart** to clear the chart created in the previous exercise.

◆ **2**   Click on **Create chart** and **XY** and then **High/Low/Close** or press ⒈ and ⒊ and then ⑺ to display the XY chart worksheet and X Data Type menu.

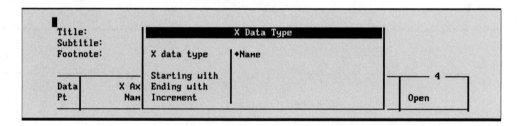

◆ **3**   Enter the X Data Type information on the following screen.

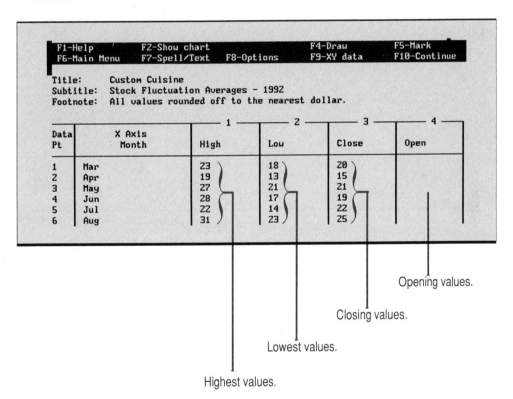

		X Data Type	
Title:			
Subtitle:	X data type	Month	
Footnote:			
	Starting with	Mar	
Data	X Ax	Ending with	Aug
Pt	Nam	Increment	1_

✦ **4**   Click on **F10-Continue** or press ⌨ or ⏎ to return to your worksheet and enter the title, subtitle, footnote, and values on the following screen.

F1-Help	F2-Show chart		F4-Draw	F5-Mark
F6-Main Menu	F7-Spell/Text	F8-Options	F9-XY data	F10-Continue

Title: Custom Cuisine
Subtitle: Stock Fluctuation Averages - 1992
Footnote: All values rounded off to the nearest dollar.

Data Pt	X Axis Month	High	Low	Close	Open
		— 1 —	— 2 —	— 3 —	— 4 —
1	Mar	23	18	20	
2	Apr	19	13	15	
3	May	27	21	21	
4	Jun	28	17	19	
5	Jul	22	14	22	
6	Aug	31	23	25	

Opening values.

Closing values.

Lowest values.

Highest values.

◆ **5**   Click on **F2-Show chart** or press F2 to view the current status of your
high/low/close chart.

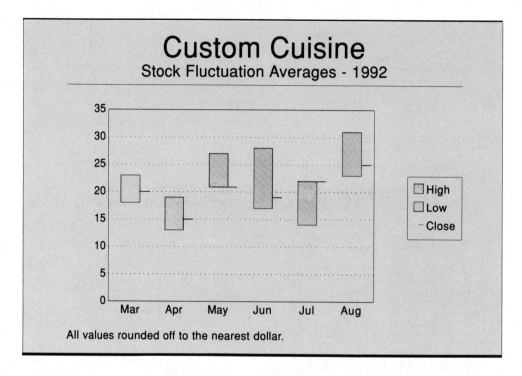

◆ **6**   Click the right mouse button or press ESC to return to your worksheet.

✦**7** Click on **F6-Main Menu** and **File** and then **Save chart** or press F6 and 4 and then 4 to save your high/low/close chart with the Filename CUISINE.

✦ Enhancing Your XY Charts

Many of the enhancement options you learned in previous chapters, such as text attributes, also apply to XY charts. This section teaches you some new options to improve the appearance of your XY charts.

Titles and Footnotes

The Titles/Footnotes option allows you to assign and edit the titles on your chart's X and Y axes and legend.

✦**1** Display the Main Menu and click on **File** and then **Get chart** or press 4 and then 1 to retrieve your AUTOSALE.CH3 chart.

Title:	Motor Vehicle Factory Sales				
Subtitle:	A Twentieth Century Explosion				
Footnote:	Source: Motor Vehicle Manufacturers Association				

		— 1 —	— 2 —	— 3 —	— 4 —
Data Pt	X Axis Year	Trucks and	Passenger	Series 3	Series 4
1	1920	321789	1905560		

✦ **2**   Click on **F8-Options** or press F8 to display the Options menu.

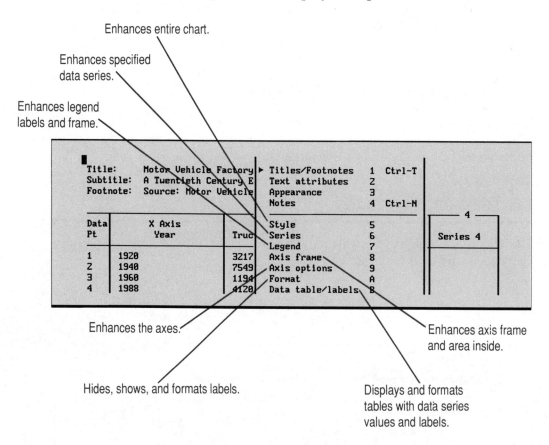

Enhances entire chart.

Enhances specified data series.

Enhances legend labels and frame.

Enhances the axes.

Enhances axis frame and area inside.

Hides, shows, and formats labels.

Displays and formats tables with data series values and labels.

✦ **3**   Click on **Titles/Footnotes** or press 1 to display the Titles/Footnotes options menu.

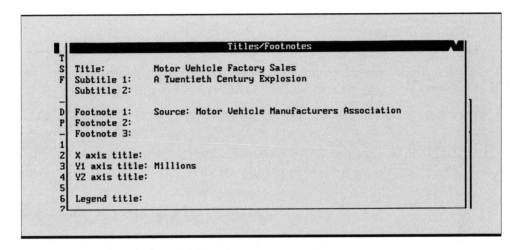

✦ **4** Move the cursor to the X axis title and type **YEAR**, at the Y1 axis title type **Number of Vehicles (Millions)**, and type **Motor Vehicles** at the Legend title.

```
1|
2| X axis title:  YEAR
3| Y1 axis title: Number of Vehicles (Millions)
4| Y2 axis title:
5|
6| Legend title:  Motor Vehicles_
7|
```

✦ **5** Click on **F2-Show chart** or press F2 to view your changes.

✦ **6** Click the right mouse button twice or press ESC twice to return to your worksheet.

Style Options

The Style Options menu lets you select a variety of shapes, widths, styles, and 2D or 3D effects. The style options you select affect your entire chart.

Let's see how some of these options modify the appearance of your XY chart.

♦ 1   Click on **F8-Options** and then **Style** or press ⎡F8⎦ and ⎡5⎦ to display the Style Options menu. The diamond symbol should be set at the Bar style option.

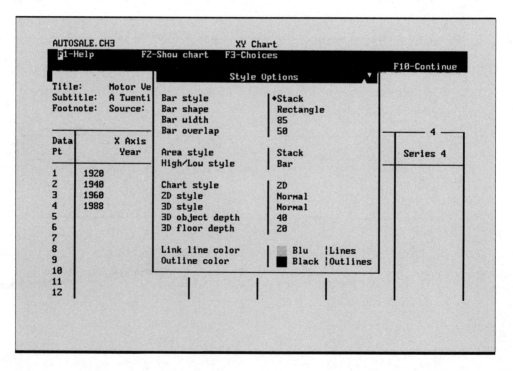

The following list describes the items on the Style Options menu.

Bar style	Selects styles such as cluster, overlap, stack, 100%, step, and paired. The 100% style displays percents on the Y axis. Used with another style, percents appear on one Y axis and the other style values on the second Y axis.
Bar shape	Selects bar shapes such as rectangle, pyramid, octagon, and cylinder.
Bar width/ Bar overlap	Enter a number between 0 and 100 to select the bar width or percentage of bar overlap.
Area style	Selects area styles such as stack, overlap, and 100%.
High/Low style	Selects area styles such as bar, area, and error bar.
Chart style	Changes between two dimensions and three dimensions.
2D style/3D style	Selects 2D normal, shadow, link, or horizontal displays, and 3D vertical or horizontal display.
3D object depth/ 3D floor depth	Sets the projected depth of chart objects such as bars and lines, or the floor on which the chart objects rest.
Link line color/ Outline color	Selects the color for the dotted lines which link bars, or the color for bar outlines.

✦ **2**   Click on **Bar style** or press F3 and select **Overlap**.

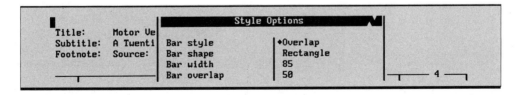

◆ **3**   Double-click on **Bar shape** or move the diamond symbol to **Bar shape** and press F3. Select **Pyramid**.

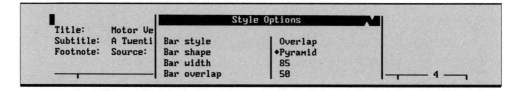

```
          ┌────────────────── Style Options ──────────────────▼
 Title:    Motor Ve│
 Subtitle: A Twenti│ Bar style        │ Overlap
 Footnote: Source: │ Bar shape        │ ◆Pyramid
                   │ Bar width        │ 85
           ┬       │ Bar overlap      │ 50          ┬──── 4 ────┬
```

◆ **4**   Double-click on **Chart style** or move the diamond symbol to **Chart style** and press F3. Select **3D**.

```
   2  │ 1940 │   Chart style    │ ◆3D
   3  │ 1960 │   2D style       │ Normal
   4  │ 1988 │   3D style       │ Normal
   5  │      │   3D object depth │ 40
   6  │      │   3D floor depth  │ 20
```

Note

3D Option Benefits and Limitations   In the 3D mode, bar shapes which would normally appear as flat rectangles or triangles take on a whole new dimension. If you use the 3D option, be sure to enter your series data with the smallest values in the first series and the largest in the last series. A larger data series can obscure a smaller one. Do not use the 3D option if your chart contains more than two data series. The series values can become difficult to decipher.

◆ **5**   Click on **3D object depth** or use the arrow keys to place the cursor at **3D object depth** and type **75**. Press ↵ to move to **3D floor depth** and type **50**.

```
  2  │ 1940       Chart style        3D
  3  │ 1960       2D style           Normal
  4  │ 1988       3D style           Normal
  5  │            3D object depth    75
  6  │            3D floor depth     50_
  7  │
```

✦ **6**   Select **F2-Show chart** to view your 3D pyramid chart.

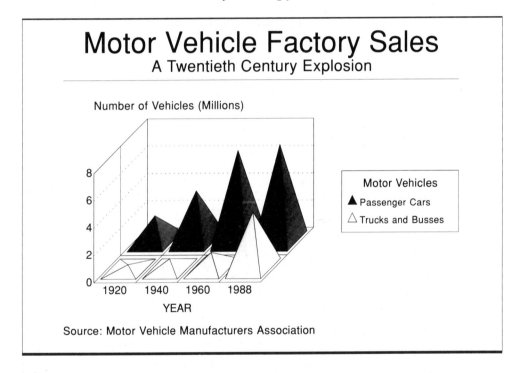

✦ **7**   Click the right mouse button twice or press ⎋ twice to return to the worksheet.

The XY chart style options you select can radically alter the appearance of your original chart. Some of the options you choose may deliver surprising results. Experiment with all the options until you find the style which meets your needs. Be sure to retain a version of your original 3D pyramid chart for use in the next exercise.

Series Options

Series options let you alter the appearance of a single data series. You can display one series as bars, another as a line, and another as points.

Let's select some series options using your 3D pyramid chart.

♦ 1   Click on **F8-Options** and then **Series** or press F8 and 6 to display the Series Options menu.

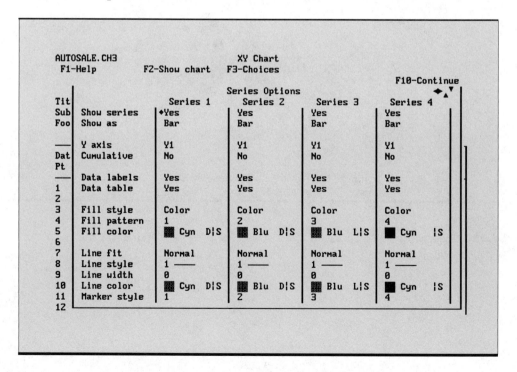

The following list describes the items on the Series Options menu.

Show series	**Yes** shows and **No** hides a series. Hidden data remains in the worksheet.
Show as	Displays a data series in bar, line, point, area, or high/low/close formats. Charts must have at least two series to use the high/low/close option. Open and close must follow low, as in series 1 set at High, 2 to Low, 3 to Close, and 4 to Open.
Y axis	Selects data series display on the Y1 or Y2 axis.
Cumulative	Displays a cumulative total series value at each X axis label when set to **Yes**.
Data labels	Displays data labels, which show each value in a data series, when this option and the **Show data labels** option on the Data Table/Data Labels pop-up menu are set to **Yes**. This option does not work with 100% bars or areas.
Data table	Displays tables with the value of each item in a data series when this option and the **Show data table** option on the Data Table/Data Labels pop-up menu are both set to **Yes**.
Fill style/Fill pattern/ Fill Color	Selects styles, pattern types and colors which fill each data series.
Line fit	Fits lines to a series of data points to show trends or averages, plot lines in a curve, display exponential progressions, or log and power regressions. **Show as** must be set to the Line option.
Line style/Line Width/Line Color	Selects styles such as dashed, dotted, or solid, and the line color or width in increments of 0 to 250.
Marker style	Selects one of 13 symbols to represent each data point.

✦ **2**   Select the options indicated by the highlighted areas on the following screen.

```
Tit|              Series 1        Series 2        Series 3        Series 4
Sub| Show series   ◆Yes           Yes             Yes             Yes
Foo| Show as       Bar            Area            Bar             Bar

 ── | Y axis        Y1             Y2              Y1              Y1
Dat| Cumulative    No             No              No              No
Pt |
 ── | Data labels   Yes            Yes             Yes             Yes
 1 | Data table    Yes            Yes             Yes             Yes
 2 |
 3 | Fill style    Pattern        Pattern         Color           Color
 4 | Fill pattern  9              11              3               4
 5 | Fill color      Cyn  D|S       Blu  D|S        Blu  L|S        Cyn   |S
```

✦ **3**   Click on **F2-Show chart** or press ⬚ to view your chart with Series 2 Area, Y2 axis and Pattern selections.

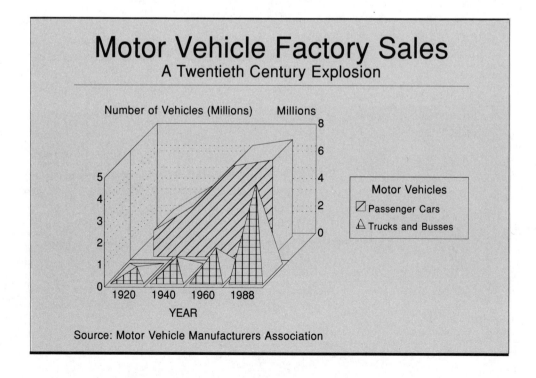

Motor Vehicle Factory Sales
A Twentieth Century Explosion

Number of Vehicles (Millions)   Millions

Motor Vehicles
◪ Passenger Cars
△ Trucks and Busses

YEAR

Source: Motor Vehicle Manufacturers Association

◆ **4**   Click the right mouse button or press ⌜ESC⌝ to return to the Series
Options menu.

Axis Options

Axis options allow you to modify the appearance of the X, Y1, and Y2 axes. You
can select the axes you want displayed, change their color, add tick marks, scale
their values, and select various styles.

Let's use your AUTOSALE.CH3 chart to explore some of these options. The
Series Options menu should be displayed.

◆ **1**   Press ⌜PG DN⌝ twice to display the Axis Frame menu.

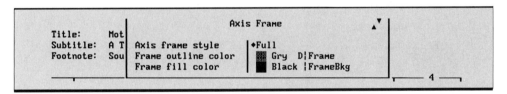

The following list describes the Axis Frame menu options.

Axis frame style	Selects five styles which frame the entire chart, the X and Y axes only, the X axis only, the Y axes only, or hides all axes.
Frame outline color	Changes the chart frame color.
Frame fill color	Changes the background color within the frame border.

You can experiment with some of these options and view your changes with
F2-Show chart. Be sure to return the options to their original settings before
continuing with this exercise.

◆ **2**   Press PGDN to move to the Axis Options menu.

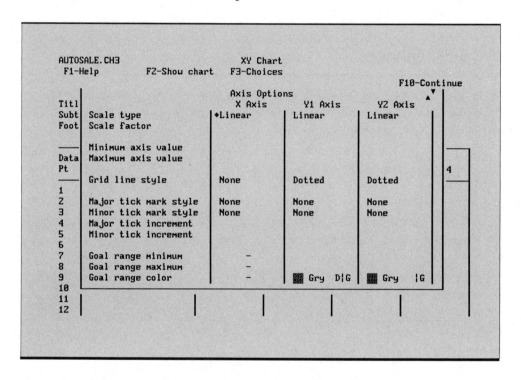

The following list describes each of the items on the Axis Options menu.

Scale type	Selects linear or logarithmic scales for charts with an equal distance between data points, or for data which requires logarithmic scaling.
Scale factor	Selects scale factors such as 10 so values like 2000 are displayed as 200 on your chart.
Minimum axis value/ Maximum axis value	Displays specified portions of an X axis data series, or specifies minimum and maximum ranges for Y1 and Y2 axes values.
Grid line style	Displays three styles such as solid, dotted, or none.

Major tick mark style/ Minor tick mark style	Displays four styles such as in, out, both, or none. Tick marks are small lines on an axis showing a value or data point. Major tick marks have axis labels. Minor tick marks are fractional values of major tick marks.
Major tick increment/ Minor tick increment	Sets the interval between major and minor tick marks. Selecting a major increment such as 3, displays every third X axis label. Minor increments can be selected to indicate the location of labels which are not displayed.
Goal range minimum/ Goal range maximum	Selects and adjusts a shaded, rectangular goal range area behind a chart data series to display comparative values such as production versus goals.
Goal range color	Selects goal range rectangle color.

✦ **3** Select the Grid line style options for the X and Y1 axes indicated by the highlighted areas on the following screen.

```
      ─────┐  Grid line style    [Solid]    [♦Solid]    Dotted      │ ┌─
    1       │
    2       │  Major tick mark style   None       None       None     │ │
    3       │  Minor tick mark style   None       None       None     │ │
    4       │  Major tick increment                                   │ │
    5       │  Minor tick increment                                   │ │
```

✦ **4** Change the Major and Minor tick mark style options for the X, Y1, and Y2 axes indicated on the following screen.

```
    2       │  Major tick mark style   [Out]      [Out]      [Out]     │ │
    3       │  Minor tick mark style   [Out]      [Out]      [♦Out]    │ │
    4       │  Major tick increment                                   │ │
    5       │  Minor tick increment                                   │ │
    6       │                                                         │ │
```

✦ **5** Click on **F2-Show chart** or press F2 to view your chart with solid X and Y1 axis grid lines and major and minor tick marks added.

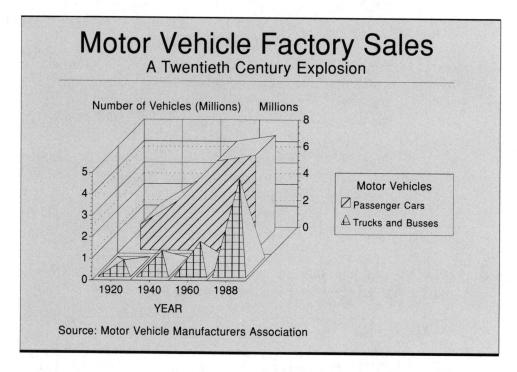

✦ **6** Click the right mouse button or press ESC to return to the Axis Options menu.

Format Options

Formatting options allow you to display numbers as percentages, with a designated number of decimal places, currency symbols, a variety of thousands separators, or text.

Using the chart from the previous exercise, let's experiment with some numerical formatting options. The Axes Options menu should be displayed on your screen.

✦**1** Press ⌜PG DN⌟ once to move to the Format Options menu.

```
AUTOSALE.CH3                      XY Chart
  F1-Help          F2-Show chart  F3-Choices
                                                        F10-Continue
                              Format Options                ▲▼
 Title|                      X Axis        Y1 Axis      Y2 Axis
 Subti| Show axis labels    ✦Yes          Yes          Yes
 Footn|
       | Percent             No            No           No
       | Currency            No            No           No
 Data|
 Pt  | Scientific notation  No            No           No              4
       | Decimal places
 1   | Thousands separator  Yes           Yes          Yes
 2
 3     | Leading text
 4     | Trailing text
 5
```

The following list describes how each option affects your chart.

Show axis labels	**Yes** displays and **No** hides axis labels.
Percent	**Yes** displays axis labels with percent signs and **No** hides percent signs.
Currency	**Yes** displays and **No** hides axis labels with currency signs selected from the Main Menu Setup option or the International formats option.
Scientific notation	**Yes** displays chart data and axis labels in scientific notation. All numbers over 10,000,000 are automatically displayed in scientific notation.
Decimal places	Selects axis label decimal places from 0 to 9 rounded off to the nearest selected decimal. Decimal separator types are selected from the Main Menu Setup option or the International formats option.

Thousands separator	**Yes** places a separator between every three digits of all axis label numbers. Separator types are selected from the Main Menu Setup option or the International formats option. **No** hides all thousands separators.
Leading text/ Trailing text	Selects up to 12 characters of entered text to lead or trail the X and Y axis labels, or Y axis data labels. You may also include characters from the Special Characters pop-up menu, displayed with the speed keys ⊏CTRL⊐ B .

For information on selecting Main Menu Setup, International Formats, or Special Characters options, refer to the appropriate sections in Chapter 3.

✦ **2**   Move the cursor to Decimal places in the Y1 axis column and type **1**.

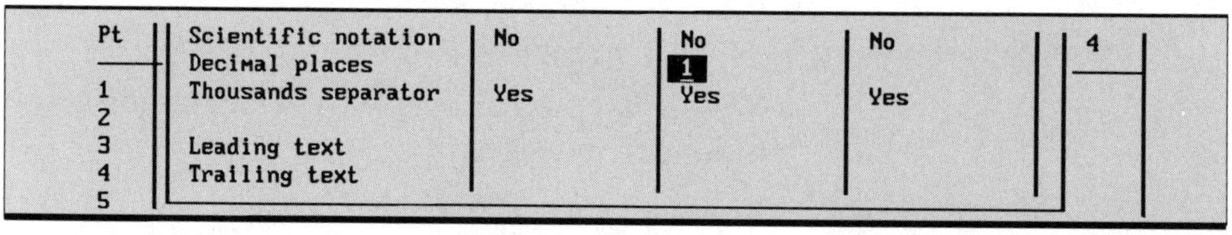

Pt					
	Scientific notation	No	No	No	4
	Decimal places		**1**		
1	Thousands separator	Yes	Yes	Yes	
2					
3	Leading text				
4	Trailing text				
5					

✦ **3**   Move the cursor to Trailing text in the Y2 axis column, press the spacebar and type **mil.** as shown on the following screen.

Pt	Scientific notation	No	No	No		4
	Decimal places		1			
1	Thousands separator	Yes	Yes	Yes		
2						
3	Leading text					
4	Trailing text			mil.		

✦ **4** Click on **F2-Show chart** or press F2 to view your chart with one
decimal place on the Y1 axis labels and trailing text on the Y2 labels.

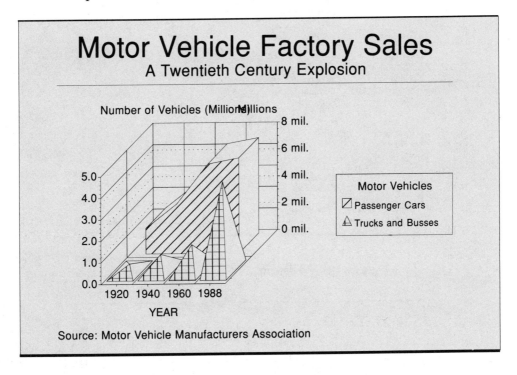

Since legends do not automatically change size when you add data to the axis labels, the other portion of your chart has narrowed, and your Y1 and Y2 titles overlap. Let's use some creative editing techniques to correct the situation.

♦ **5**   Click the right mouse button or press [ESC] to return to the Format Options menu and press [PG DN] twice to display the Titles/Footnotes menu.

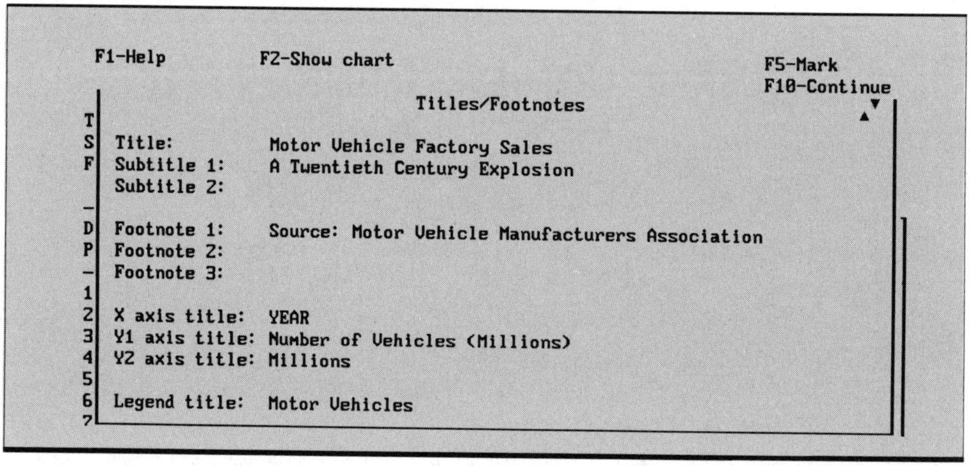

```
     F1-Help              F2-Show chart                          F5-Mark
                                                                 F10-Continue
   T                              Titles/Footnotes                        ▼
   S   Title:        Motor Vehicle Factory Sales                          ▲
   F   Subtitle 1:   A Twentieth Century Explosion
       Subtitle 2:

   D   Footnote 1:   Source: Motor Vehicle Manufacturers Association
   P   Footnote 2:
   ─   Footnote 3:
   1
   2   X axis title: YEAR
   3   Y1 axis title: Number of Vehicles (Millions)
   4   Y2 axis title: Millions
   5
   6   Legend title:  Motor Vehicles
   7
```

♦ **6**   Delete the Y2 axis title **Millions** as shown on the following screen.

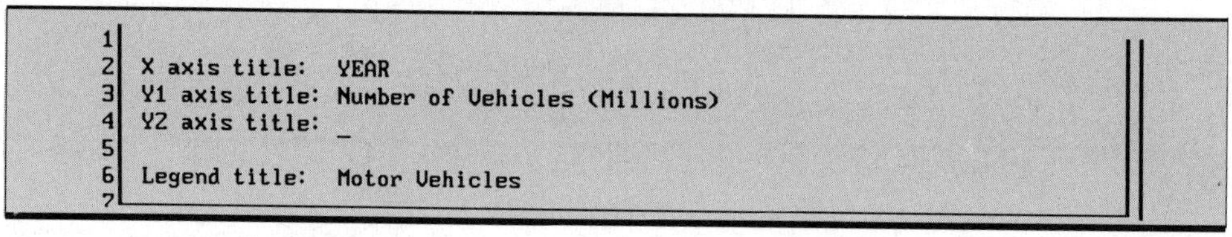

```
   1
   2   X axis title: YEAR
   3   Y1 axis title: Number of Vehicles (Millions)
   4   Y2 axis title: _
   5
   6   Legend title:  Motor Vehicles
   7
```

✦ **7**   Select **F2-Show chart** to view your edited chart without the Y2 axis
title. Click the right mouse button or press ⎋ to return to the
Titles/Footnotes menu.

Data Tables

To display the exact numerical value of the bars on your chart, you can create
data tables or labels. Data tables display this information in a table format,
and data labels place it on your chart next to each bar.

Let's create a data table for your AUTOSALE chart. The Titles/Footnotes menu
should be displayed.

✦ **1**   Press ⇞ to move to the Data Table/Data Labels menu.

```
┌──────────────────────────────────────────────────────────────────┐
│                         Data Table/Data Labels    ▲▼             │
│   Title:    Motor Ueh│                                            │
│   Subtitle: A Tuentie│ Show data table       ✦No                 │
│   Footnote: Source: M│ Table grid lines      Vertical            │
│                      │                                3─────4───  │
│                      │ Show data labels      No                  │
│   ─────────────────  │                                           │
│   Data    Y Axis     │                                           │
└──────────────────────────────────────────────────────────────────┘
```

The following list describes the options on the Data Table/Data Labels menu.

Show data table	**No** hides tables, **With chart** displays tables with charts, and **Table only** displays tables only. These options work only when the Data table option on the Series Options menu is set to **Yes**.
Table grid lines	Selects data table grid line options such as vertical, horizontal, both or none.
Show data labels	**Yes** displays labels above each chart bar when the Data table option on the Series Options menu is also set to **Yes**.

For information on using the Data table option, refer to the Series Options section in this chapter.

✦ **2**   Click on **Show data table** or press F3 to display the Show data table pop-up menu.

✦ **3**   Select **With chart**.

✦ **4**   Double-click on **Table grid lines** or move the diamond symbol to **Table grid lines** and press F3 to display the grid line options.

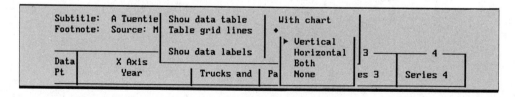

✦ **5**   Select **Both**.

To fully display your data table, let's place the legend below the graph.

⋆**6**   Press [PGUP] four times to display the Legends Options menu. Click
on the center dot under the legend box or move the menu arrow
to **Location** and press the space bar to move the arrow to the correct dot.

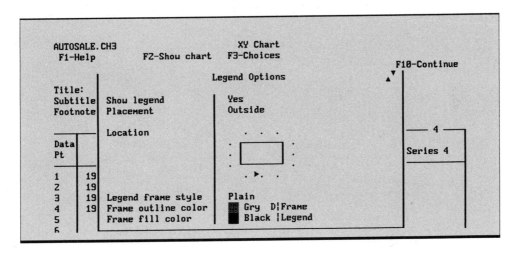

Let's also modify some text sizes to improve your chart's appearance.

⋆**7**   Press [PGUP] five times to display the Text Attributes Labels menu, and
make the size changes shown in the highlighted areas on the following screen.

✦ **8** Click on **F2-Show chart** or press F2 to view your chart with a data table, repositioned legend, and smaller text size. The trailing text you selected for the Y1 axis also appears in the data tables.

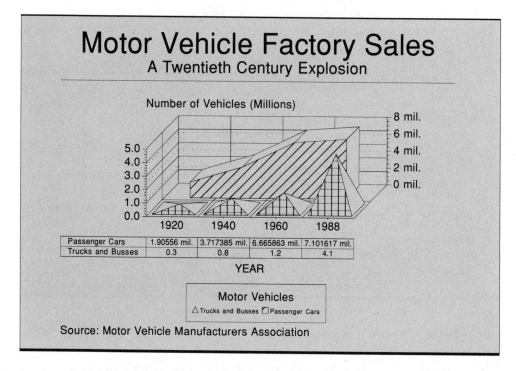

✦ **9** Click the right mouse button twice or press ESC twice to return to the worksheet.

✦ **10** Save your chart with the Filename AUTOSALE and exit Harvard Graphics.

✦ Summary

In this chapter you taught yourself the basic steps for constructing, converting and enhancing a variety of XY charts. Chapter 6 introduces you to organization charts.

6

Establishing a Framework
with Organization Charts

✦   Effective organization charts can be powerful additions to your presentations. Organization charts illustrate the hierarchical relationships between people, divisions, branches, or departments with interconnected groups of chart boxes.

Chapter 6 teaches you to create masterful organizational charts with a wide variety of functions, options and enhancements.

- ✦ Creating Organization Charts
- ✦ Working with Chart Boxes
- ✦ Working with Chart Displays
- ✦ Enhancing Your Charts

✦ Creating Organization Charts

In this section you can learn to enter and edit data, add, delete and reorganize chart boxes.

The Organization Chart Worksheet

The Organization Chart worksheet contains a series of interconnected chart boxes. Harvard Graphics organizes chart boxes in groups, with individual boxes categorized as managers, subordinates, and peers.

Let's begin by displaying a worksheet and exploring its format. Start Harvard Graphics and display the Main Menu.

✦ **1**   Click on **Create chart** or press ⌊**1**⌋ to display the Chart menu.

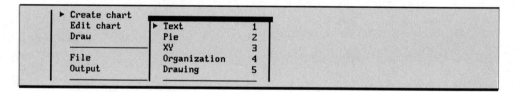

✦ **2**   Click on **Organization** or press ⌊**4**⌋ to display the worksheet.

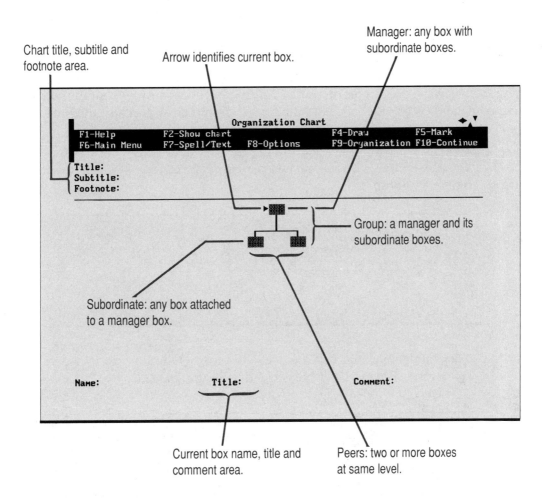

Chart title, subtitle and footnote area.

Arrow identifies current box.

Manager: any box with subordinate boxes.

Group: a manager and its subordinate boxes.

Subordinate: any box attached to a manager box.

Current box name, title and comment area.

Peers: two or more boxes at same level.

The top box on your worksheet is a manager box. The two attached boxes are subordinates, and also peers since they are on the same level. All three boxes form a group, which is automatically displayed on each new worksheet.

Entering Data

Let's enter some data and create a chart which shows the hierarchical relationship between the executives of a small company. The box arrow should indicate the manager box on level one, and the cursor should be at the chart title line.

⋆ **1**   Type the title, subtitle, and footnote shown on the following screen. You are limited to 100 characters per entry. Do not press ↵ after typing the footnote.

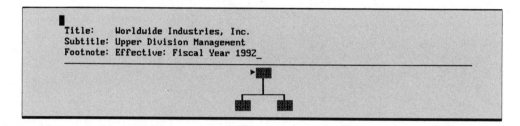

⋆ **2**   Click on the manager box on level 1 or press ↓ to move into the data box region. The manager box should be highlighted.

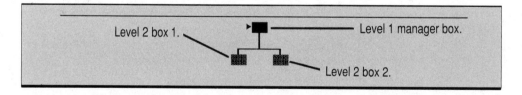

⋆ **3**   Click on the highlighted box or press ↵ to display the Add/Edit Box Text pop-up menu.

♦ 4   Type the information shown on the following screen. You are limited to 22 characters per line.

```
                                                    F10-Continue
                                            Add/Edit Box Text
  Title:    Worldwide Industries, Inc.
  Subtitle: Upper Division Management    Name:    Robert Thompson
  Footnote: Effective: Fiscal Year 1992  Title:   CEO
                                         Comment: Europe_
                                    ▶■
```

♦ 5   Click on **F10-Continue** or press ⏎ to enter your text. Your box text appears in the name, title, and comment area at the bottom of the screen.

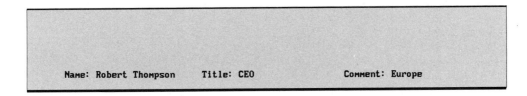

Name: Robert Thompson   Title: CEO   Comment: Europe

♦ 6   Click on subordinate box 1 on level 2 or press ⏎ to move the box arrow. The box should be highlighted.

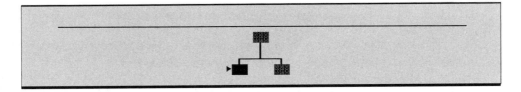

✦ **7**   Click on the highlighted box or press ⏎ to display the Add/Edit Box Text menu and type the text shown on the following screen.

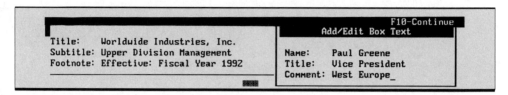

✦ **8**   Select **F10-Continue** or press ⏎ to enter your data.

✦ **9**   Click on subordinate box 2 or press ⏎ to move the box arrow. Press ⏎ to display the Add/Edit Box Text menu and type the text shown on the following screen.

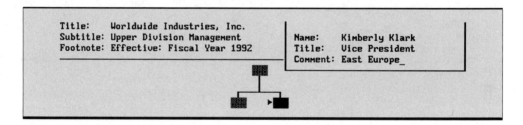

✦ **10**   Select **F10-Continue** or press ⏎ to enter your data.

✦ **11**   Select **F2-Show chart** to display the current status of your chart. At this stage in the chart construction process, comments do not automatically appear in the boxes, and boxes on the lowest level are without box frames, titles, or comments.

Worldwide Industries, Inc.
Upper Division Management

**Robert Thompson
CEO**

Paul Greene

Kimberly Klark

Effective: Fiscal Year 1992

Note

Box Size and Text Editing   Box sizes automatically adjust to fit the longest line of text. You cannot change the text size, but you can change the box size by splitting, or editing lines of text. To edit box text, select the appropriate box and press ⏎ to display the Add/Edit Box Text menu. Make your edits, which change the box size according to the text line length, and press ⏎ to enter the data.

For more information on splitting lines of text, and forcing chart data and box frames to appear, refer to the later sections in this chapter on chart displays and enhancements.

✦ **12**   Click the right mouse button or press ᴇsᴄ to return to your worksheet.

At this point you probably aren't satisfied with the appearance of your chart. The following sections demonstrate many of the ways you can make your charts more attractive, persuasive and presentable.

✦ Working with Chart Boxes

This section teaches you to add, delete, and move chart boxes.

Adding Boxes

The three boxes displayed on your worksheet can be increased up to 210 boxes. The two types of boxes you can add to your chart are called subordinate and staff. Subordinate boxes identify key individuals, and can also serve as manager boxes when subordinate boxes are attached. Staff boxes identify people outside the normal structure such as assistants or secretaries. You cannot add a subordinate box to a staff box.

Let's add subordinate and staff boxes to the chart you created in the previous exercise. Your worksheet should be displayed.

⋅**1**   Move the box arrow to the manager box on level 1.

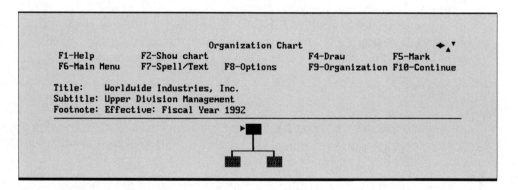

✦ **2**   Click on **F9-Organization** or press ⒡⑨ to display the Organization menu.

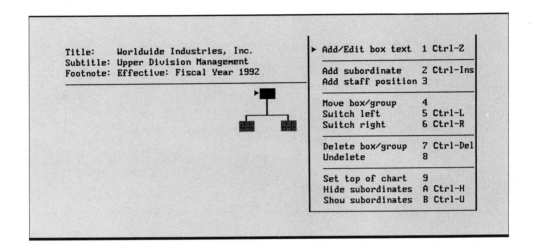

✦ **3**   Click on **Add subordinate** or press ⑵ to add a new box. You can
also bypass the Organization menu and add a new box by pressing
the speed keys ⌨CTRL⌨INS.

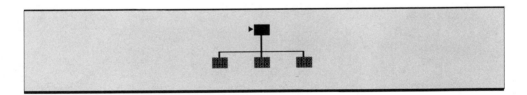

✦ **4** Move the box arrow to the new subordinate box, which is box 3 on level 2, and select **F9-Organization**. Click on **Add/Edit box text** or press ⬚1️⃣ and type the information shown on the following screen.

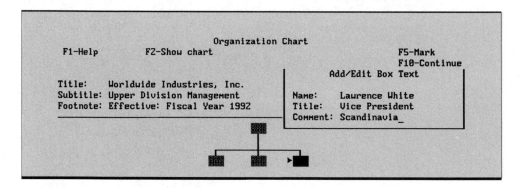

✦ **5** Press ⏎ to enter your data.

✦ **6** To add a staff box, move the box arrow to the manager box on level 1 and click on **F9-Organization** or press 🄵9️⃣ to display the Organization menu.

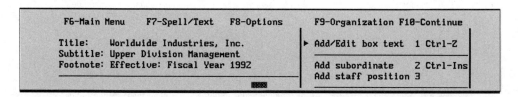

✦ **7** Click on **Add staff position** or press 3️⃣ to add a staff box between the manager box and its subordinates.

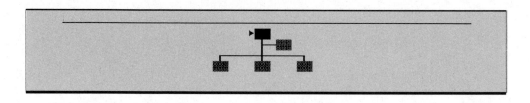

Note

Staff Box Limitations   You can only add two staff boxes to each manager box. The staff boxes appear below and to the right and left sides of the manager box.

Deleting and Undeleting

With Harvard Graphics you can delete any box or group of boxes except the level 1 manager box. You can also restore the last box or group you deleted using the undelete function.

Let's practice these functions with the chart you created in the last exercise. Your worksheet should be displayed.

✦ **1**   Move the box arrow to the staff box.

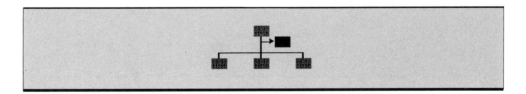

✦ **2**   Select **F9-Organization** to display the Organization menu and click on **Delete box/group** or press Ⓩ to delete the staff box. The speed keys ⒸⓉⓇⓁ ⒹⒺⓁ also delete any box or group indicated by the box arrow.

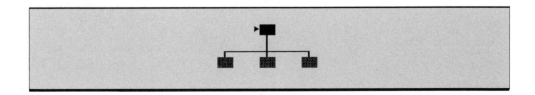

✦ **3** Move the box arrow to box 3 on level 2 and press CTRL INS to add a subordinate box. These two boxes are a group. Remember the level 1 manager box cannot be deleted.

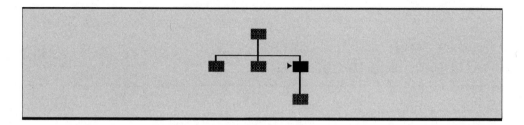

✦ **4** With the box arrow on box 3 on level 2, select **F9-Organization** to display the Organization menu and click on **Delete box/group** or press 7 to delete the two-box group. When deleting a group, the box arrow must indicate the box on the highest level.

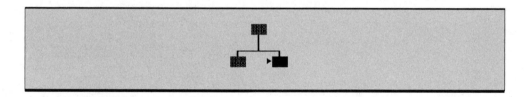

✦ **5** Select **F9-Organization** and click on **Undelete** or press 8 to restore the deleted group.

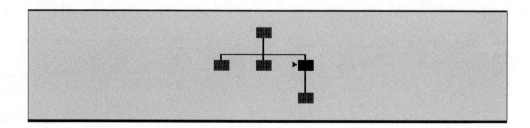

Note

Undelete Features and Limitations   A deleted box or group is stored in memory until another box or group is deleted. Undelete does not function if too many boxes are added after a box or group is deleted. Harvard Graphics warns you when the limit is reached.

Moving Boxes

You can move a box or a group of boxes to new locations, and switch box positions on the same level. Let's explore these possibilities with your chart from the previous exercise. The worksheet should be displayed.

♦ **1**   Move the box arrow to the box on level 3.

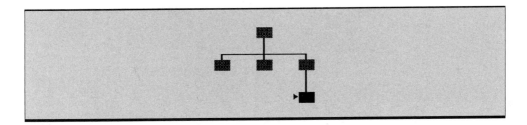

♦ **2**   Select **F9-Organization** and click on **Move box/group** or press ④ to display the pop-up menu.

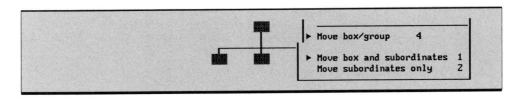

♦ **3** Click on **Move box and subordinates** or press ①. The indicated box shifts slightly and the stem is highlighted. If subordinate boxes were attached, they would also shift as part of the group.

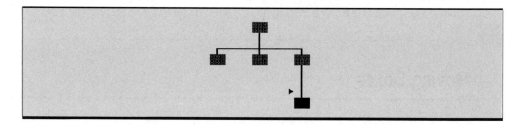

♦ **4** Press ① once and ⊟ twice to move the highlighted box to box 1 on level 2. Notice the name, title, and comment, information you entered for box 1 level 2 is visible at the bottom of your screen.

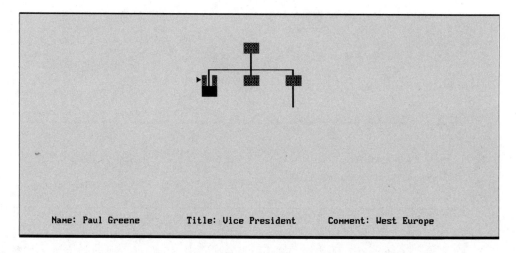

Name: Paul Greene   Title: Vice President   Comment: West Europe

♦ **5** Press ⊡ to attach the box at its new location. The name, title and comment area is now blank since you have not entered any data for the relocated box.

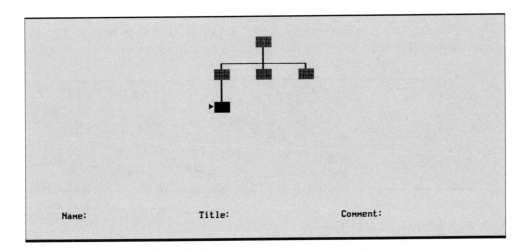

✦ **6**   Move the box arrow to box 1 on level 2.

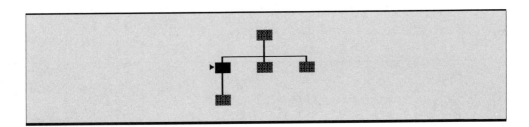

✦ **7**   Click on **F9-Organization** and **Move box/group** or press ⌨F9 and ⌨4 to display the pop-up menu. Select **Move subordinates only** to change the subordinate box below to an inverted T symbol.

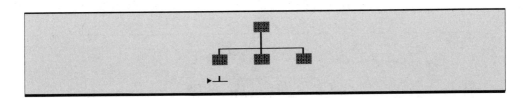

✦ **8**   Press ⊡ twice to move the selected subordinate box to box 3 on level 2. Press ⊡ to attach the box at its new location.

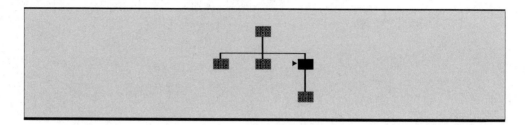

Switching Positions

Now let's switch box locations on the same level using your worksheet from the previous exercise.

✦ **1**   Move the box arrow to box 2 on level 2.

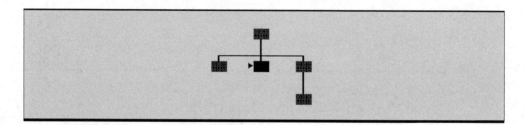

✦ **2**   Select **F9-Organization** and click on **Switch right** or press ⑥ to switch the positions of box 2 and the pair on the right.

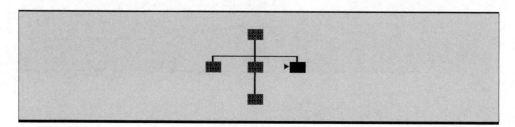

✦ **3**   Select **F9-Organization** and click on **Switch left** or press ⑤ to switch
the boxes to their original positions.

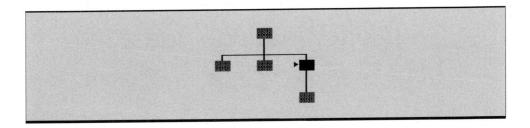

Note

Switch Speed Keys   To bypass the Organization menu, press the speed keys
CTRL R to switch right and CTRL L to switch left. Use the speed keys for faster
movement along several boxes on the same level.

✦ Working with Chart Displays

As your organization chart grows toward the 210 box limit, it can become ex-
tremely unwieldy. Harvard Graphics solves this problem by allowing you to display or output selected parts of your chart. You can select a box for temporary
display at the top of your chart, and temporarily show or hide selected boxes.

Setting Top of Chart

Using your worksheet from the previous exercise, let's temporarily select a new
top box.

✦ **1**   Click on **F2-Show chart** or press F2 to display the current status of your chart.

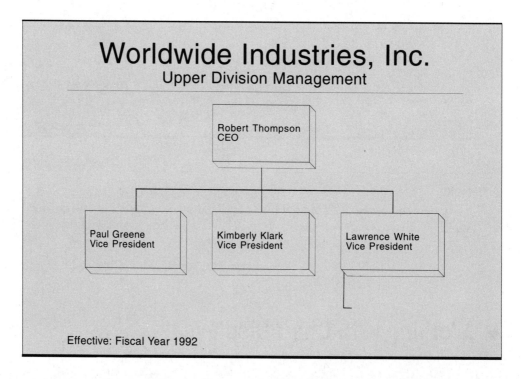

Since no data has been entered for the level 3 box, it is indicated by a line extending below the third box on level 2. With the addition of a third level, the subordinate boxes on level 2 now have borders and title text.

✦ **2**   Click the right mouse button or press ESC to return to your worksheet. Make sure the box arrow indicates box 3 on level 2, and click on **F9-Organization** or press F9 to display the Organization menu.

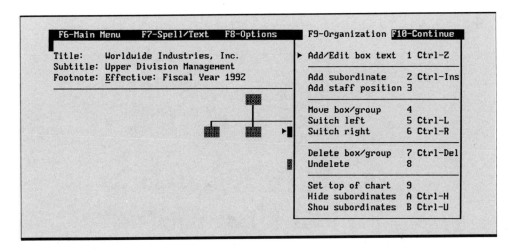

✦ **3**   Click on **Set top of chart** or press ⑨ and return to the worksheet.

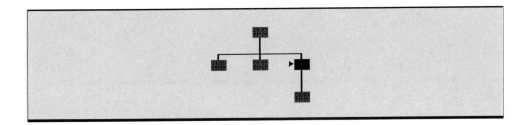

Those boxes not selected are inactive and appear dim on the worksheet. You can
still add, delete, and move the inactive boxes.

✦ **4**   Click on **F2-Show chart** or press F2 to view your selected box.

The selected box, which was originally a subordinate box, is now on level 1, and the subordinate box line appears below it. The inactive boxes do not appear. Harvard Graphics automatically enlarges active boxes to fill the chart area. What you produce on your output device is also resized accordingly.

✦ **5**   Click the right mouse button or press ESC to return to your worksheet and move the box arrow to the manager box on level 1.

✦ **6**   Click on **F9-Organization** and **Set top of chart** or press F9 and 9 to select a new top of chart.

✦ **7**   Select **F2-Show chart** to view a full complement of boxes, and then return to your worksheet.

Showing and Hiding

You can also show and output particular parts of your chart by temporarily hiding selected subordinate boxes. Your worksheet should still be displayed.

✦ **1**   With the box arrow on the manager box on level 1, select **F9-Organization** and click on **Hide subordinates** or press Ⓐ to hide all the subordinate boxes. The dotted line below the manager box indicates hidden boxes.

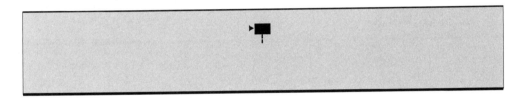

✦ **2**   Click on **F2-Show chart** or press F2 to view your chart with hidden subordinate boxes, and then return to your worksheet.

✦ **3**   To restore the hidden boxes, select **F9-Organization** and click on **Show subordinates** or press Ⓑ.

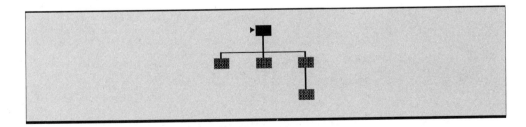

Note

Show and Hide Speed Keys   You can bypass the Organization menu by selecting the appropriate box and pressing the speed keys [CTRL][H] to hide and [CTRL][U] to restore boxes.

✦ Enhancing Your Charts

The enhancement options you taught yourself in previous chapters also apply to organization charts. This section covers some new options which are particular to organization charts.

Box Options

The Box Options menu lets you select various box frame styles and box colors, show and hide titles and comments, align text within a box, and change the appearance of low level boxes.

Let's explore some of these options with your organization chart. Your worksheet should be displayed.

✦ **1**   Click on **F8-Options** or press [F8] to display the Options menu.

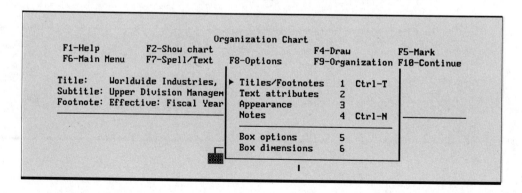

♦ **2**   Click on **Box options** or press ⑤ to display the Box Options menu.

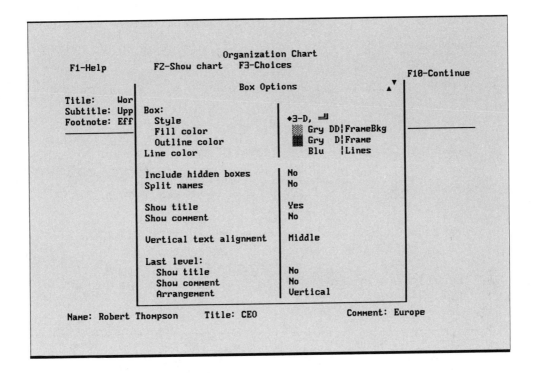

The following list explains each item on the Box Options menu.

Box:

Style	Select one of sixteen box frame styles or **None** to hide the frame.
Fill color	Select box interior color.
Outline color	Select frame line color.
Line color	Select box-connecting line color.
Include hidden boxes	Display and produce boxes hidden by the Organization menu Hide subordinates option.

Split names	Selects automatic splitting of long names, titles, and comments.
Show title	**Yes** displays all chart box titles and **No** hides them.
Show comment	**Yes** displays all chart box comments and **No** hides them.
Vertical text alignment	Places box text in top, middle, bottom, or spreads it evenly.
Last level:	
Show title	**Yes** displays last level box titles and **No** hides them.
Show comment	**Yes** displays last level box comments and **No** hides them.
Arrangement	Places boxes vertically without frames, or horizontally with frames.

◆ **3**   Select the options indicated by the highlighted areas on the following screen.

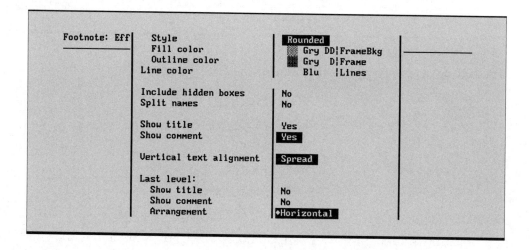

◆ **4**   Click on **F2-Show chart** or press F2 to view your chart with rounded boxes, comment text, and even text spread. The third level box, with no data entered, is displayed horizontally.

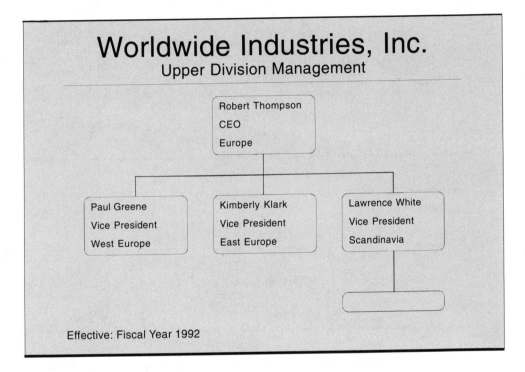

◆ **5**   Click the right mouse button or press ESC until you return to the worksheet.

Box Dimensions

Harvard Graphics can automatically size your chart boxes to suit the amount of text and number of boxes. You can also manually set the dimensions.

Let's use your organization chart to explore some Box Dimensions options. Your worksheet should be displayed.

◆ **1**   Select **F8-Options** to display the Options menu.

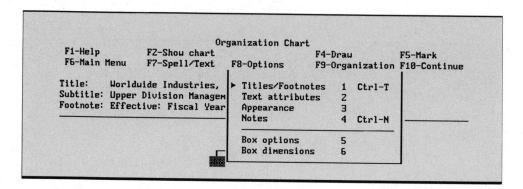

◆ **2**   Click on **Box dimensions** or press 6 to display the Box Dimensions pop-up menu.

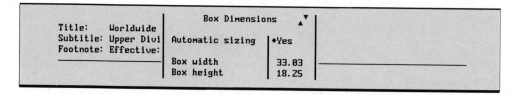

◆ **3**   Select **Automatic sizing** and then **No** to turn automatic sizing off.

◆ **4**   To manually change your dimensions, select **Box width** and type **25** and then select **Box height** and type **10** using the spacebar to delete unwanted numbers .

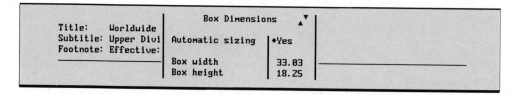

Note

Manual Box Sizing Features and Limitations   When sizing chart boxes, you can type any number between 0 and 400. If you attempt to create a box size too large for the worksheet, Harvard Graphics warns you and provides screen instructions to correct the situation.

✦ **5**   Select **F2-Show chart** to view your dimension changes.

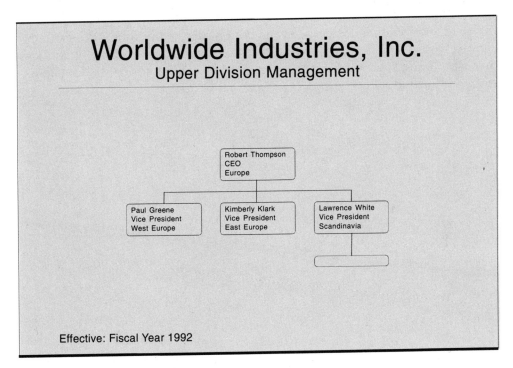

✦ **6**   Click the right mouse button or press ⒺⓈⒸ to return to your worksheet.

Take some time to experiment with various manual box dimension settings. To return to automatic sizing, set Automatic sizing to **Yes** on the Box Dimensions pop-up menu. Select **F2-Show chart** to view your changes.

✦ **7**   Click the right mouse button or press <kbd>ESC</kbd> until you return to the Main Menu.

✦ **8**   Select **Exit** to exit Harvard Graphics and a pop-up warning box tells you the current chart has not been saved. Click on **F10-Continue** or press <kbd>F10</kbd> to exit the program without saving your chart.

✦ Summary

In this chapter you taught yourself the basic skills for building masterful organization charts. Chapter 7 further advances your capabilities with valuable lessons on customizing Harvard Graphics, and working with templates and macros to suit your individual needs.

7

Customizing the Program to Suit Your Style

◆   In the first six chapters you learned to build and output masterful charts. Now it's time to teach yourself some advanced techniques to streamline your work.

Templates and macros can simplify many of the tasks you perform on a regular basis, and give your charts a uniform, professional look. This chapter also teaches you to customize Harvard Graphics so it performs more effectively on your system, and supports your individual work style.

- ◆ Working with Templates
- ◆ Working with Macros
- ◆ Customizing Your Program

✦ Working with Templates

If you are building a series of charts with similar data and options, such as titles, colors and frame styles, Harvard Graphics allows you to accelerate the process by creating your charts with a template.

Creating Templates

Creating a template is as easy as creating a new chart. You simply build in some basic options, with or without data, and save your new chart as a template. You can also retrieve existing charts and save them as templates.

Let's retrieve one of your charts, select a new palette and background drawing, and save it as a template. Start Harvard Graphics and display the main menu.

✦ **1**   Retrieve your CONSUMER.CH3 bullet chart and display the worksheet.

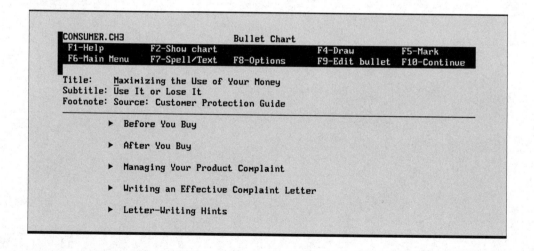

```
CONSUMER.CH3                    Bullet Chart
  F1-Help           F2-Show chart              F4-Draw         F5-Mark
  F6-Main Menu      F7-Spell/Text   F8-Options    F9-Edit bullet  F10-Continue

Title:    Maximizing the Use of Your Money
Subtitle: Use It or Lose It
Footnote: Source: Customer Protection Guide

    ▶  Before You Buy

    ▶  After You Buy

    ▶  Managing Your Product Complaint

    ▶  Writing an Effective Complaint Letter

    ▶  Letter-Writing Hints
```

✦ **2**   Select **F8-Options** and **Appearance** to display the Appearance
Options menu.

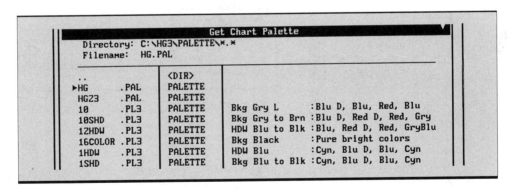

```
┌──────────────────────────────────────────────────────────────┐
│ ■■            Appearance Options            ▼│
│                                                              │
│  Chart orientation   ◆Landscape                              │
│  Chart proportions   A  (8.5 in. x 11 in.)                   │
│                                                              │
│  Chart palette:      C:\HG3\PALETTE\HG3.PL3                   │
│  Background drawing:                                         │
│                                                              │
│                    Titles        Bullet text      Footnotes  │
│                  ┌───────────┬───────────────┬─────────────┐ │
│  Text overflow   │Shrink-to-fit│Shrink-to-fit │Shrink-to-fit│ │
│                  │           │               │             │ │
│  Region frame style│Line      │None           │None         │ │
│  Frame outline color│  Blu ¦Lines│   Blu ¦Lines │   Blu ¦Lines│ │
│  Frame fill color │ Gry DD¦Frame│ Gry DD¦Frame │ Gry DD¦Frame│ │
│                  └───────────┴───────────────┴─────────────┘ │
└──────────────────────────────────────────────────────────────┘
```

✦ **3**   Click on **Chart palette** or place the diamond symbol and select **F3-Choices** to display a list of palettes.

```
┌──────────────────────────────────────────────────────────────┐
│ ■■              Get Chart Palette              ▼│
│     Directory:  C:\HG3\PALETTE\*.*                            │
│     Filename:   HG.PAL                                        │
│    ─────────────────────────────────────────────────────────  │
│      ..          <DIR>                                        │
│    ►HG      .PAL  PALETTE                                     │
│     HG23    .PAL  PALETTE                                     │
│     10      .PL3  PALETTE   Bkg Gry L      :Blu D, Blu, Red, Blu│
│     10SHD   .PL3  PALETTE   Bkg Gry to Brn :Blu D, Red D, Red, Gry│
│     12HDW   .PL3  PALETTE   HDW Blu to Blk :Blu, Red D, Red, GryBlu│
│     16COLOR .PL3  PALETTE   Bkg Black      :Pure bright colors│
│     1HDW    .PL3  PALETTE   HDW Blu        :Cyn, Blu D, Blu, Cyn│
│     1SHD    .PL3  PALETTE   Bkg Blu to Blk :Cyn, Blu D, Blu, Cyn│
└──────────────────────────────────────────────────────────────┘
```

◆ **4**   Select **16COLOR.PL3** to change the colors your monitor displays or the shades and patterns your output device produces. This palette change only affects this chart.

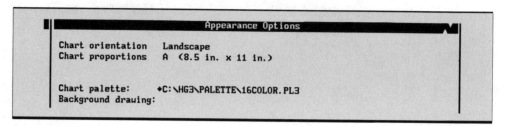

◆ **5**   Click on **Background drawing** or place the diamond symbol and select **F3-Choices** to display a list of background files.

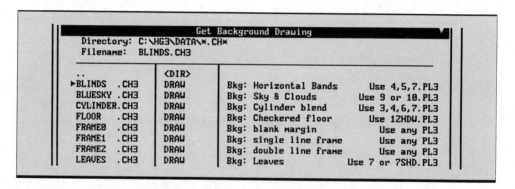

◆ **6**   Select **FRAME2.CH3** to place a frame around your chart data.

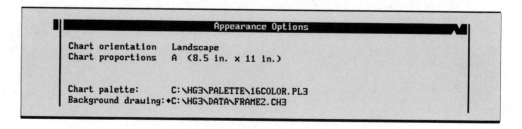

✦**7**   Click the right mouse button or press ⎋ to return to the worksheet.

✦**8**   Select **F2-Show chart** to display your chart with triangle bullets, the 16COLOR.PL3 palette, and a frame background. The bullets are also indented, a format option you selected when you first created this chart.

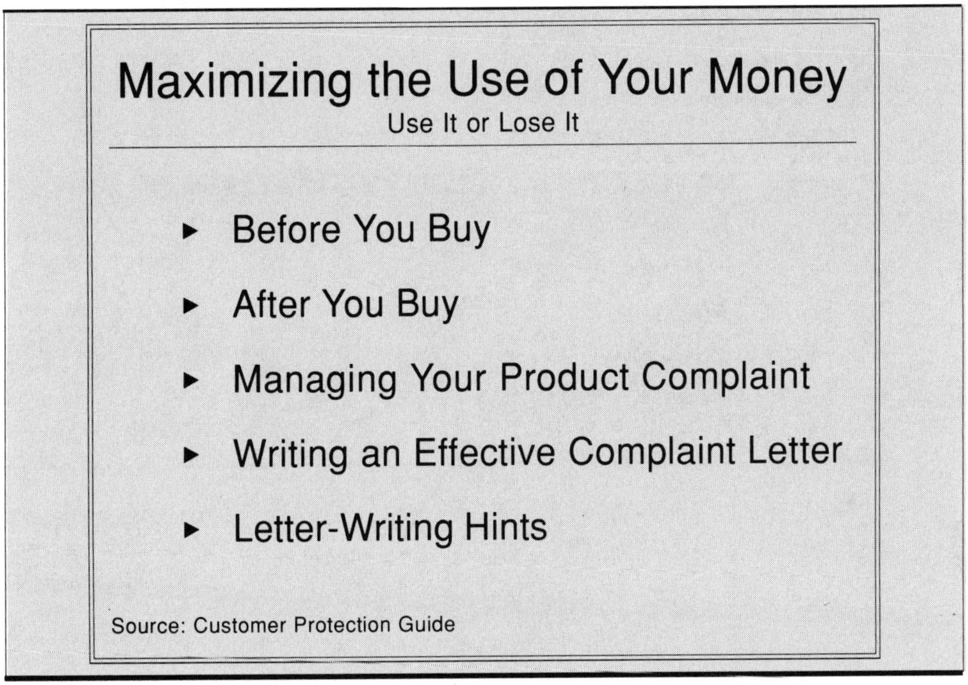

Maximizing the Use of Your Money
Use It or Lose It

▸ Before You Buy

▸ After You Buy

▸ Managing Your Product Complaint

▸ Writing an Effective Complaint Letter

▸ Letter-Writing Hints

Source: Customer Protection Guide

✦**9**   Return to your worksheet and select **F6-Main Menu** and then **File**.

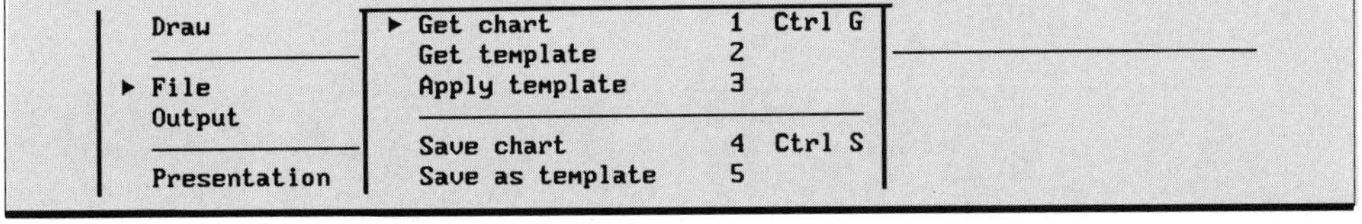

Draw	▸ Get chart	1	Ctrl G
	Get template	2	
▸ File	Apply template	3	
Output			
	Save chart	4	Ctrl S
Presentation	Save as template	5	

♦ **10** Click on **Save as template** or press ⑤ to display the Save Template menu.

Enter up to an
eight-character Filename
without extension.

Enter directory path
to store template.

Enter up to a
40-character description.

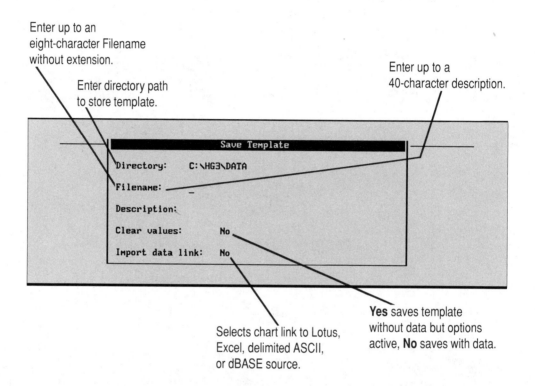

```
                        Save Template
Directory:      C:\HG3\DATA

Filename:       _

Description:

Clear values:       No

Import data link:   No
```

Selects chart link to Lotus,
Excel, delimited ASCII,
or dBASE source.

Yes saves template
without data but options
active, **No** saves with data.

♦ **11** Type the Filename **BULLET#1**.

```
Filename:       BULLET#1

Description:

Clear values:       No
```

⋆ **12** Select **Description** and type **Bullet chart with double-line frame**.

```
Filename:     BULLET#1

Description:  Bullet chart with double-line frame._

Clear values:    No
```

Note

Saving a Template With or Without Data   You can save your template with or without data. If you save a template with data, it's easier to observe the options you've selected. To keep a record of the data when you don't want it to appear in your template, save your worksheet as a chart first.

⋆ **13** Double-click on **Clear values** or place the diamond symbol and press F3. Select **Yes** and Click on **F10-Continue** or press F10. Harvard Graphics warns you your latest changes have not been saved. Select **F10-Confirm** to save your template without data.

Creating Charts with Templates

Let's create a new chart with the BULLET#1.TP3 template you created in the previous exercise.

⋆ **1** Select **F6-Main Menu** and **Create chart** and then select **Clear chart**. You are warned that your latest changes have not been saved. To clear the CONSUMER.CH3 worksheet from your screen, click on **F10-Confirm** or press F10.

✦ **2** From the Main Menu, select **File** to display the File menu.

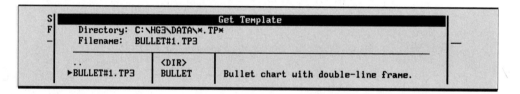

```
        Draw          ▶ Get chart         1   Ctrl G
                        Get template      2
      ▶ File            Apply template    3
        Output
                        Save chart        4   Ctrl S
        Presentation    Save as template  5
```

✦ **3** Click on **Get template** or press ⌊**2**⌋ to display a list of template filenames.

```
 S|                       Get Template
 F|   Directory:  C:\HG3\DATA\*.TP*
 —|   Filename:   BULLET#1.TP3                                        —
   |              <DIR>
   | ▶BULLET#1.TP3  BULLET    Bullet chart with double-line frame.
```

✦ **4** Click on or place the menu arrow to highlight **BULLET#1.TP3** and press ⌊F10⌋ or ⌊↵⌋ to display the worksheet. Select **F2-Show chart** to view your template. Only the frame appears.

✦ **5** Click the right mouse button or press ⌊ESC⌋ to return to your worksheet. Enter the data shown on the following screen.

```
 ■
 Title:    Atlas Air Conditioning Tips
 Subtitle: A Guide to Saving Energy
 Footnote: See Atlas representative for estimate.

        ▶  Clean or replace dirty filters

        ▶  Keep windows and doors closed

        ▶  Shade windows to block sun's heat

        ▶  Insure ducting is properly insulated_
```

✦ **6**   Select **F2-Show chart** to view your data formatted by the template.

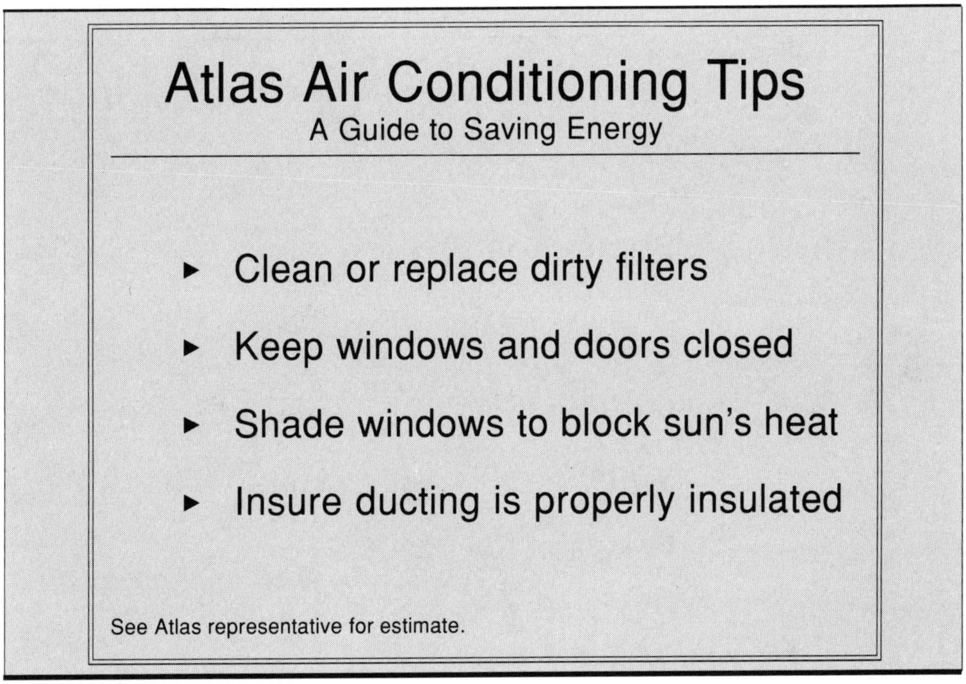

Atlas Air Conditioning Tips
A Guide to Saving Energy

- ▶ Clean or replace dirty filters

- ▶ Keep windows and doors closed

- ▶ Shade windows to block sun's heat

- ▶ Insure ducting is properly insulated

See Atlas representative for estimate.

✦ **7**   Click the right mouse button or press ⎋ to return to your worksheet.

Applying Templates to Charts

Existing charts can be modified with templates. Current chart data is not changed, but template options replace existing chart options.

✦ **1**   Select **F6-Main Menu** and **Create chart** and then **Clear chart** to clear your chart from the previous exercise.

✦ **2**   Click on **File** and **Get chart** or press ⎣4⎦ and ⎣1⎦ to display a list of filenames. Select **CONSUMER.CH3** to view your original chart.

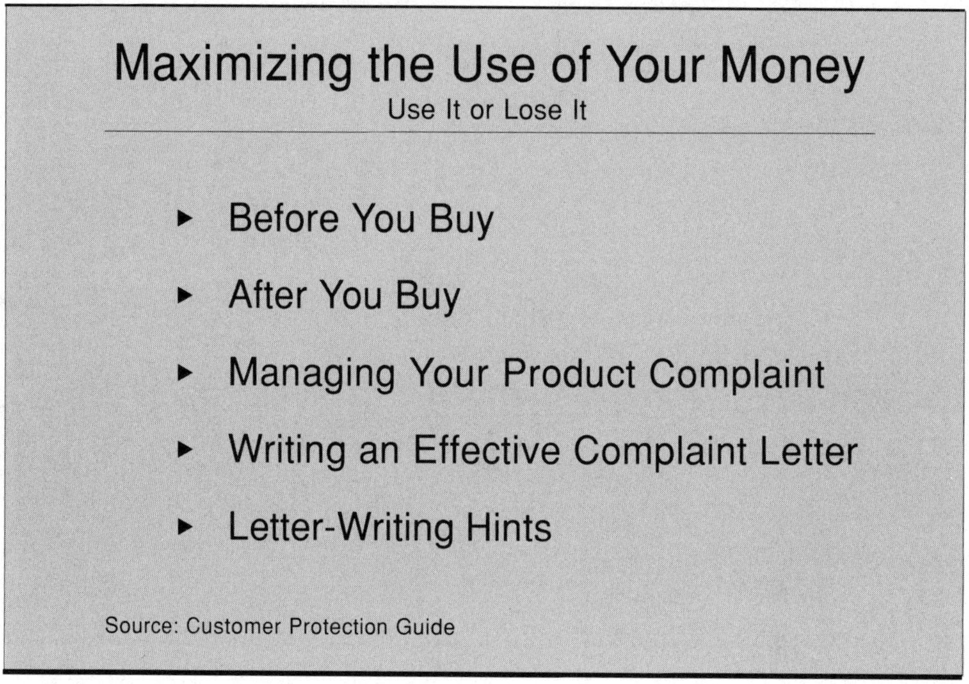

Maximizing the Use of Your Money
Use It or Lose It

- ▶ Before You Buy

- ▶ After You Buy

- ▶ Managing Your Product Complaint

- ▶ Writing an Effective Complaint Letter

- ▶ Letter-Writing Hints

Source: Customer Protection Guide

✦ **3**   Return to your worksheet and select **F6-Main Menu** and **File** to display the File menu.

✦ **4**   Click on **Apply template** or press ⎣3⎦ to display the template list. Select **BULLET#1**.

✦ **5**   Click on **F2-Show chart** or press ⎣F2⎦ to view your chart with the template options.

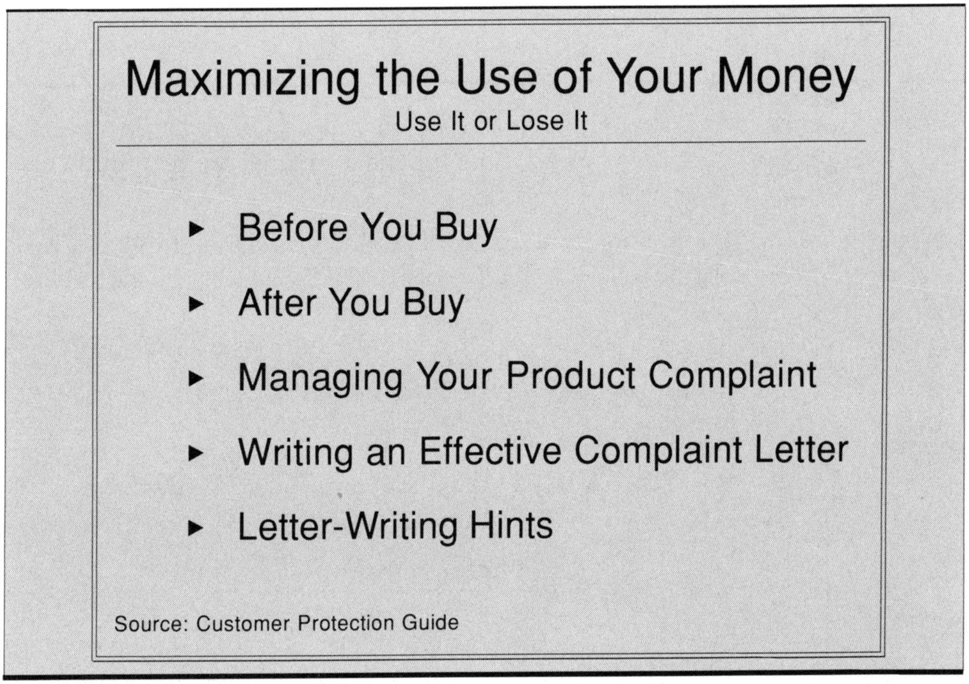

Maximizing the Use of Your Money
Use It or Lose It

- ▶ Before You Buy

- ▶ After You Buy

- ▶ Managing Your Product Complaint

- ▶ Writing an Effective Complaint Letter

- ▶ Letter-Writing Hints

Source: Customer Protection Guide

✦ **6**   Click the right mouse button or press ⎋ to return to your worksheet.

Note

Templates and Compatible Charts   Templates can only be applied to compatible charts. For example, a template created from one type of XY chart can be applied to any other XY chart, but not to text or pie charts.

✦ Working with Macros

A macro is an automated sequence of keystrokes and menu options which is activated by pressing two macro keys or typing a short macro name. Macros are an excellent way to streamline and accelerate routine procedures.

Recording

Macro sequences are recorded in a macro file and assigned a name. When you press the appropriate macro keys or type the macro name, the recorded sequence is performed.

Let's record a macro to print a chart. The methods you learn in this exercise can be applied to any routine task. The CONSUMER.CH3 worksheet should be displayed on your screen.

✦ **1**   Click on **F6-Main Menu** or press F6 to display the Main Menu.

```
 F6-Main Menu   F7-Spell/Text   F8-Options      F9-Edit bullet  F10-Continue

    ▶ Create chart    1    of Your Money
      Edit chart      2
      Draw            3    rotection Guide

      File            4
      Output          5

      Presentation    6
                           oduct Complaint
      Macros          7
      Setup           8    tive Complaint Letter
```

✦ **2**   Click on **Macros** or press 7 to display the Macros pop-up menu.

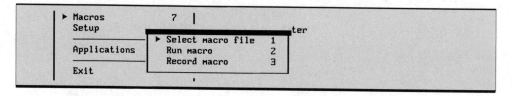

```
    ▶ Macros          7  |
      Setup                              ter
                        ▶ Select macro file   1
      Applications        Run macro            2
                          Record macro         3
      Exit
```

✦ **3**   Click on **Record macro** or press ③ to display the Start Recording menu.

Enter directory path where macro file stored.

Enter up to an eight-character macro Filename without extension. Up to 50 macros in each file.

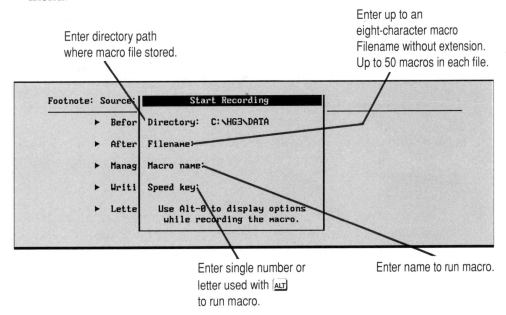

Enter single number or letter used with ⌐ALT⌐ to run macro.

Enter name to run macro.

✦ **4**   Type the Filename, Macro name, and Speed key shown on the following screen.

```
    ▶ Befor  Directory:  C:\HG3\DATA

    ▶ After  Filename:   MACRO#1

    ▶ Manag  Macro name: PRINT

    ▶ Writi  Speed key:  P
```

♦ **5**   Click on **F10-Continue** or press 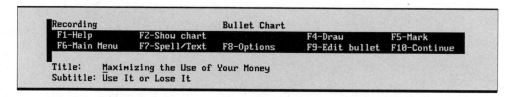 to return to your worksheet and begin the macro recording process.

```
Recording                      Bullet Chart
  F1-Help        F2-Show chart                F4-Draw       F5-Mark
  F6-Main Menu   F7-Spell/Text  F8-Options    F9-Edit bullet F10-Continue

  Title:    Maximizing the Use of Your Money
  Subtitle: Use It or Lose It
```

The current status of your recording session is displayed in the upper left corner of your screen. While you are in the Recording mode, every keystroke is recorded in your macro.

♦ **6**   To record a macro for printing a chart from a worksheet, press F6 to display the Main Menu, press 5 to display the Output menu, and press 1, or the number for your output device, to display the Output to Printer menu.

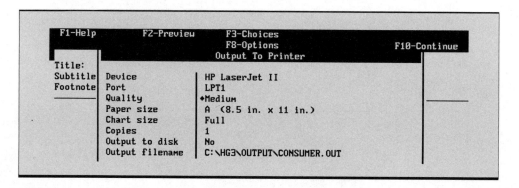

```
  F1-Help        F2-Preview     F3-Choices
                                F8-Options                 F10-Continue
                                Output To Printer
  Title:
  Subtitle  Device           HP LaserJet II
  Footnote  Port             LPT1
            Quality          ♦Medium
            Paper size       A  (8.5 in. x 11 in.)
            Chart size       Full
            Copies           1
            Output to disk   No
            Output filename  C:\HG3\OUTPUT\CONSUMER.OUT
```

♦ **7**   Press [ALT][0] (zero) to display the Recording Options menu.

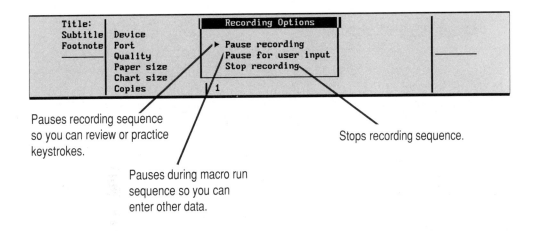

Pauses recording sequence so you can review or practice keystrokes.

Pauses during macro run sequence so you can enter other data.

Stops recording sequence.

Note

Pause Recording and Keystroke Limitations   To pause the recording process and practice or review your keystrokes, select **Pause recording**. The pause message is displayed in the upper left corner of your screen. To resume recording, press [ALT] [O] (zero). Select menu items by pressing their speed keys or menu numbers only. Using a mouse or the menu arrow, diamond symbol and [↵] method can cause your macro to improperly execute. All keystrokes are acceptable except those which exit Harvard Graphics, or load, run, or record other macros.

✦ **8**   Select **Stop recording** and press [ESC] to complete your PRINT macro and return to the worksheet.

When you run your macro, it automatically stops at the Output to Printer menu. This allows you to make selections such as paper size and number of copies before you begin printing.

✦ **9**   To prepare for the next exercise, click on **F6-Main Menu** and **Exit** or press [F6] and [E] to exit Harvard Graphics. Do not save the latest changes.

Loading and Running

To run your macro, the macro file must be loaded into Random Access Memory (RAM). The macro file stays in RAM until you exit Harvard Graphics. You can load up to 50 macros at a time.

♦ **1**   Start Harvard Graphics and retrieve the CONSUMER.CH3 worksheet.

♦ **2**   To load your macro file, select **F6-Main Menu** and **Macros** to display the Macro pop-up menu.

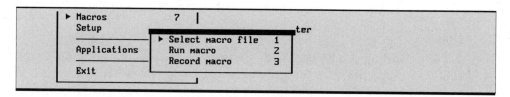

♦ **3**   Click on **Select macro file** or press ⌊**1**⌋ to display the Load Macros menu.

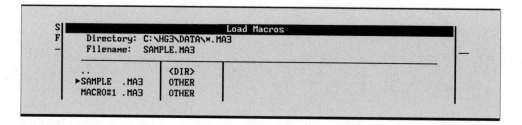

♦ **4**   Click on **MACRO#1** or place the menu arrow and press ⌷ to load the file into memory and return to your worksheet.

You can now run any macro stored in the MACRO#1 file. The fastest way to run a macro is to press ⒜ and the designated macro speed key. This method lets you run the macro from anywhere in the program. The PRINT macro you created in the previous exercise is the only macro presently available.

Let's print the CONSUMER.CH3 chart using the PRINT macro. Turn your printer on and display the CONSUMER worksheet.

◆ **5**   Press your designated speed keys ⒜⒫ to run the PRINT macro and display the Output to Printer menu.

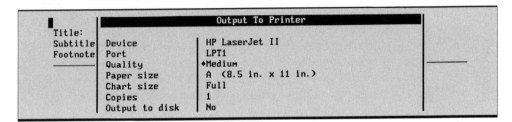

◆ **6**   Select the print options you want and then **F10-Continue** to begin printing.

Note

Running Macros by Name   The alternate way to run your macro is to select it by name. This method is slower, but it allows you to confirm the macro's function. The PRINT macro prints your charts.

Display the CONSUMER worksheet on your screen.

◆ **7**   Select **F6-Main Menu** and **Macros** to display the Macros pop-up menu.

✦ **8**   Select **Run macro** to display the Run Macro menu.

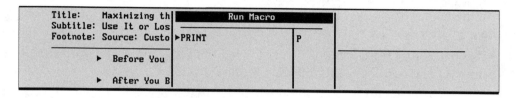

Note

Macro Playback Options   While your macro is running, you can press
ALT O (zero) to interrupt the process and display the Playback Options menu.
This allows you to select **Step playback** and run your macro one step at a time
by pressing any key on your keyboard. You can also select **Pause playback**
and **Stop playback**. If you select the Pause option, press ALT O (zero) to display
the Pause Options menu and then select either **Continue playback** or **Step
playback** to resume running your macro.

✦ **9**   Click on **PRINT** or place the menu arrow and press ⏎ to run your
macro and display the Output to Printer menu.

✦ **10**   After you have selected your print options, click on **F10-Continue** or
press F10 to begin printing.

Here are some helpful hints for creating and running error-free macros.

✦ Limit your files to 50 macros.

✦ Save your chart before you run a macro.

✦ Play back your macro from the same place you recorded it.

✦ Start recording your macro at the Main Menu with **Create chart** highlighted. Press ESC five to six times to make sure the macro returns to the
Main Menu before executing important keystrokes.

✦ Macros you create for some worksheets may not work with other worksheets.

✦ Customizing Your Program

The Setup selection on the Main Menu allows you to customize Harvard Graphics to suit your individual needs. You used some of the Setup menu options to configure your output device. This section introduces the remaining ones.

Program Defaults

The standard default settings are activated when you start Harvard Graphics. If you use alternative settings on a regular basis, you may want to establish them as the defaults.

Display the Main Menu on your screen.

✦ **1** Click on **Setup** or press ⑧ to display the Setup menu.

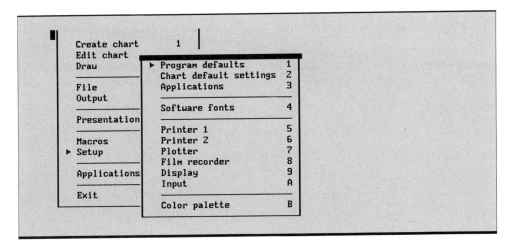

✦ **2**   Click on **Program defaults** or press ⬚1⬚ to display the Program
Defaults menu.

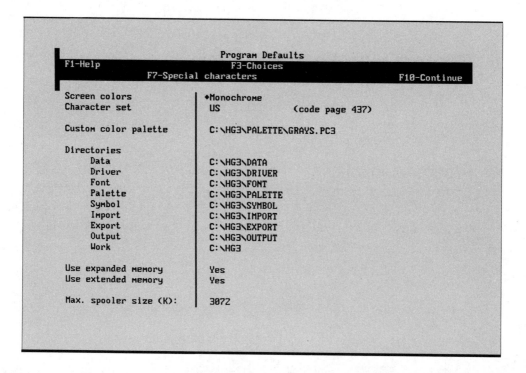

The following list explains each option. When you select an option, click on **F3-Choices** or press ⬚F3⬚ to display a pop-up menu of further choices.

Screen colors	Select color Scheme 1, Scheme 2, Scheme 3, or Monochrome palettes.
Character set	Select country name for creating charts in other languages.
Custom color palette	Enter a custom palette name or select one from the pop-up menu.
Directories	Select the path and enter the name for file directories.

Use expanded/ extended memory	Configure Harvard Graphics for these memory types.
Max. spooler size (K)	Enter the output spooler disk storage capacity in kilobytes. The default setting is 3072K.

✦ **3** Enter your changes and press F10 to return to the Setup menu.

Chart Defaults

These default options only affect your charts.

✦ **1** From the Setup menu, click on **Chart default settings** or press 2 to display the Chart Defaults Settings menu.

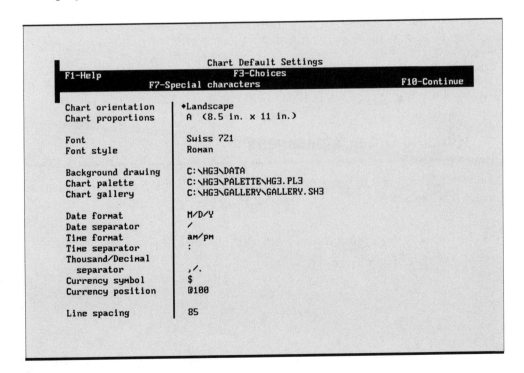

```
                          Chart Default Settings
 F1-Help                      F3-Choices
                     F7-Special characters                    F10-Continue

   Chart orientation      ◆Landscape
   Chart proportions       A  (8.5 in. x 11 in.)

   Font                    Swiss 721
   Font style              Roman

   Background drawing      C:\HG3\DATA
   Chart palette           C:\HG3\PALETTE\HG3.PL3
   Chart gallery           C:\HG3\GALLERY\GALLERY.SH3

   Date format             M/D/Y
   Date separator          /
   Time format             am/pm
   Time separator          :
   Thousand/Decimal
     separator             ,/.
   Currency symbol         $
   Currency position       @100

   Line spacing            85
```

The following list explains each option. When you select an option, select **F3-Choices** to display a pop-up menu of further choices.

Chart orientation	Select **Landscape** or **Portrait**.
Chart proportions	Select a proportion equal to or smaller than the size you plan to output.
Font/Font style	Select the default font and style for all charts.
Background drawing	Select the default background drawing for all charts.
Chart palette	Select the default color palette for all charts.
Chart gallery	Select the default Screen show or alternative gallery file.

Refer to Chapter 3 for information on the international formats for dates, times, thousand/decimal separators, currency, and line spacing options.

⋆ **2**   Enter any changes you want to make and press F10 to return to the Setup menu.

Running Other Applications

The Application option lets you set up and run additional programs, such as Lotus 1-2-3 and WordPerfect, without exiting Harvard Graphics.

⋆ **1**   From the Setup menu, click on **Applications** or press ③ to display the Applications menu.

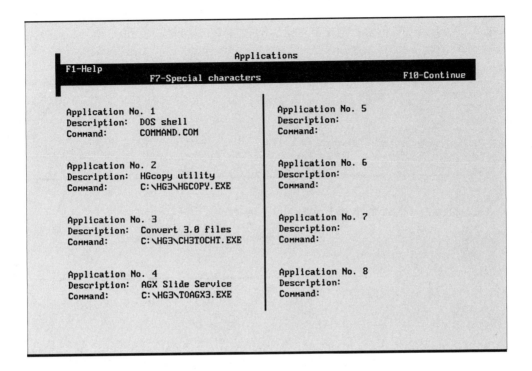

The following default applications are set up and ready to run.

DOS shell	Shells out to DOS so you can perform DOS functions.
HGcopy utility	Copies Harvard Graphics files to other directories.
Convert 3.0 files	Converts 3.0 files to 2.x files.
AGX Slide Service	Creates ToAGX3 slides.

Refer to your Harvard Graphics documentation for detailed instructions on running these applications.

♦ **2**   To set up WordPerfect so it runs within Harvard Graphics, move your cursor to Application No. 5 Description: and type **WordPerfect**. At Command: type **C:\WP51\WP.EXE** or your WordPerfect directory.

```
 ▌

       Application No. 1                    Application No. 5
       Description:   DOS shell             Description:   Wordperfect
       Command:       COMMAND.COM           Command:       C:\WP51\WP.EXE_
```

♦ **3**   Press F10 to return to the Setup menu.

Working with Fonts

Hardware fonts are selected when you set up your output device. Software fonts are selected when you install Harvard Graphics.

Software Fonts   Software fonts can be active, idle, or assigned to the system. Active fonts use valuable RAM, but are immediately available for use. Active fonts appear on the Font Name and Font Styles pop-ups within the Text Attributes menu. Idle fonts are installed on your disk, but are not available for immediate use.

Refer to Chapter 3 for information on changing fonts and font styles with F8-Options and Text attributes.

Note

Freeing Up RAM with Idle Fonts   Active fonts can use up large portions of Random Access Memory (RAM) and may restrict the quantity of data and options you can enter into your charts. Change the fonts you are not planning to use from Active to Idle. This frees up RAM for other uses.

Let's change a font from active to idle and back again. The Setup menu should be displayed on your screen.

✦ **1**   Click on **Software fonts** or press ④ to display a list of Harvard Graphics software fonts.

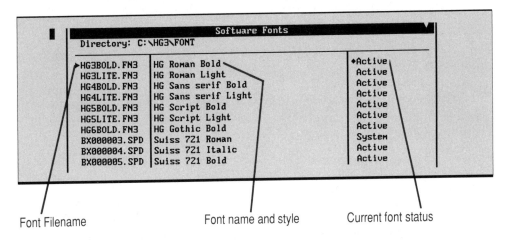

Font Filename   Font name and style   Current font status

✦ **2**   Place the menu arrow on **HG Roman Bold** and click on **F3-Choices** or press F3 to display the Status pop-up menu.

✦ **3**   Select **Idle** to make the font inactive.

```
┌─┬────────────────────────Software Fonts────────────────────▼──┐
│ │ Directory:  C:\HG3\FONT                                      │
│ │                                                              │
│ │ ►HG3BOLD.FN3 │ HG Roman Bold        │ ♦Idle                 │
│ │  HG3LITE.FN3 │ HG Roman Light       │  Active               │
│ │  HG4BOLD.FN3 │ HG Sans serif Bold   │  Active               │
│ │  HG4LITE.FN3 │ HG Sans serif Light  │  Active               │
└─┴──────────────────────────────────────────────────────────────┘
```

✦ **4**   Repeat steps 2 and 3 and select **Active** to return HG Roman Bold to active status.

The System Font   The system font provides substitute characters for active fonts which lack those characters. There can be only one system font at a time. Harvard Graphics recommends Swiss 721 or Dutch 801.

Let's select a new system font. The Software Fonts menu should be displayed.

✦ **5**   Press ⌜PG DN⌝ or ⌜PG UP⌝ to place the menu arrow on **Dutch 801 Roman**.

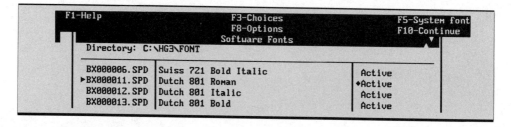

```
┌─ F1-Help ──────────────F3-Choices───────────────F5-System font ┐
│                         F8-Options                 F10-Continue │
│                       Software Fonts              ▼             │
│    Directory:  C:\HG3\FONT                                      │
│                                                                 │
│     BX000006.SPD │ Swiss 721 Bold Italic │ Active              │
│    ►BX000011.SPD │ Dutch 801 Roman       │ ♦Active             │
│     BX000012.SPD │ Dutch 801 Italic      │ Active              │
│     BX000013.SPD │ Dutch 801 Bold        │ Active              │
└─────────────────────────────────────────────────────────────────┘
```

✦ **6**   Click on **F5-System font** or press ⌜F5⌝ to change the status to System. The original system font changes to Active.

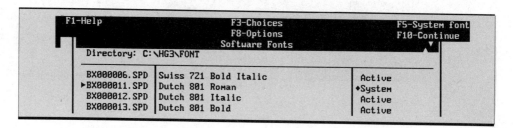

```
┌─ F1-Help ──────────────F3-Choices───────────────F5-System font ┐
│                         F8-Options                 F10-Continue │
│                       Software Fonts              ▼             │
│    Directory:  C:\HG3\FONT                                      │
│                                                                 │
│     BX000006.SPD │ Swiss 721 Bold Italic │ Active              │
│    ►BX000011.SPD │ Dutch 801 Roman       │ ♦System             │
│     BX000012.SPD │ Dutch 801 Italic      │ Active              │
│     BX000013.SPD │ Dutch 801 Bold        │ Active              │
└─────────────────────────────────────────────────────────────────┘
```

Note

System Font Limitations   Harvard Graphics refuses to let you select a system font without bullet characters. A more complete font is automatically selected.

. **7**   Click on **F10-Continue** or press 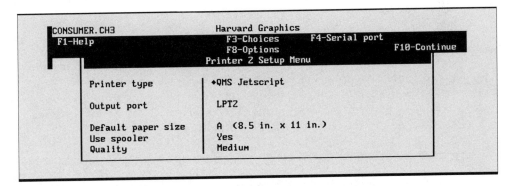 to install your new system font and return to the Setup menu.

Hardware Fonts   Hardware fonts are installed with your output device drivers when you set up your printer or film recorder. Plotters do not have hardware fonts. When you select one of these fonts it appears on your printer or film recorder output, but it cannot be displayed on your screen. Harvard Graphics substitutes the most closely matched software font. Your output text may be slightly different than the text you see displayed on your screen.

Let's select some hardware fonts. The Setup menu should be displayed.

. **8**   Select the output device which contains your hardware fonts. In the following example, Printer 2 is selected and set up for a QMS Jetscript printer.

```
CONSUMER.CH3              Harvard Graphics
 F1-Help                     F3-Choices      F4-Serial port
                             F8-Options                    F10-Continue
                          Printer 2 Setup Menu


      Printer type          ◆QMS Jetscript

      Output port           LPT2

      Default paper size    A (8.5 in. x 11 in.)
      Use spooler           Yes
      Quality               Medium
```

. **9**   Select **F8-Options** to display the Printer Options menu.

```
 F1-Help                          F3-Choices
                                                      F10-Continue
                          Printer 2 Setup Menu
                            Printer Options
  Printer t
               Actual size                   ◆No
  Output po    Pause between pages            No
               Reverse black and white       Yes
  Default p    Black text                     Yes
  Use spool    Draw background color          No
  Quality      Use hardware fonts only        Yes
              ✕Special option                 None
               ✕ = not available
```

The QMS Jetscript printer default is set at internal hardware fonts. If hardware fonts are not available for your output device, an asterisk appears at the **Use hardware fonts only** option.

✦ **10** To turn hardware fonts printing on or off, double-click on **Use hardware fonts only** or place the diamond symbol and press F3. Select **No** to turn them off and **Yes** to turn them back on.

✦ **11** Click on **F10-Continue** twice or press F10 twice to configure your program selection and return to the Setup menu.

Note

Viewing Hardware Fonts   To view the available hardware fonts for your printer or film recorder, display a chart worksheet and select **F8-Options** and **Text attributes** to display the Text Attributes menu. Select **Font name** and press F3. A list of font names appears, and available hardware fonts are preceded by the symbols: O for Printer 1; • for Printer 2; Δ for Film Recorder. Select the font for the output device you are using.

✦ **12** Click the right mouse button or press ESC to return to the Main Menu and click on **Exit** to exit Harvard Graphics.

✦ Summary

In this chapter you learned to customize Harvard Graphics and work with some of its more advanced features. Chapter 8 teaches you to build your charts into masterful presentations.

8

Building Masterful Presentations

◆ A presentation is a group of up to 175 related charts stored in a single presentation file. Harvard Graphics lets you add, remove, edit, reorganize, and enhance single charts or groups of charts within each presentation file. You can also automatically display the charts in your presentation with the ScreenShow feature.

◆ Creating Presentations

◆ Editing Your Presentation

◆ Enhancing Your Presentation

◆ Creating ScreenShows

✦ Creating Presentations

A presentation is created by adding chart files to a presentation list and saving it as a presentation file. This section teaches you to create a presentation file with the title, bullet, table, and XY charts you created earlier in this book.

Adding Files

You can add single files or groups of up to 50 files to your presentation list. Start Harvard Graphics and display the Main Menu.

✦ **1** Click on **Presentation** or press ⑥ to display the Presentation pop-up menu.

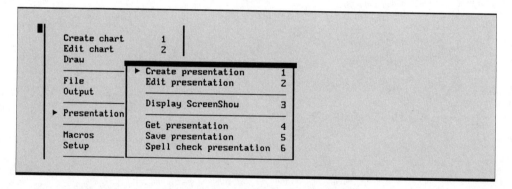

✦ **2** Click on **Create presentation** or press ⑴ to display the Edit Presentation worksheet.

```
                           Edit Presentation
 F1-Help            F2-Preview                F4-Effects      F5-Mark block
 F6-Main Menu       F7-Add/Edit    F8-Options  F9-HyperShow   F10-Continue

  #  │  Filename  │  Type  │         Description/Directory

  ►                  DRAW     Background drawing for presentation

  1
  2
  3
  4
  5
```

✦ **3**   Click on **F7-Add/Edit** or press [F7] to display the Add/Edit menu.

```
 F1-Help            F2-Preview                F4-Effects      F5-Mark block
 F6-Main Menu       F7-Add/Edit    F8-Options  F9-HyperShow   F10-Continue

  #  │  Filename │ ► Add file        1  Ctrl-Ins  │ ectory
                    Remove file      2  Ctrl-Del
  ►                 Duplicate file   3             │ entation

  1                 Move file up     4  Ctrl-↑
  2                 Move file down   5  Ctrl-↓
  3                 Jump to file     6  Ctrl-J
  4
  5                 Edit chart data  7  Ctrl-E
  6                 Edit notes       8  Ctrl-N
  7                 Edit descriptions 9
  8
  9                 Add blank chart  A
 10                 Add blank template B
 11
```

✦ **4**   Click on **Add file** or press [1] to display a list of files in the current directory. You can also press the speed keys [CTRL] [INS] from anywhere in the
program. Type a new directory name if your files are stored elsewhere.

```
┌─┬─────────────────────────────────────────────────────────────────┬─┐
│ ─ │        Add File (Press F5 to mark multiple files)          ▼ │ ─ │
│ ► │   Directory: C:\HG3\DATA\*.*                                  │   │
│ ─ │   Filename:  BULLET#1.TP3                                    │ ─ │
│   │                                                              │   │
│   │            .  .          <DIR>                               │   │
│   │          ►BULLET#1.TP3   BULLET    Bullet chart with double-line frame. │
│   │           AUTOSALE.CH3   XY        Motor Vehicle Factory Sales │
│   │           BESTSALE.CH3   TITLE     Regional Sales Conference  │
│   │           BLINDS  .CH3   DRAW      Bkg: Horizontal Bands    Use 4,5,7.PL3 │
└───┴─────────────────────────────────────────────────────────────────┴───┘
```

✦ **5**   Click on **AUTOSALE.CH3** or move the menu arrow to
AUTOSALE.CH3 and press ↵ to add the file to your Edit
Presentation worksheet.

#	Filename	Type	Description/Directory
		DRAW	Background drawing for presentation
►1	AUTOSALE.CH3	XY	Motor Vehicle Factory Sales
2			

✦ **6**   Select **F7-Add/Edit** and **Add file** to display the file list.

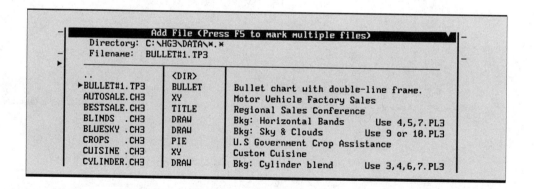

```
┌─┬─────────────────────────────────────────────────────────────────┬─┐
│ ─ │        Add File (Press F5 to mark multiple files)          ▼ │ ─ │
│   │   Directory: C:\HG3\DATA\*.*                                  │   │
│ ─ │   Filename:  BULLET#1.TP3                                    │ ─ │
│ ► │                                                              │   │
│   │            .  .          <DIR>                               │   │
│   │          ►BULLET#1.TP3   BULLET    Bullet chart with double-line frame. │
│   │           AUTOSALE.CH3   XY        Motor Vehicle Factory Sales │
│   │           BESTSALE.CH3   TITLE     Regional Sales Conference  │
│   │           BLINDS  .CH3   DRAW      Bkg: Horizontal Bands    Use 4,5,7.PL3 │
│   │           BLUESKY .CH3   DRAW      Bkg: Sky & Clouds    Use 9 or 10.PL3 │
│   │           CROPS   .CH3   PIE       U.S Government Crop Assistance │
│   │           CUISINE .CH3   XY        Custom Cuisine            │
│   │           CYLINDER.CH3   DRAW      Bkg: Cylinder blend    Use 3,4,6,7.PL3 │
└───┴─────────────────────────────────────────────────────────────────┴───┘
```

✦**7**   Click on **F8-Sort files** or press F8 to sort your files alphabetically.

✦**8**   Move the menu arrow to BESTSALE.CH3, CONSUMER.CH3, CROPS.CH3, and CUISINE.CH3, clicking **F5-Mark file** or pressing F5 after each selection. The marked files are highlighted.

```
               Add File (Press F5 to mark multiple files)          ▼
    Directory: C:\HG3\DATA\*.*
    Filename:  CUISINE.CH3
  ►
    ..            <DIR>
    AUTOSALE.CH3   XY        Motor Vehicle Factory Sales
    BESTSALE.CH3   TITLE     Regional Sales Conference
    BLINDS  .CH3   DRAW      Bkg: Horizontal Bands      Use 4,5,7.PL3
    BLUESKY .CH3   DRAW      Bkg: Sky & Clouds          Use 9 or 10.PL3
    BULLET#1.TP3   BULLET    Bullet chart with double-line frame.
    CONSUMER.CH3   BULLET    Maximizing the Use of Your Money
    CROPS   .CH3   PIE       U.S Government Crop Assistance
   ►CUISINE .CH3   XY        Custom Cuisine
```

Harvard Graphics automatically adds the filename indicated by the menu arrow to your presentation list. To keep an unmarked filename from being added, place the menu arrow next to a marked filename. To unmark a filename, place the menu arrow and select **F5-Mark file**.

✦**9**   Select **F10-Continue** to add the marked filenames to your Edit Presentation worksheet.

```
                          Edit Presentation
  F1-Help         F2-Preview              F4-Effects       F5-Mark block
  F6-Main Menu    F7-Add/Edit    F8-Options    F9-HyperShow  F10-Continue

   #    Filename     Type         Description/Directory

                     DRAW      Background drawing for presentation

   1    AUTOSALE.CH3 XY        Motor Vehicle Factory Sales
  ►2    BESTSALE.CH3 TITLE     Regional Sales Conference
   3    CONSUMER.CH3 BULLET    Maximizing the Use of Your Money
   4    CROPS   .CH3 PIE       U.S Government Crop Assistance
   5    CUISINE .CH3 XY        Custom Cuisine
```

Note

Viewing File Directories and Printing Your Presentation List   Your presentation files can be stored in several different directories. The View description/directory option lets you display the directory for every file in the presentation list. Select **F7-Add/Edit** and **Edit descriptions** to display the Edit Descriptions pop-up menu and click on **View description/directory** or press 3 to display the directory for each file on your list. To print your presentation list, display the Main Menu and select **Output**, **Presentation list** and **Printer 1** or **Printer 2** and then press F10. Some printers will not support this option.

Refer to your Harvard Graphics documentation for additional information on printer compatibility.

Saving, Retrieving and Previewing

The methods for saving, retrieving and previewing your presentations are similar to those you taught yourself for charts. Let's begin by displaying your Edit Presentation worksheet.

✦ **1**   Select **F6-Main Menu** and **Presentation** to display the Presentation pop-up menu.

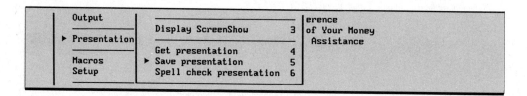

◆ **2**   Click on **Save presentation** or press ⑤ to display the Save Presentation pop-up menu and type the filename and description, up to 40
characters, as shown on the following screen. Harvard Graphics
automatically assigns the extension .SH3.

◆ **3**   Select **F10-Continue** to save the presentation with the filename
SHOW.SH3 and return to your worksheet.

◆ **4**   Click the right mouse button or press ⟨ESC⟩ to return to the Main Menu.

◆ **5**   To retrieve your presentation, select **Presentation** and click on **Get
presentation** or press ④ to display the Get Presentation file list
which shows all the .SH3 filenames.

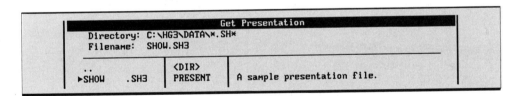

◆ **6**   Click on **SHOW.SH3** or place the menu arrow and press ꜰ10 or ↵ to display your Edit Presentation worksheet.

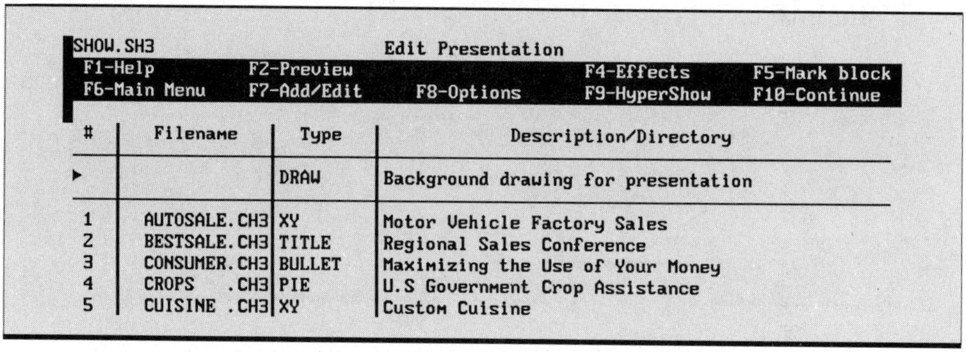

```
SHOW.SH3                        Edit Presentation
  F1-Help          F2-Preview                    F4-Effects        F5-Mark block
  F6-Main Menu     F7-Add/Edit     F8-Options     F9-HyperShow     F10-Continue

  #  │  Filename   │ Type │          Description/Directory
 ────┼─────────────┼──────┼─────────────────────────────────────────────
  ►  │             │ DRAW │ Background drawing for presentation
     │             │      │
  1  │ AUTOSALE.CH3│ XY   │ Motor Vehicle Factory Sales
  2  │ BESTSALE.CH3│ TITLE│ Regional Sales Conference
  3  │ CONSUMER.CH3│ BULLET│ Maximizing the Use of Your Money
  4  │ CROPS   .CH3│ PIE  │ U.S Government Crop Assistance
  5  │ CUISINE .CH3│ XY   │ Custom Cuisine
```

Note

Locating Presentation Files   When you retrieve a presentation, Harvard Graphics looks on your disk for each file on the presentation list. If a file is not found, the File Not Found pop-up menu appears and offers you three options. You can select an alternative file, continue without the file, or quit the operation.

◆ **7**   To preview your presentation, place the menu arrow on the first chart you want to preview and select **F2-Preview**. Click the right mouse button or press any key to preview the next chart on your list.

◆ Editing Your Presentation

Harvard Graphics lets you duplicate your presentation files, change their order, jump from one file to another, and remove files. Let's edit your SHOW.SH3 presentation list.

Duplicating and Removing Files

You can easily duplicate or remove single files or groups of files in your presentation. Display your Edit Presentation worksheet.

♦ **1** To duplicate a single file, click on **CROPS.CH3** or place the menu arrow on CROPS.CH3 and then click on **F7-Add/Edit** or press ⏎ to display the Add/Edit menu.

```
 F1-Help          F2-Preview                        F4-Effects      F5-Mark block
 F6-Main Menu     F7-Add/Edit      F8-Options        F9-HyperShow    F10-Continue

    #      Filename  ▶ Add file          1  Ctrl-Ins   ectory
                       Remove file       2  Ctrl-Del
                       Duplicate file    3             entation
```

♦ **2** Click on **Duplicate file** or press ③ to display a second copy of CROPS.CH3 on your worksheet.

```
    1      AUTOSALE.CH3 XY       Motor Vehicle Factory Sales
    2      BESTSALE.CH3 TITLE    Regional Sales Conference
    3      CONSUMER.CH3 BULLET   Maximizing the Use of Your Money
    4      CROPS   .CH3 PIE      U.S Government Crop Assistance
   ▶5      CROPS   .CH3 PIE      U.S Government Crop Assistance
    6      CUISINE .CH3 XY       Custom Cuisine
```

♦ **3** To duplicate a group of files, place the menu arrow on the first file, in this case the new CROPS file at row 5, click on **F5-Mark block** or press ⑤ to mark the file, and then press ⬇ to move the menu arrow to CUISINE.CH3 which is automatically marked.

```
    1      AUTOSALE.CH3 XY       Motor Vehicle Factory Sales
    2      BESTSALE.CH3 TITLE    Regional Sales Conference
    3      CONSUMER.CH3 BULLET   Maximizing the Use of Your Money
    4      CROPS   .CH3 PIE      U.S Government Crop Assistance
    5      CROPS   .CH3 PIE      U.S Government Crop Assistance
   ▶6      CUISINE .CH3 XY       Custom Cuisine
```

Note

Marking and Unmarking Consecutive Files   All the files between the first file you mark with **F5-Mark block** and the last file you select with the menu arrow are automatically marked. This procedure also works when reordering and removing files. To unmark a block of files, select **F5-Unmark**.

◆ **4**   Select **F7-Add/Edit** and **Duplicate file** to add both files to your worksheet.

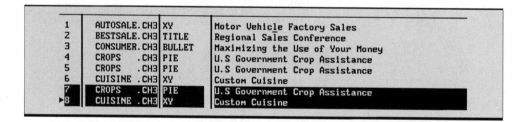

```
1   AUTOSALE.CH3 XY       Motor Vehicle Factory Sales
2   BESTSALE.CH3 TITLE    Regional Sales Conference
3   CONSUMER.CH3 BULLET   Maximizing the Use of Your Money
4   CROPS   .CH3 PIE      U.S Government Crop Assistance
5   CROPS   .CH3 PIE      U.S Government Crop Assistance
6   CUISINE .CH3 XY       Custom Cuisine
7   CROPS   .CH3 PIE      U.S Government Crop Assistance
▶8  CUISINE .CH3 XY       Custom Cuisine
```

◆ **5**   Click on **F5-Unmark** or press F5 to unmark your files.

◆ **6**   To remove your duplicate files, click on **CROPS.CH3** in row 5 or place the menu arrow and select **F5-Mark block** to highlight the filename.

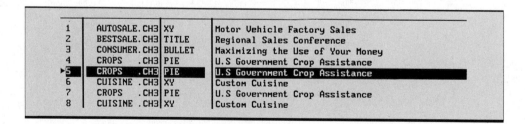

```
1   AUTOSALE.CH3 XY       Motor Vehicle Factory Sales
2   BESTSALE.CH3 TITLE    Regional Sales Conference
3   CONSUMER.CH3 BULLET   Maximizing the Use of Your Money
4   CROPS   .CH3 PIE      U.S Government Crop Assistance
▶5  CROPS   .CH3 PIE      U.S Government Crop Assistance
6   CUISINE .CH3 XY       Custom Cuisine
7   CROPS   .CH3 PIE      U.S Government Crop Assistance
8   CUISINE .CH3 XY       Custom Cuisine
```

٠**7** Click on **CUISINE.CH3** in row 8 or move the menu arrow until files 5 through 8 are highlighted.

```
 1     AUTOSALE.CH3 XY      Motor Vehicle Factory Sales
 2     BESTSALE.CH3 TITLE   Regional Sales Conference
 3     CONSUMER.CH3 BULLET  Maximizing the Use of Your Money
 4     CROPS   .CH3 PIE     U.S Government Crop Assistance
 5     CROPS   .CH3 PIE     U.S Government Crop Assistance
 6     CUISINE .CH3 XY      Custom Cuisine
 7     CROPS   .CH3 PIE     U.S Government Crop Assistance
▶8     CUISINE .CH3 XY      Custom Cuisine
```

٠**8** Select **F7-Add/Edit** and click on **Remove file** or press 2 to delete the filenames from the presentation list. You can also press the speed keys CTRL DEL to remove selected files from your worksheet.

```
                    DRAW    Background drawing for presentation

 1     AUTOSALE.CH3 XY      Motor Vehicle Factory Sales
 2     BESTSALE.CH3 TITLE   Regional Sales Conference
 3     CONSUMER.CH3 BULLET  Maximizing the Use of Your Money
▶4     CROPS   .CH3 PIE     U.S Government Crop Assistance
```

Reordering Files

You can reorganize the files in your presentation list by moving single files or groups of files. Display your worksheet.

٠**1** Place the menu arrow on BESTSALE.CH3 and select **F7-Add/Edit** to display the Add/Edit menu.

```
 #     ·Filename  ▶ Add file         1  Ctrl-Ins  ectory
                    Remove file      2  Ctrl-Del
                    Duplicate file   3            entation

 1     AUTOSALE.   Move file up      4  Ctrl-↑
▶2     BESTSALE.   Move file down    5  Ctrl-↓
 3     CONSUMER.   Jump to file      6  Ctrl-J    Money
 4     CROPS   .                                  nce
```

♦ **2**   Click on **Move file up** or press ④ to move BESTSALE up one line. You can also use the speed keys [CTRL][↑] to move a selected File up your list.

```
|                | DRAW   | Background drawing for presentation  |
|----------------|--------|--------------------------------------|
| ►1 BESTSALE.CH3| TITLE  | Regional Sales Conference            |
| 2  AUTOSALE.CH3| XY     | Motor Vehicle Factory Sales          |
| 3  CONSUMER.CH3| BULLET | Maximizing the Use of Your Money     |
| 4  CROPS   .CH3| PIE    | U.S Government Crop Assistance       |
```

♦ **3**   Place the menu arrow on AUTOSALE.CH3 and select **F7-Add/Edit** and then click on **Move file down** or press ⑤ to move AUTOSALE down one line. The speed keys [CTRL][↓] also move selected files down your list.

```
|                | DRAW   | Background drawing for presentation  |
|----------------|--------|--------------------------------------|
| 1  BESTSALE.CH3| TITLE  | Regional Sales Conference            |
| 2  CONSUMER.CH3| BULLET | Maximizing the Use of Your Money     |
| ►3 AUTOSALE.CH3| XY     | Motor Vehicle Factory Sales          |
| 4  CROPS   .CH3| PIE    | U.S Government Crop Assistance       |
```

Note

Jumping to a File   When your presentation list has a large number of files, it's helpful to be able to jump from one file to another without using the cursor keys. Select **F7-Add/Edit** and click on **Jump to file** or press ⑥ to display the Jump to File pop-up. You can also press the speed keys [CTRL][J] to display the pop-up directly from your worksheet. Type the row number of the file you want to jump to and press [↵] or [F10]. The menu arrow moves to the selected file on your worksheet.

Editing Chart Data and Descriptions

You can edit any or all the data on the individual charts in your presentation. You can also edit the chart descriptions on your presentation list without changing them on your original chart. This lets you create new descriptions for your presentation.

Display your Edit Presentation worksheet and place the menu arrow on CROPS.CH3.

◆ **1** Select **F7-Add/Edit** to display the Add/Edit menu.

```
   1  │  BESTSALE.│  Move file up         4  Ctrl-↑  │
   2  │  CONSUMER.│  Move file down       5  Ctrl-↓  │ Money
   3  │  AUTOSALE.│  Jump to file         6  Ctrl-J  │
  ►4  │  CROPS  . │ ─────────────────────────────────│ nce
   5  │           │  Edit chart data      7  Ctrl-E  │
   6  │           │  Edit notes           8  Ctrl-N  │
   7  │           │  Edit descriptions    9           │
   8  │           │ ─────────────────────────────────│
   9  │           │  Add blank chart      A           │
```

◆ **2** Click on **Edit chart data** or press **7** to display the CROPS.CH3 chart worksheet. You can also press the speed keys [CTRL][E] to display your current chart worksheet from anywhere in the program.

```
■
  Title:     U.S Government Crop Assistance
  Subtitle:  States of Alabama & Colorado - 1988
  Footnote:  Source: U.S. Department of Agriculture
  Pie title: Alabama


  Slice        Label        │   Value   │  Cut  │  Color  │ Pattern
         └                  │           │       │         │
```

◆ **3** Delete the word **Government** in the title and press [CTRL][S] to display the Save Chart pop-up menu. Select **F10-Continue** to save the edits and return to your chart worksheet.

◆ **4**   Press ⟨CTRL⟩⟨E⟩ to return to your Edit Presentation worksheet, place the menu arrow on BESTSALE.CH3 and click on **F7-Add/Edit** or press ⟨F7⟩ to display the Add/Edit menu.

```
 ►1    BESTSALE.   Move file up        4  Ctrl-↑
  2    CONSUMER.   Move file down      5  Ctrl-↓    Money
  3    AUTOSALE.   Jump to file        6  Ctrl-J
  4    CROPS   .                                    nce
  5                Edit chart data     7  Ctrl-E
  6                Edit notes          8  Ctrl-N
```

◆ **5**   Click on **Edit descriptions** or press ⟨9⟩ to display the Edit description pop-up menu.

```
  5                Edit chart data     7  Ctrl-E
  6                Edit notes          8  Ctrl-N
  7              ► Edit descripti
  8              ─────────────────  ► Edit description           1
  9                Add blank char     Update all descriptions    2
 10                Add blank temp     View description/directory 3
 11
```

◆ **6**   Click on **Edit description** or press ⟨1⟩ to display the Edit description pop-up with your current chart description.

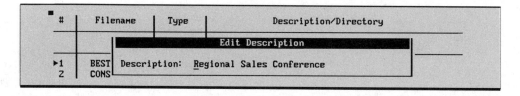

◆ **7**   Type the description shown on the following screen. You can enter up to 40 characters.

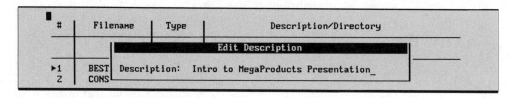

.**8**   Select **F10-Continue** to place the new description on your Edit
Presentation worksheet.

			DRAW	Background drawing for presentation
▶1	BESTSALE.CH3	TITLE	Intro to MegaProducts Presentation
2	CONSUMER.CH3	BULLET	Maximizing the Use of Your Money
3	AUTOSALE.CH3	XY	Motor Vehicle Factory Sales
4	CROPS .CH3	PIE	U.S Government Crop Assistance

.**9**   To return your edited BESTSALE description to its original form,
select **F7-Add/Edit** and **Edit descriptions** to display the Edit Descriptions pop-up. Click on **Update all descriptions** or press **2**.

			DRAW	Background drawing for presentation
▶1	BESTSALE.CH3	TITLE	Regional Sales Conference
2	CONSUMER.CH3	BULLET	Maximizing the Use of Your Money
3	AUTOSALE.CH3	XY	Motor Vehicle Factory Sales
4	CROPS .CH3	PIE	U.S Government Crop Assistance

Note

Spell Checking Your Presentation   To spell check the charts on your presentation list, select **F6-Main Menu** and **Presentation** and then **Spell check
presentation**. Each chart's filename appears in the upper-left corner of your
screen as it is checked.

For a complete discussion of the spell checking function, refer to Chapter 3.

✦ Enhancing Your Presentation

Various enhancement options let you create a consistent look for your presentation. You can change chart titles and footnotes, text attributes, and the overall

appearance of all your charts. You can also apply the templates you learned to create in Chapter 7.

The Presentation titles/footnotes option can change every type of chart in your presentation except title and draw charts. Display your SHOW.SH3 worksheet.

◆ **1**   Click on **F8-Options** or press 🖸 to display the Options menu.

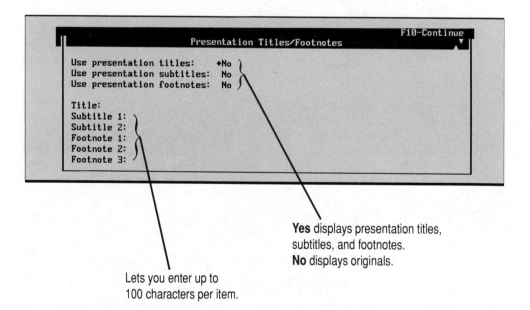

◆ **2**   Click on **Presentation titles/footnotes** or press ⒈ to display the Presentation Titles/Footnotes menu.

Yes displays presentation titles, subtitles, and footnotes.
No displays originals.

Lets you enter up to 100 characters per item.

.**3** Change the Use presentation items to **Yes** and enter any changes you
want to make at the appropriate title, subtitle, and footnote prompts.
Select **F10-Continue** to return to your worksheet.

Changing the text attributes for your entire presentation is similar to working
with individual charts.

.**4** Select **F8-Options** to display the Options menu and click on **Presentation text attributes** or press ⎡**2**⎤ to display the Presentation Text
Attributes menu.

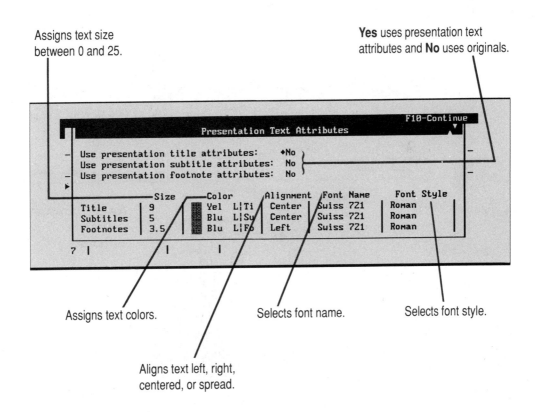

Assigns text size
between 0 and 25.

Yes uses presentation text
attributes and **No** uses originals.

Assigns text colors.

Selects font name.

Selects font style.

Aligns text left, right,
centered, or spread.

◆ **5**   Change the Use presentation items to **Yes** and change the attribute
options to suit your needs. Select **F10-Continue** to return to your
presentation worksheet.

Presentation appearance options let you assign the same palette colors or background drawing to all the charts in your presentation.

◆ **6**   Select **F8-Options** to display the Options menu and click on
Presentation appearance or press ⦗**3**⦘ to display the Presentation
Appearance menu.

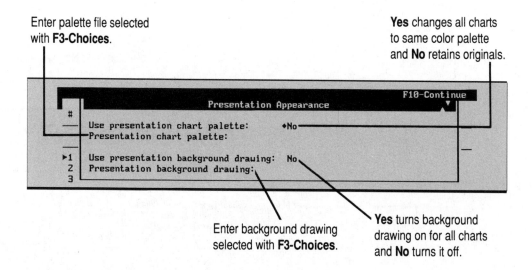

Enter palette file selected
with **F3-Choices**.

Yes changes all charts
to same color palette
and **No** retains originals.

Enter background drawing
selected with **F3-Choices**.

Yes turns background
drawing on for all charts
and **No** turns it off.

◆ **7**   Make your selections and click on **F10-Continue** or press ⦗**F10**⦘ to
return to your worksheet.

◆ **8**   Place the menu arrow on BESTSALE.CH3 and select **F2-Preview** to
see how the enhancements you selected affect this chart. Click the
right mouse button or press any key to move to the next chart in
your presentation.

Now let's apply the BULLET#1.TP3 template you created in Chapter 7 to your CONSUMER.CH3 bullet chart.

✦ **9**   Move the menu arrow to BESTSALE.CH3 and select **F7-Add/Edit** and **Add file** to display a list of filenames. Click on the down scroll arrow or press `PGDN` until the BULLET#1.TP3 file is revealed.

```
  -|   Filename:  SHADE3.CH3                                          |-
     ▸   SHADE2  .CH3   DRAW    Bkg: Gray to center Blk  Use 3,4,6,7.PL3
         ▸SHADE3  .CH3   DRAW    Bkg: Blend float rect.  Use 5,7,8,12.PL3
         SHADE4  .CH3   DRAW    Bkg: Diagonal Use 1,2,3,4,5,6,7,8,12.PL3
         WORLD   .CH3   DRAW    Bkg: World    Use 1,2,3,4,5,6,7,8,12.PL3
         WORLDINC.CH3   ORG     Worldwide Industries, Inc.
         FLOOR   .PCC   OTHER
         ROCKTOP .PCC   OTHER
         LOGOBKG1.PCX   OTHER
         SHOW    .SH3   PRESENT A sample presentation file.
         BULLET#1.TP3   BULLET  Bullet chart with double-line frame.
```

✦ **10**   Select **BULLET#1.TP3** and return to your worksheet. BULLET#1.TP3 is now inserted before CONSUMER.CH3 on your presentation list.

```
                        DRAW    Background drawing for presentation
     1    BESTSALE.CH3 TITLE   Regional Sales Conference
    ▸2    BULLET#1.TP3 BULLET  Bullet chart with double-line frame.
     3    CONSUMER.CH3 BULLET  Maximizing the Use of Your Money
     4    AUTOSALE.CH3 XY      Motor Vehicle Factory Sales
```

✦ **11**   Select **F2-Preview** to display your presentation. CONSUMER.CH3 should now have a frame around it. Press `ESC` to return to your worksheet.

> **Note**
>
> **Controlling Template Effects**   When you place a particular type of template in your presentation worksheet, such as a bullet chart template, it affects all the following bullet charts on your list. To cancel the template effects for similar charts, move the menu arrow to the file before the first chart you don't want to change and select **F7-Add/Edit**. Select **Add blank template** and then the template type to insert a blank template in your worksheet. The following charts of that type now maintain their original settings.

✦ Creating ScreenShows

The F2-Preview option you taught yourself earlier, lets you manually display your presentation charts. The Harvard Graphics ScreenShow feature lets you show your presentation automatically in a variety of creative ways.

Display your SHOW.SH3 Edit Presentation worksheet.

✦ **1**   Click on **F4-Effects** or press F4 to display the Effects menu.

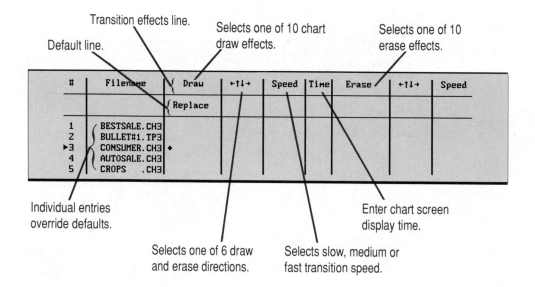

Note

The HyperShow Feature   The Harvard Graphics HyperShow Feature lets
you create interactive presentations which jump from one related chart to
another. This feature is not covered in this book.

For detailed information on creating HyperShow presentations, consult your
Harvard Graphics documentation.

Let's select some transition options which affect all the charts in your presentation. These steps also apply to options selected for individual charts.

٠ **2**   Double-click on **Replace**, on the defaults line in the Draw column, or
place the diamond symbol and press ⬛F3⬛ to display the Draw pop-up
menu.

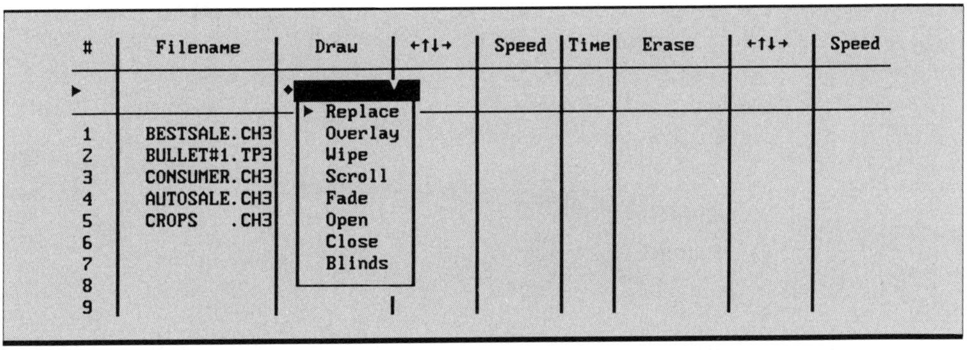

#	Filename	Draw	←↑↓→	Speed	Time	Erase	←↑↓→	Speed
		► Replace						
1	BESTSALE.CH3	Overlay						
2	BULLET#1.TP3	Wipe						
3	CONSUMER.CH3	Scroll						
4	AUTOSALE.CH3	Fade						
5	CROPS .CH3	Open						
6		Close						
7		Blinds						
8								
9								

٠ **3**   Select **Fade** and then press ⬛TAB⬛ to move the diamond symbol to each
option along the defaults line. Select **F3-Choices**, and from each
pop-up menu, select the items shown on the following screen. Enter
Ø:Ø5 in the time column.

#	Filename	Draw	←↑↓→	Speed	Time	Erase	←↑↓→	Speed
▸		Fade	In	Slow	0:05	Scroll	Right	◆Slow
1	BESTSALE.CH3							
2	BULLET#1.TP3							
3	CONSUMER.CH3							
4	AUTOSALE.CH3							
5	CROPS .CH3							

◆ **4**　Select **F2-Preview** to see your transition effects in action. Press any key if you want to display the next chart before the set display time has elapsed. Press ⌜ESC⌟ at any time to cancel the preview and return to the Effects menu.

Note

Pausing a ScreenShow　　To pause your ScreenShow, press the spacebar or press and hold either mouse button. When you are ready to continue, press any key or release the mouse button. You can also automatically pause your presentation by placing a blank chart in your list. Move the menu arrow on your worksheet to the file you want the pause to follow, and select **F7-Add/Edit** and **Add blank chart**. Enter the pause length you want in the Time column opposite the individual entry for your blank chart. Your other charts are still displayed according to your default line time selection.

◆ **5**　Select **F4-Descriptions** to return to your Edit Presentations worksheet.

◆ **6**　Select **F6-Main Menu** and **Presentations** and then **Save presentation**. Press ⌜F10⌟ to save your presentation file with the current name.

◆ **7**　Click on **F6-Main Menu** and **Exit** or press ⌜F6⌟ and ⌜E⌟ to exit Harvard Graphics.

✦ Summary

This chapter covered the basic skills for building and presenting masterful presentations. In Chapter 9 you can teach yourself to use the powerful Harvard Graphics Draw feature.

9

Enhancing Your Presentations with Draw

◆　　The Harvard Graphics Draw feature lets you create charts from scratch, or import existing charts into Draw and modify them with various objects and drawings. Draw's graphical environment allows you to see exactly how your chart is going to look as you create it.

Harvard Graphics comes with a standard library of over 500 symbols, and Draw provides more than 35 drawing and editing tools to let you move, resize, copy, paste, flip, rotate, zoom, animate, and skew these symbols and other chart objects. You can also change their color and shape, and place symbols and logos on your charts.

The Draw feature has so many powerful options an entire book could be devoted to the subject. This chapter is designed to teach you the basics, so you can begin building masterful Draw charts right away.

- ◆ Getting Started
- ◆ Working with Objects
- ◆ Creating Original Draw Charts

✦ Getting Started

Let's begin by starting Draw and exploring the various areas and items on your Draw screen. Once you've started Draw, you can import an existing chart, and retrieve some standard symbols into your drawing area.

Starting Draw

This section teaches you to start Draw and display a blank drawing area. In addition to the direct method shown in the following exercise, you can also start Draw by selecting Create chart from the Main Menu and the Drawing function from the Chart menu.

✦**1**   Start Harvard Graphics and display the Main Menu.

```
┌──────────────────────────────────────────────────────────────────────┐
│ F6-Main Menu  │ F7-Spell check                              F10-Continue │
│                                                                        │
│    ▶ Create chart      1                                               │
│      Edit chart        2                                               │
│      Draw              3                                               │
│     ─────────────                                                      │
│      File              4                                               │
│      Output            5                                               │
└──────────────────────────────────────────────────────────────────────┘
```

✦**2**   Click on **Draw** or press ③ to display a Draw screen with a blank drawing area.

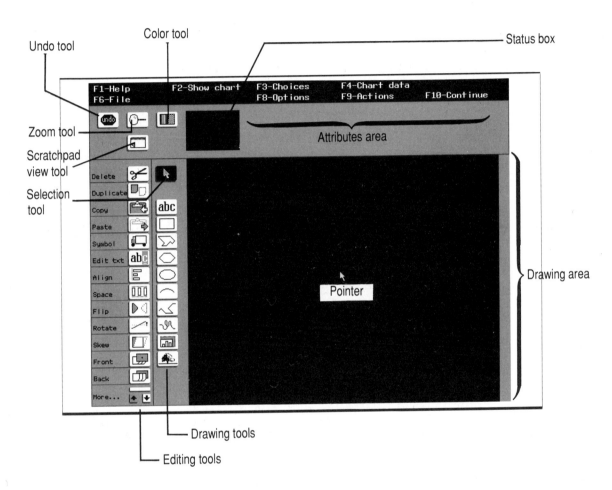

The following list describes the areas and items displayed on your Draw screen.

Attributes area   Displays icons to change the color, pattern, and
                       style of objects, text and lines.

Undo tool   Cancels the last action and reverses undo when
                       selected again.

Zoom tool	Magnifies selected portion of a chart.
Color tool	Selects colors and patterns for text and objects.
Scratchpad view tool	Displays a temporary drawing area for experiments which can be copied to a chart.
Status box	Displays currently selected tool or object.
Editing tools	Various tools for modifying objects, and scroll arrows for switching between a second column of tools.
Selection tool	Activates the pointer as the selection tool for choosing chart objects for modification.
Drawing tools	Various tools for free-hand drawing, to add background canvases, and import bitmap images.
Drawing area	Area for creating original draw charts or working on existing charts.
Pointer	Selects options, icons, and function keys to create, resize, and move objects.

Note

Using the Mouse or Keyboard   The instructions for the exercises in this chapter are primarily written for a mouse. To select icons or objects with the keyboard, use the arrow keys to place the pointer on the item and press ⏎.

Importing Charts

Importing one of your existing charts into Draw is a simple process. You can retrieve a chart from the Main Menu before you start Draw by selecting the Get chart option from the File menu. Choose a chart from the file list and then select

F4-Draw from your worksheet. Draw starts and the chart you retrieved is displayed on the Draw screen.

Once in Draw, you can also use the Get subchart option to import any previously saved chart as part of your current Draw chart. You can manipulate subcharts just like any other chart object, but you cannot enhance them.

You may want to modify the text or data on an existing chart, either before or after you import it, to make it more compatible with the design of your Draw chart. If you're already in Draw, press F4 to display your original chart worksheet and modify the chart as needed.

Let's import one of your existing charts into the drawing area. Your blank Draw screen should still be displayed.

⋆ 1   Click on **F6-File** or press F6 to display the File menu.

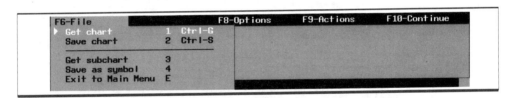

⋆ 2   Click on **Get chart** or press 1 to display a list of chart filenames.

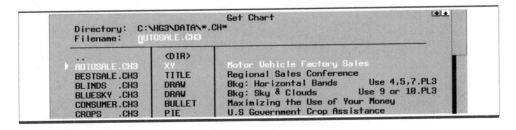

✦ **3**   Select **F8-Sort files** and select **CONSUMER.CH3** to display a copy
of the bullet chart on your screen and then click the right mouse button or press ESC to return to your chart worksheet.

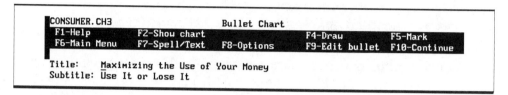

✦ **4**   Click on **F4-Draw** or press F4 to display the Draw screen with the
CONSUMER.CH3 chart in the drawing area.

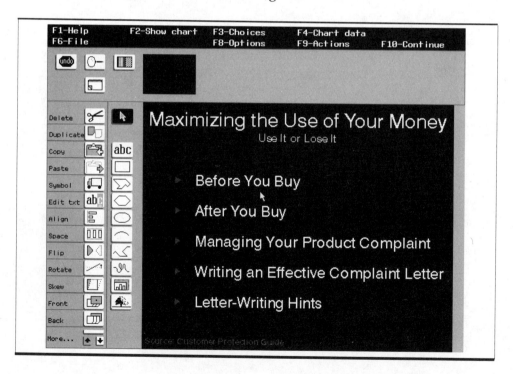

Retrieving Symbols

Now let's retrieve some of Harvard Graphics' standard symbols and place them in your Draw chart. Your Draw screen with the CONSUMER.CH3 chart should still be displayed.

✦ 1   Click on the **Symbol** (truck) icon to display a submenu of Symbol icons.

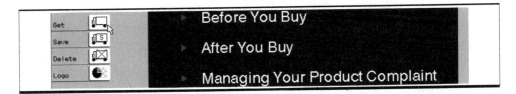

✦ 2   Click on the **Get** icon to display the symbol file list and then press
`PG DN` twice.

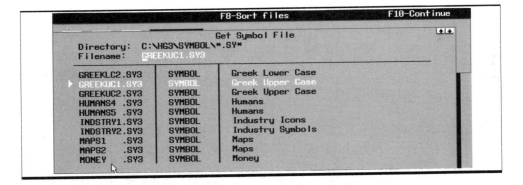

✦ **3**   Select **MONEY.SY3** to display the standard money symbols.

✦ **4**   Click on and highlight the names of the green bill and the tilted currency symbol.

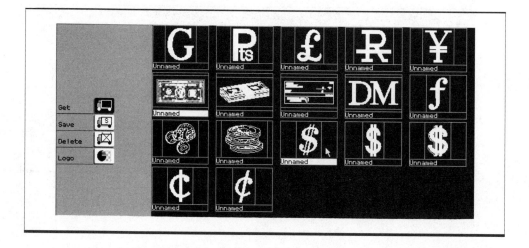

✦ **5**   Select **F10-Continue** to place these symbols on your chart.

✦ **6**   Click the right mouse button or press ⌷ESC⌷ to return to the Draw screen.

✦ Working with Objects

The Draw function has a wide array of editing tools which allow you to place objects such as text and symbols on your charts and modify them to suit your needs. The exercises in this section are designed to provide you with some basic skills so you may explore Draw's more advanced editing features on your own.

Moving and Resizing

Symbols or objects are placed in the center of your chart. They can then be moved and resized for proper fit. An object must be selected before you can move or resize it. The eight small boxes which surround selected objects are called handles, and these are used to expand or contract the object area in the resizing process. To activate the pointer as your selection tool, click on and highlight the Selection icon.

Your Draw screen with the CONSUMER.CH3 chart and the dollar sign and green bill should be displayed. Let's move these symbols to uncover the chart text and then resize them to suit the proportions of your chart.

◆ **1**   Click on and highlight the Selection icon, place the pointer anywhere in the drawing area and click the right mouse button or press ᴱˢᶜ to deselect both objects.

◆ **2**   Place the pointer on the dollar sign and click the left mouse button or or press ↵ to select it as a single object.

✦ 3 With the pointer on the dollar sign, not one of the handles, press and hold the left mouse button or press the spacebar to change the pointer to a four-directional arrow.

✦ 4 Continue to hold the mouse button or spacebar and drag the mouse or press the arrow keys to move a box outline of the dollar sign to the location shown on the following screen.

✦ **5**   Release the mouse button or spacebar and press ⏎ to draw the dollar sign in its new location.

✦ **6**   Repeat steps 2 through 5 with the green bill to move it to the location shown on the following screen.

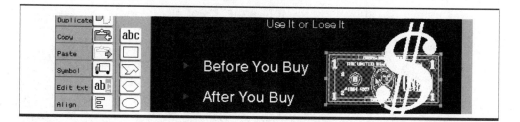

✦ **7**   Place the pointer on the upper-right handle of the green bill and click and hold the left mouse button or press the spacebar to change the pointer to a two-directional arrow.

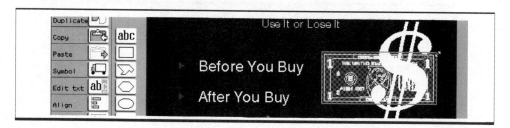

٠ **8**   Continue to hold the left mouse button or use the spacebar and arrow keys method to move and resize the green bill image box as shown on the following screen.

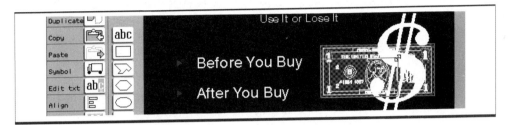

٠ **9**   Release the mouse button or the spacebar and press ⏎ to redraw the green bill in a smaller size.

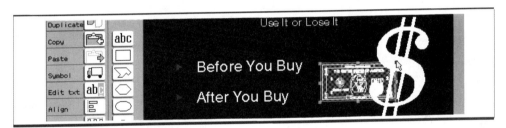

٠ **10**   Repeat steps 7 through 9 to resize the dollar sign and move it to the location shown on the following screen.

Note

Editing Shortcuts with Shift and Group   You can select more than one object at a time by pressing and holding the shift key as you use the selection method described in step 2 in this section. When you have more than one object selected and you want to deselect an individual object, press and hold the shift key, place the pointer on the object you want to deselect, and click the left mouse button or press ⏎. You can also maintain the original proportions of an object while resizing it by pressing and holding the shift key as you drag the object's handle. The Group icon on the second column of editing tools, accessed with the down scroll arrow, allows you to group individual objects and move or resize them as a unit. Simply select the objects you want to group using the shift key method described above, and click on the Group icon. To release the objects from a group, click on the Ungroup icon.

Copying, Duplicating and Deleting

When you copy an object, a copy of it is placed in RAM in an area called the clipboard. The contents of the clipboard can then be pasted in other locations. Your most recently copied object remains in the clipboard until you replace it with the next item you copy.

Duplicating is a quick way to place copies of an object on top of the original to create a cascading effect. The offset between the original and each duplicate is set by default, but you can alter the offset distance by moving the duplicate to a new offset position.

Deleting objects is as simple as selecting them and clicking on the Delete icon.

Your Draw screen should be displayed with the dollar sign selected.

✦ **1**   Click on the **Copy** (clipboard) icon to copy the dollar sign to the clipboard and then click on the **Paste** icon to place a copy of the dollar sign over the original.

◆ **2**   Place the pointer on the dollar sign and move the copy to the left as shown on the following screen.

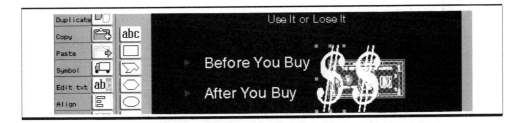

◆ **3**   Select the original dollar sign and click on the **Duplicate** icon.

◆ **4**   Move the duplicate dollar sign to the right to establish a new offset distance as shown on the following screen.

◆ **5** Click on the **Duplicate** icon and another dollar sign appears at your new offset distance. You can repeat this process, with the default offset or a new offset, to achieve cascading effects with any of your chart objects.

◆ **6** Click on the **Delete** (scissors) icon to remove the selected dollar sign. When you click on Delete, all selected objects are removed simultaneously.

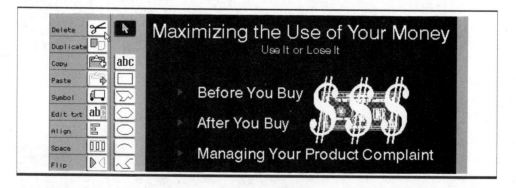

◆ **7** To restore your deleted dollar sign, click on the **undo** icon at the upper left corner of your Draw screen. You can only undo the last object you deleted.

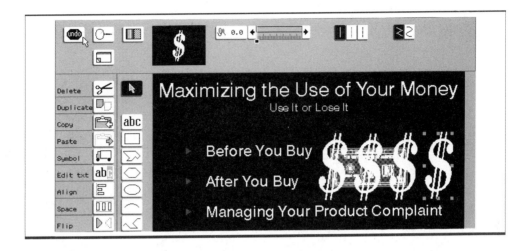

Note

Deleting Symbols   To delete unwanted symbols from your symbol files, click on the **Symbol** icon to display a submenu of Symbol icons, and click on the **Delete** icon to display the symbol file list. Select the appropriate file to display those symbols on your Draw screen. Select the symbols you want deleted and click the right mouse button and then **F10-Confirm** to complete the process.

Positioning Layered Objects

Draw lets you position layered objects, like those you just learned to create, in front of or behind other layered objects. Your Draw screen should still be displayed from the last exercise.

◆ **1**   Select the green bill and click on the **Front** icon to display a submenu of Front icons.

◆ **2**   Click on the **Front 1** icon to bring the green bill forward one layer. The Front submenu icon brings the selected object to the front of all layered objects.

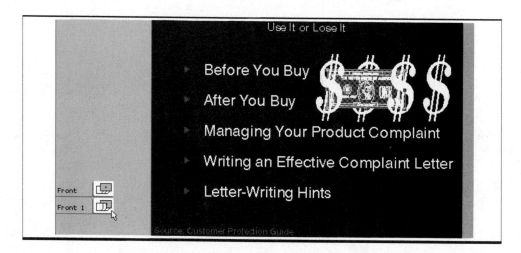

✦ **3**   Click the right mouse button or press ⟨ESC⟩ to exit the Front options and click on the **Back** icon to display a submenu of Back icons.

✦ **4**   Click on **Back 1** to move the green bill back one layer. The Back submenu icon moves the selected object to the back of all layered objects.

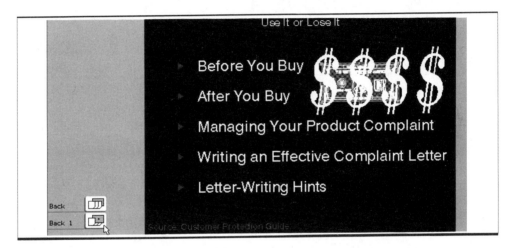

✦ **5**   Click the right mouse button or press ⟨ESC⟩ to return to your Draw screen.

Saving Charts and Objects as Symbols

The procedure for saving a Draw chart is the same as other Harvard Graphics charts. An entire Draw chart or an individual object on a chart can be saved as a symbol, retrieved into another Draw chart and manipulated like any other object.

Display your Draw screen, and let's save your entire chart and then one of the chart objects as symbols.

◆ **1**   Select **F6-File** to display the File menu and click on **Save as symbol** or press **4** to display the Save Symbol File menu.

◆ **2**   Type the Filename, Description and Symbol name shown on the following screen. Harvard Graphics automatically assigns the .SY3 extension.

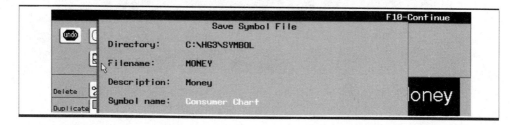

◆ **3**   Select **F10-Continue** to save the chart as a symbol in the MONEY.SY3 file and return to your Draw screen.

◆ **4**   To save an object as a symbol, select the green bill and overlapping dollar signs. All the objects should appear in the status box.

✦**5** Click on the **Symbol** icon to display the submenu of Symbol icons and then click on the **Save** icon to display the Save Symbol File menu. Type the Symbol name shown on the following screen.

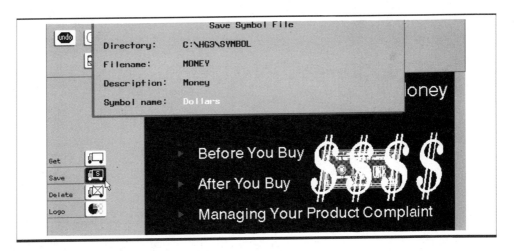

✦ **6** Select **F10-Continue** to save the object as a symbol in the
MONEY.SY3 file and return to your Draw screen.

✦ **7** Click the right mouse button or press ⎋ until you return to the
Main Menu.

✦ **8** Select **Create chart** and **Clear chart** and then **F10-Confirm** to clear
the CONSUMER.CH3 chart from memory.

Note

Creating a Logo Symbol File Selecting the Logo icon automatically
retrieves a symbol saved in a special file named HG3LOGO.SY3. To create this
file, retrieve a symbol or create a new symbol and save it with this Filename.

For information on deleting unwanted symbols from your symbol files, see the Note
at the end of the Copying, Duplicating and Deleting section in this chapter.

✦ Creating Original Draw Charts

In the first part of this chapter you taught yourself some basic skills for enhancing existing charts with Draw. This section teaches you to create original Draw
charts, enter, edit and enhance text, and draw objects such as triangles, polygons,
boxes and circles.

Entering and Editing Text

Draw chart text can be resized, moved, duplicated, copied, and manipulated like
any other object. Start Draw and display a blank drawing area.

◆ **1**   Click on the **Text** (abc) icon to change your pointer to a cross-hair, and place your cross-hair pointer as shown on the following screen.

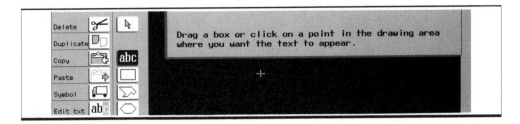

◆ **2**   Hold the left mouse button or press the spacebar, and drag the mouse or press the arrow keys to create the box shown on the following screen. Release the mouse button, or release the spacebar and press ⏎ to complete your box and display the text screen.

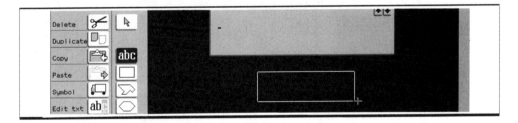

◆ **3**   Type **DRAWING SYMBOLS**.

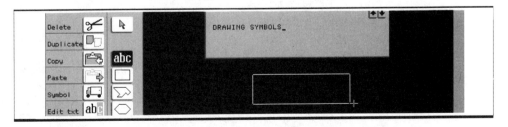

✦ **4**   Click the right mouse button or press ⟨F10⟩ to place your text in the drawing area.

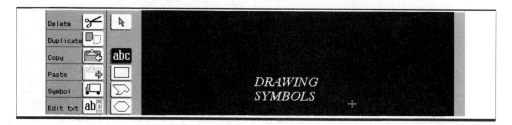

✦ **5**   Click on the Select icon and move your text to the location shown on the following screen.

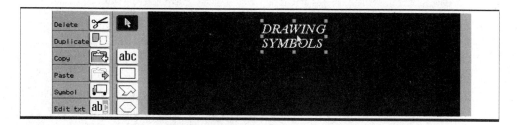

✦ **6**   Click on the **Edit txt** icon to display a submenu of Edit text icons and click on the **Edit txt** icon to display the text screen.

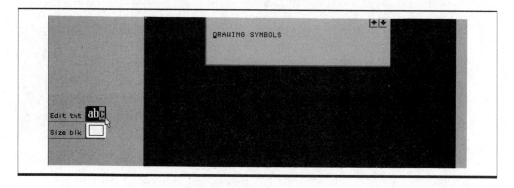

✦**7**   Edit the text to read **HAVING FUN WITH SYMBOLS**.

✦**8**   Click on **F10-Continue** or press ⌨ and then click the right mouse
button or press ⌨ to return to your Draw screen.

✦**9**   To resize your text block, click on the **Edit txt** icon to display the submenu of Edit text icons and click on the **Size blk** icon to change the
handles to triangle shapes.

◆ **10**   Place your pointer on the right-center handle, press and hold the left mouse button or press the space bar, and use the mouse or arrow keys to drag the text box to the right edge of the screen.

◆ **11**   Release the mouse button, or release the spacebar and press ⏎.Click the right mouse button twice or press ⟨ESC⟩ twice to display your text on one line, and then move your text to the location shown on the following screen.

Note

Using Special Characters   To enter a special character on your Draw chart, display the text screen and place the cursor where you want the character to appear. Select **F7-Special char** to display the Special Character menu, and choose the desired character. You can also select a special character by pressing and holding ⟨ALT⟩ while you type the character's decimal value.

Enhancing Text

Draw text can be enhanced in a variety of ways from three enhancement menus. Let's access each menu and explore its options. Display your Draw screen from the previous exercise with the text block selected.

✦**1**   Click on the **Edit txt** icon to display the submenu of Edit text icons. Select **Edit txt** to display the first enhancement menu.

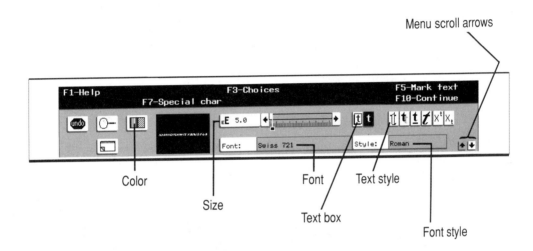

The following list describes each option on the first enhancement menu.

Color	Changes text color, pattern or text shadow.
Size	Enter text size between 0 and 100 by clicking on size box and typing number, clicking on slider bar and dragging slider, or clicking on arrows.
Font	Displays menu of fonts when you click on Font.
Font style	Displays list of font styles when you click on Style.
Text box	Creates or removes text box.
Text style	Selects styles other than regular such as outline, shadow, underline, slant, superscript, and subscript.
Menu scroll arrows	Scrolls between three enhancement menus.

Note

Enhancing Part of Your Text   To enhance a portion of your text, place the
pointer on the first character, click and hold the left mouse button or press F5
and then drag the mouse or use the arrow keys to highlight the desired characters. To deselect highlighted text, click the right mouse button or press F5
before you select your enhancement options.

✦ **2**   Click on the down scroll arrow to display the second enhancement
menu.

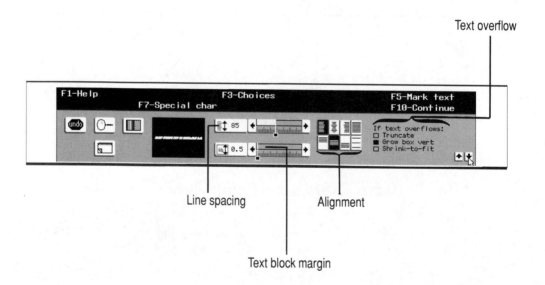

Text overflow

Line spacing   Alignment

Text block margin

The following list describes each option on the second enhancement menu.

Line spacing   Enter value between 0 and 200 by typing number in
                          line spacing box, dragging slider bar, or clicking on
                          arrows. Single space value is 85 and 170 equals double
                          space.

Text block margin	Enter value between 0 and 25 by typing number in margin box, dragging slider bar, or clicking on arrows to determine space between text and text block boundary.
Alignment	Selects horizontal text alignment such as left, right, centered, or justified, and vertical alignment such as top, bottom, middle, or spread.
Text overflow	Select **Truncate** to cut text extending over block boundary, **Grow block vert** to expand block to fit text, and **Shrink-to-fit** to change text size to fit block.

✦ **3**   Click on the down scroll arrow to display the third enhancement menu.

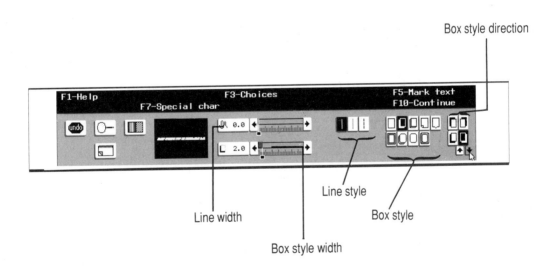

Box style direction

Line width

Box style width

Line style

Box style

This menu lets you select text box attributes. You must select the text box option on the first enhancement menu to activate these options.

The following list describes each option on the third enhancement menu.

Line width	Enter value between 0 and 25 by typing number in line box, dragging slider bar, or clicking on arrows.
Line style	Selects line styles such as solid, dotted, or dashed.
Box style	Chooses box styles such as plain, shadow, 3D, page, caption, frame, rounded shadow, rounded, and button.
Box style width	Enter value between 0 and 25 by typing number in style box, dragging slider bar, or clicking on arrows.
Box style direction	Changes shadow direction of 3D, page, caption, and rounded box styles.

Take time to experiment with the options on these menus, and use F2-Show chart to view the results of your changes. Be sure to return your chart to its original settings before continuing with the next exercise.

Drawing Objects

This section teaches you to use the drawing tools to create objects such as boxes, polygons, regular polygons, ovals, arcs, lines, and freehand drawings. To display a list of drawing tool speed keys, press CTRL F1.

Display your draw screen with the original settings from the last exercise.

◆ **1**   Click on the **Box** icon and place your cross-hair pointer as shown on the following screen.

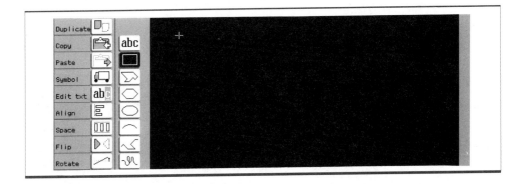

⋆ **2** Click the left mouse button and move the pointer to create a box shape. To create a square, hold the spacebar as you move the pointer.

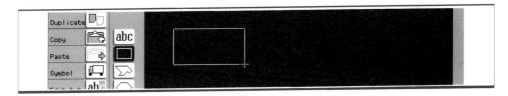

⋆ **3** Click the right mouse button or press ⏎ to form the box.

The following screen shows examples of what you can do with the other Draw tools. See if you can duplicate these objects or create some new ones of your own. To begin, click on the tool icon. To draw an object, click the left mouse button and move the cross-hair pointer as you taught yourself in the previous example.

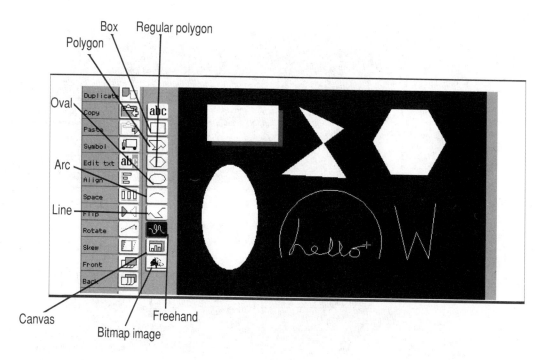

The following list covers some specific guidelines for using each of the Draw tools. After you draw an object, click the right mouse button to complete the process.

Polygon
Creates multi-sided objects in segments by placing the pointer, clicking the left mouse button and moving the pointer in a diagonal direction, clicking the left button again and moving the pointer in another direction.

Regular Polygon
Creates objects with 3 to 15 sides by clicking on the **Number of sides** box just above the draw area and typing the number of sides. Place the pointer where you want the object centered, click the left mouse button and move the pointer to where you want the outer edge.

Oval	Creates oval objects by placing the pointer where you want to center your object, clicking the left mouse button and moving the pointer to form the shape. To draw a perfect circle, hold the shift key as you move the pointer.
Arc	Creates arc shaped lines by placing the pointer where you want the arc to begin. Click the left mouse button, move the pointer to where you want the arc to end, and click the left mouse button again. Shape the arc by moving the mouse, and click the left mouse button one more time.
Line	Draws straight lines in segments by placing the pointer at the starting position, clicking the left mouse button, and moving the pointer to draw each line. To draw horizontal and vertical lines, hold the shift key as you move the pointer. To undo line segments in reverse order, press `CTRL` `U` or press the backspace key.
Freehand	Draws freehand lines by holding down the left mouse button and moving the mouse in any direction you want. To stop drawing, release the left mouse button.

For information on using the Canvas and Bitmap image drawing tools, consult your Harvard Graphics documentation.

Draw and Action Options

Draw has a variety of options which allow you to display a ruler and grid, change the pointer size and movement speed, redraw the screen in draft or high quality, and customize the program to suit your needs.

◆ **1**   Display your Draw screen and click on **F8-Options** to display the
Options menu.

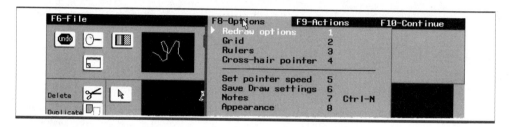

The following list describes each option on the Options menu.

Redraw options   Select **High** to redraw charts in greater detail but at a
                     slower rate. You can also show or hide various
                     objects as the screen is redrawn.

Grid   Displays dot grid and lets you select grid display in
                     inches, centimeters, or percents, modify interval
                     between horizontal and vertical dots, and select how
                     objects move to grid dots.

Rulers   Display or hide rulers on left and top edge of
                     drawing area, and select ruler display in inches,
                     centimeters, or percents.

Cross-hair pointer   Select default pointer, or larger pointer which tracks
                     along top and bottom edge of drawing area.

Set pointer speed   Set pointer tracking speed or distance pointer moves
                     when arrow key pressed.

Save Draw settings   Save current text and object enhancements, and F8-
                     Option selections.

Notes   Record current chart comments.

Appearance   Display charts in portrait or landscape orientation,
                     modify chart proportions, and select new palette or
                     background drawing.

✦ **2**   Click on **F9-Actions** or press [F9] to display the Actions menu.

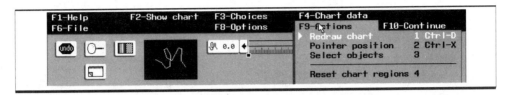

The following list describes each option on the Actions menu.

Redraw chart	Redraws your chart. Press [ESC] to stop redraw.
Pointer position	Moves pointer to selected location entered in inches, centimeters or percents.
Select objects	Selects and deselects all objects, similar objects or HyperShow buttons.
Reset chart regions	Resets chart regions which have been resized or moved.

✦ **3**   Click the right mouse button or press [ESC] to return to the Draw screen.

✦ **4**   Exit Harvard Graphics without saving your chart.

✦ Summary

In this final chapter you taught yourself some basic skills for building more masterful charts with the Draw feature. If you've completed all nine chapters in this book, you have built a solid foundation for creating persuasive and visually exciting presentations with Harvard Graphics.

A

Installing
Harvard Graphics

This appendix imparts some basic computer knowledge, and teaches you to install and prepare Harvard Graphics 3.0 to run on your computer system. Be sure to read the introduction before you begin. It contains important information on how to gain maximum benefit from the step-by-step format of this book.

✦ Computer Basics

The information in this section is designed to lay a basic foundation for beginning users, and to remind intermediate users of some important concepts.

Software and Hardware Software refers to the programs which perform various tasks on your computer such as DOS, Harvard Graphics, Lotus 1-2-3, Word-Perfect, and dBASE. Computer hardware refers to the computer itself and the components you need to operate your software such as a monitor, display card, hard and floppy disk drives, and output devices.

Monitors A monitor is the screen which displays the data generated by your software. Monitors come in a variety of shapes, sizes, and resolution qualities. Harvard Graphics can display data on monochrome, composite or color monitors.

Display Cards The display card is the hardware component in your computer system which links your computer and monitor. It processes software data and the documents you create and displays them on your monitor screen. Each monitor requires a specific type of display card. Be sure your system is set up properly.

Disks and Disk Drives   There are two types of disks and disk drives. Floppy disks come in 5¼ or 3½ inch sizes and are used for external data storage. Your computer usually labels floppy disk drives with the letters A and B. Your hard drive, installed inside your computer, is normally labeled with the letter C. External hard drives are also available.

Output Devices   Harvard Graphics can produce printer, plotter, and film recorder output. High-quality dot-matrix and laser printers work well with Harvard Graphics. Daisy-wheel printers are unacceptable since they do not print graphics. Plotters produce charts of excellent quality, and can also make overhead transparencies. Film recorders produce high quality charts in 35mm slide format.

The Disk Operating System   The Disk Operating System (DOS) is the master program which operates your computer system. Once you've installed DOS on your hard drive, it is automatically loaded into Random Access Memory each time you start your computer. It allows you to load and run Harvard Graphics and other software programs installed on your hard drive or accessed from floppy disks.

Computer Memory   Computers have two types of memory. Random Access Memory (RAM) temporarily stores the current software and the documents you are creating and working with. RAM provides fast data access, but when you turn your computer off or you accidentally lose power, the data stored in RAM is lost. Permanent memory is the term used for the software and data you install or save on your hard or floppy disks. To avoid losing the current version of the data you have created or modified in RAM, save it as often as possible to your hard or floppy disks.

Accessing Your Data   Hard drives can hold hundreds of files organized into groups called directories and subdirectories. When you want to work with a particular file, you have to tell your computer where to find it. The route to a specific file is called a path. To retrieve a Harvard Graphics document with the Filename REPORT, you would enter **C:\HG3\REPORT.CH3** to describe the path. Your computer would go to drive C, and search the Harvard Graphics directory HG3 to retrieve the file named REPORT.CH3.

✦ The Harvard Graphics Keyboard

Harvard Graphics uses special key combinations and function keys to perform certain tasks. The following text and illustrations describe how Harvard Graphics uses these keys on three common computer keyboards.

TAB	The Tab key, in combination with the Shift key, moves the cursor, menu arrow, or diamond symbol.
↵	The Enter key, also called the Return key, enters data, selects menu items, and executes certain commands.
BKSP	The Backspace key deletes unwanted characters.
INS	The Insert key switches between Insert and Typeover modes.
SHIFT	The Shift key creates uppercase letters, and with the Tab key, moves the cursor, menu arrow, or diamond symbol.
ALT	The Alt key, with other designated keys, executes macros.
ESC	The Escape key steps backward to the previous menu, or cancels an action.
DEL	The Delete key erases the characters at the cursor position.
↑ ↓ ← →	The Arrow keys move the cursor, menu arrow, or diamond symbol.
HOME	The Home key moves the cursor back to the beginning of a line.
CTRL	The Control key, in combination with other keys, performs specific tasks.

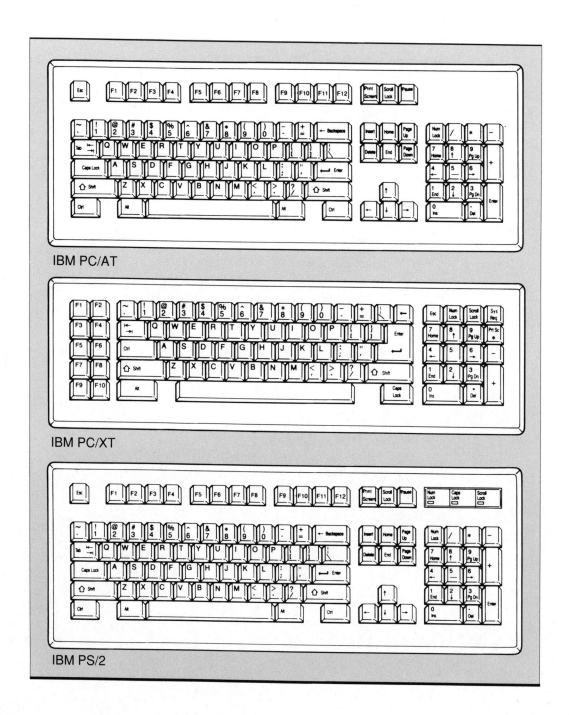

IBM PC/AT

IBM PC/XT

IBM PS/2

Function Keys   The function keys, labeled F1 through F10 or F12, are located along the top or left side of the keyboard. These keys are programmed to access specific Harvard Graphics option menus and other important functions.

Refer to the inside covers of this book for a listing of the various tasks assigned to the Harvard Graphics function keys.

The Numeric Keypad   The numeric keypad, on the right side of your keyboard, provides an alternative way to enter and manipulate numerical data. To activate the numeric keypad, press the Num Lock key.

✦ Hard Disk Installation

The Harvard Graphics program disks have an installation program which automatically installs Harvard Graphics 3.0 on your hard disk. This process creates a primary directory named HG3, which stores your main program files, and separate subdirectories for the program's supplementary files. There are no conflicts with any files created with version 2.0 of Harvard Graphics. Version 3.0 files use a new .CH3 extension.

You can install all your Harvard Graphics files at the same time, or the Program files and selected supplementary files to save space on your hard disk. Harvard Graphics also works with extended or expanded memory. If your computer system has this capability, use step 8 in the following instructions to gain its full benefit.

✦ **1**   Start your computer and display the C> prompt. Bypass any date and time prompts by pressing ⏎.

```
C>_
```

◆ **2**   Place Harvard Graphics Disk 1 in drive A, and at the C> prompt type **a:install** or **a:install /m** if you have a black and white monitor such as VGA gray scale. Press ⏎ to display the following screen.

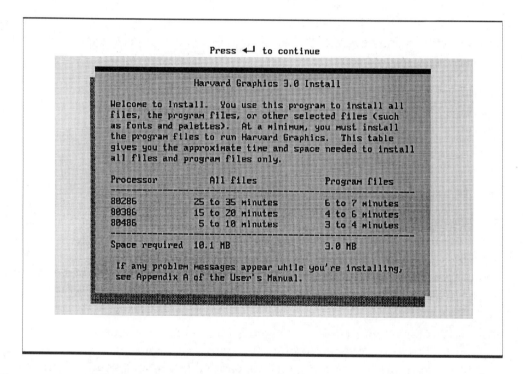

◆ **3**   Press ⏎ to continue and press ⬆ or ⬇ to select your installation drive with the menu arrow. You would normally select drive C as shown on the following screen.

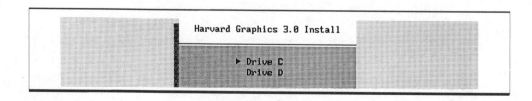

⋆ **4**   Press ⏎ to continue, and if you wish to place your files in a directory other than \HG3, observe the instructions on the following screen.

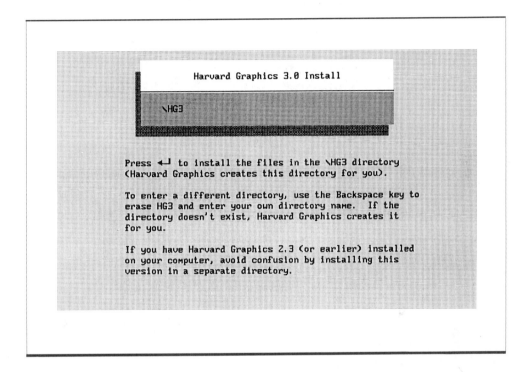

⋆ **5**   Press ⏎ to continue. To install the entire program select **All files** and press ⏎. If you choose the individual method, you must select and install **Program files** and then press ⬆ or ⬇ to select individual files for installation. Press ⏎ after each selection.

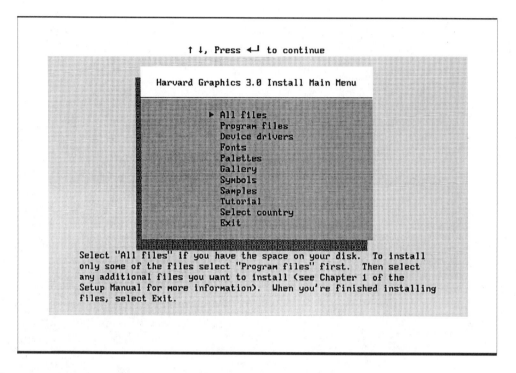

✦ **6**   Your selected file names are displayed as they are installed. When prompted, insert additional program disks in drive A and press ⏎. The following screen is displayed when installation is complete.

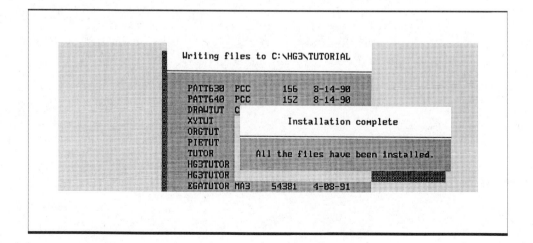

◆ **7**   Press ⏎ to return to the Install Main Menu. Do not press Esc. This interrupts the installation process.

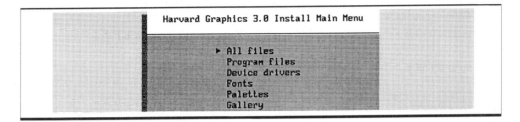

◆ **8**   If you installed your files individually, select Exit and press ⏎. To configure your system for expanded or extended memory, observe the instructions on the following screen.

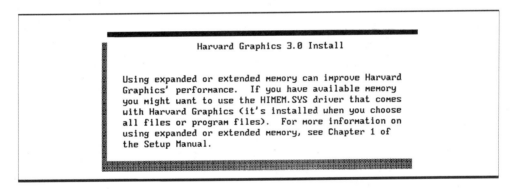

◆ **9**   Press ⏎ to continue.

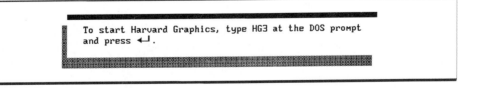

◆ **10**   Press ⏎ to exit to the DOS prompt. Harvard Graphics is now ready to run.

Note

Starting Harvard Graphics with an AUTOEXEC.BAT File   AUTOEXEC.BAT
is a file that can instruct your computer to automatically execute Harvard
Graphics at start up. You can create or edit an AUTOEXEC.BAT file with text
editors such as WordPerfect, Office PC Editor, or Microsoft Word which can
retrieve, edit, and save text in ASCII format.

Refer to your DOS manual for instructions on creating an AUTOEXEC.BAT file
containing the Harvard Graphics directory name and startup command.

✦ Installing a Mouse

A mouse can be used to display menus, select menu options, position the cursor,
execute functions, and draw chart objects. Using a mouse in conjunction with
your keyboard lets you work more quickly and efficiently.

Note

Hints for Installing Your Mouse   When installing your mouse, carefully follow the instructions in the manufacturer's documentation. You may have to install a mouse card in one of your computer's expansion slots. The software for
your mouse driver must also be installed on your hard disk. MOUSE.COM,
MOUSE.SYS, MSMOUSE.COM, and MSMOUSE.SYS are four common mouse
drivers.

Harvard Graphics is already set up for all Microsoft compatible mice. To use
another type of mouse, you need to select it with the Harvard Graphics Setup
feature.

Refer to your mouse documentation to determine the type of input port your mouse
uses and to familiarize yourself with specific installation and set up instructions.

♦ 1   At the C> prompt, type **HG3** and press ⏎ to start Harvard Graphics.

♦ 2   From the Main Menu, press ⑧ to display the Setup menu.

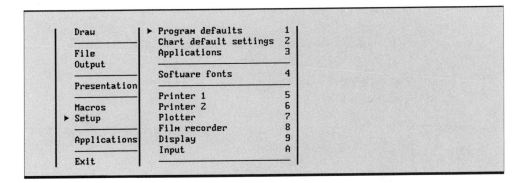

♦ 3   Press Ⓐ to display the Input Device Setup Menu.

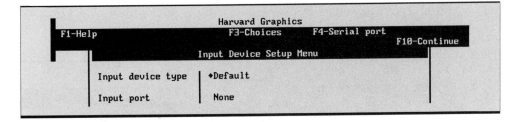

♦ 4   Press F3 to display a list of input devices. The Default setting is for Microsoft compatible mice.

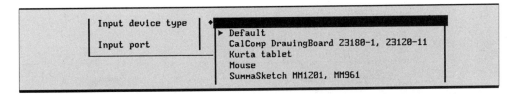

♦ 5   Press ↓ to move the menu arrow to **Mouse** and press ⏎.

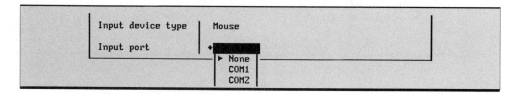

✦ **6** Press ⬇ to move the diamond symbol to **Input port** and press ⬚F3⬚ to display a list of ports.

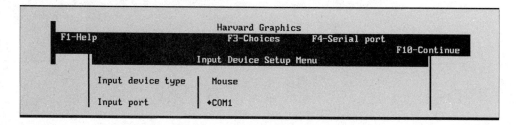

✦ **7** Press ⬇ to move the menu arrow to your mouse port. **COM 1** is selected in the example on the following screen.

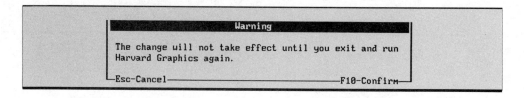

✦ **8** Press ⬚F10⬚. You are warned you must exit Harvard Graphics and restart the program.

◆9   Press F10 to save your mouse settings and return to the Setup menu.

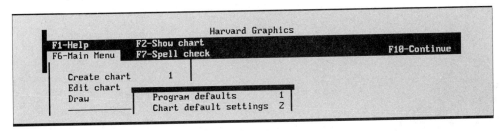

◆10   Press ESC and E to exit Harvard Graphics.

✦ Making Backup Copies of Your Disks

You should make backup floppy disk copies of your Harvard Graphics program disks to avoid the cost of replacement if your originals are damaged. It's also a good idea to back up all your other program files on a regular basis.

New floppy disks must be formatted by your system before data can be written on or read from them. To format and copy data to a new disk, locate the FORMAT.COM and DISKCOPY.COM files in your DOS program files. If you need help locating the directory which contains your DOS files, consult your computer dealer or the person who set up your system.

Before you back up your original disks, be sure to write-protect them to prevent inadvertent erasure. Write-protect your 3½ inch disks by pushing the small tab on the side until the hole is uncovered. Your 5¼ inch disks are write protected when you place one of the small rectangular stickers, provided with your disks, over the write-protect notch.

For specific details on how to format new floppy disks, and back up your Harvard Graphics disks and other program files, consult your DOS, Harvard Graphics, and system documentation.

B

Importing and Exporting Data

Harvard Graphics can import data from Lotus 1-2-3 1.A, 2.0, and 2.2, Lotus Symphony 1.0, 1.2, 2.0, and 2.2, and Microsoft Excel 2.0. You can also import ASCII and dBASE files.

Harvard Graphics data can be exported to a variety of other formats, including Professional Write, CGM metafiles, Encapsulated PostScript (EPS) files, Hewlett-Packard Graphics Language (HPGL) plotter files, and .PCX bitmap files.

Before you use this appendix, you should have a working knowledge of the first six chapters of this book, and be familiar with Lotus 1-2-3, Excel, dBASE, and ASCII formated files.

✦ Importing Lotus and Excel

Let's import a Lotus graph into Harvard Graphics. These instructions also apply to Excel charts. Simply substitute Excel menu selections.

Start Harvard Graphics and display the Main Menu.

✦ 1   Click on **File** or press ④ to display the File menu.

```
■  Create chart     1  |
   Edit chart
   Draw            ┌────────────────────────────────┐
                   │ ► Get chart        1  Ctrl G    │
                   │   Get template     2            │
   ► File          │   Apply template   3            │
   Output          │                                 │
                   │   Save chart       4  Ctrl S    │
   Presentation    │   Save as template 5            │
                   │   Save as symbol   6            │
   Macros          │                                 │
   Setup           │   Import           7            │
                   │   Export           8            │
                   └────────────────────────────────┘
```

✦ **2**   Click on **Import** or press ⑦ to display the Import menu.

```
► File        │ Apply template │ ► Import Lotus graph  1
  Output      │                │   Import Lotus data   2
              │ Save chart     │   Import Excel chart  3
  Presentation│ Save as template│  Import Excel data   4
              │ Save as symbol │
  Macros      │                │   Import ASCII data   5
```

✦ **3**   Click on **Import Lotus graph** or press ① to display the Select Lotus
Worksheet which shows the Lotus files in the Harvard Graphics Import directory. To locate files in another directory, select or type the
new directory name.

```
          ┌──────────── Select Lotus Worksheet ────────────┐
          │ Directory: C:\HG3\IMPORT\*.W*                   │
          │ Filename:  FILMS.WK1                            │
          │ ──────────────────────────────────────────────│
          │  ..          <DIR>                              │
          │ ►FILMS .WK1  OTHER                              │
          └────────────────────────────────────────────────┘
```

✦ **4**   Select **FILMS.WK1**, a Lotus worksheet in your Harvard Graphics
program files, to display the Import Lotus Graph menu. The default
setting for the Import data only selection is No. If you want to import only data from your Lotus graph, select **Import data only** and
F3-Choices and then **Yes**.

```
■
  Worksheet:     FILMS.WK1
  Named graph:  CURRENT
  Import data only:  No

  ┌──────────────────┬──────────┬─────────────────────────────────────────┐
  │  Named Graph     │   Type   │                 Title                    │
  ├──────────────────┼──────────┼─────────────────────────────────────────┤
  │ ►CURRENT         │   PIE    │ Quarterly Cost / Fiscal Year 1992       │
  │  FILM03          │ STACKED  │ Net Sales / With 1993 Projections       │
  │  FILM04          │  LINE    │ Net Sales / With 1993 Projections       │
  │  FILM05          │  LINE    │ Cost Us. Gross Sales / Fiscal Year 1992 │
  │  FILM06          │   PIE    │ Quarterly Cost / Fiscal Year 1992       │
  │  FILM07          │   PIE    │ Quarterly Gross / Fiscal Year 1992      │
  └──────────────────┴──────────┴─────────────────────────────────────────┘
```

◆**5** Leave the Import data only selection set at No and click on **FILM06**
or place the menu arrow and press ⎆ to display the imported chart.
An imported chart or graph may not look exactly like the original.
Harvard Graphics cannot translate every detail of a document
created in another program.

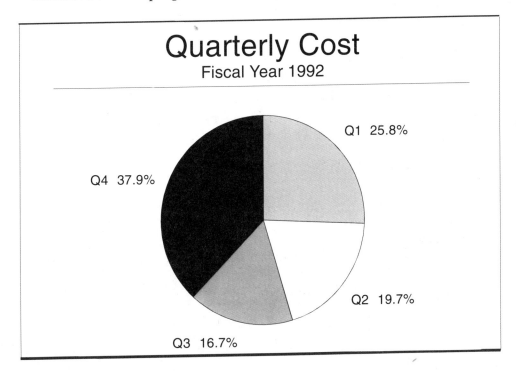

◆ **6**   Click the right mouse button or press ⌷ESC⌷ to display the chart worksheet. Your imported chart can be edited and enhanced like any other Harvard Graphics chart.

```
┌──────────────────────────────────────────────────────────────────────┐
│ FILM06.CH3                      Pie Chart 1                      ▼     │
│  F1-Help        F2-Show chart   F3-Choices     F4-Draw       F5-Mark  ▲│
│  F6-Main Menu   F7-Spell/Text   F8-Options     F9-Pie data   F10-Continue│
│                                                                        │
│  Title:      Quarterly Cost                                            │
│  Subtitle:   Fiscal Year 1992                                          │
│  Footnote:                                                             │
│  Pie title:                                                           │
│                                                                        │
│                                                                        │
│  Slice        Label           Value      Cut      Color      Pattern  │
│                                                                        │
│    1    Q4                      25        No    ■ Cyn  |S       3      │
│    2    Q3                      11        No    ▨ Blu  L|S      2      │
│    3    Q2                      13        No    ▨ Blu  D|S      1      │
│    4    Q1                      17        No    ▨ Cyn  D|S      0      │
│    5                                      No    ▨ Yel  L|S      4      │
│                                                                        │
└──────────────────────────────────────────────────────────────────────┘
```

◆ **7**   Click on **F6-Main Menu** and **Create chart** and then **Clear chart** or press ⌷F6⌷ and ⌷1⌷ and ⌷8⌷ to clear your imported chart from memory.

When you've imported one Lotus graph, and want to import a second one from another worksheet, the Import Lotus Graph menu is displayed. To display the Select Lotus Worksheet, select **F8-Worksheet**.

Note

Importing Data Only   When you select **Import data only** and then **Yes**, the Lotus graph or Excel chart you import excludes the original format options, and uses the options in the current Harvard Graphics chart. The data only method is very similar to importing an entire graph or chart, but you must first retrieve or create a Harvard Graphics chart. As you complete the process, the Lotus or Excel data is imported and displayed in your current chart. Before you import an X axis date format, make sure it matches one of the Harvard Graphics formats.

✦ Importing ASCII and dBASE Data

The following example uses Lotus worksheet data, but you can import Excel, ASCII, and dBASE files by simply substituting the appropriate menu option. Harvard Graphics accepts data for text, XY, pie and column charts. The Import Data screens vary slightly, but the process is the same.

✦**1**　From the Main Menu click on **Create chart** and **XY chart** and then **Bar** or press ⬜**1** and ⬜**3** and ⬜**1** to display a bar chart worksheet. Select **F10-Continue** to accept the default X Data Type Name.

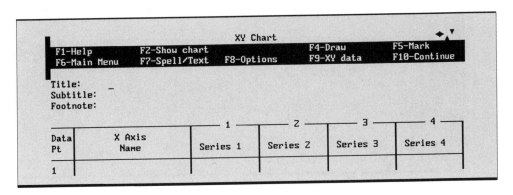

✦**2**　Click on **F6-Main Menu** and **File** and then **Import** or press ⬜**F6** and ⬜**4** and ⬜**7** to display the Import menu.

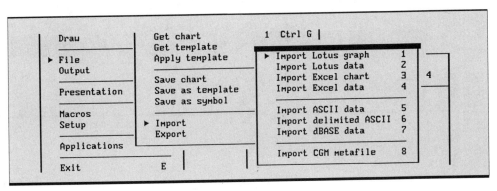

◆ **3**   Click on **Import Lotus data** or press ② to display a list of Lotus files.

```
                        Select Lotus Worksheet
          Directory: C:\HG3\IMPORT\*.W*
          Filename:  FILMS.WK1

             ..              <DIR>
          ►FILMS   .WK1      OTHER
```

◆ **4**   Select **FILMS.WK1** to display the Import Lotus Data Into XY Chart worksheet.

```
                    Import Lotus Data Into XY Chart            ◆
   F1-Help                     F3-Choices      F4-View file
                               F8-Options                   F10-Continue

   Filename:      FILMS.WK1
   Append data:   No

   Title:            _
   Subtitle:
   Footnote:
   X axis title:
   Y axis title:
   X axis data:
```

◆ **5**   At the Title line, type **Templeton Films, Ltd.** and press TAB or ⏎ to move the cursor to the Subtitle line.

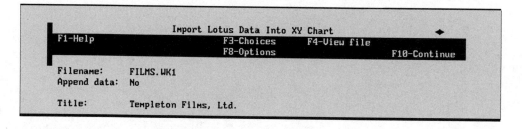

```
                    Import Lotus Data Into XY Chart            ◆
   F1-Help                     F3-Choices      F4-View file
                               F8-Options                   F10-Continue

   Filename:      FILMS.WK1
   Append data:   No

   Title:         Templeton Films, Ltd.
```

✦ **6** Click on **F4-View file** or press **F4** to display the Lotus worksheet.

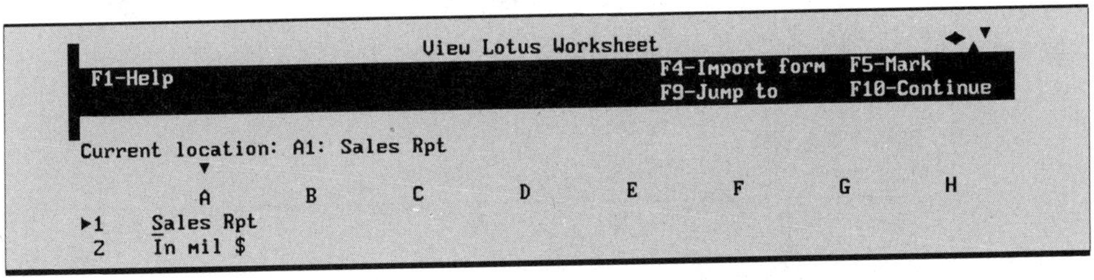

```
                        Uiew Lotus Worksheet            ◆ ▼
  F1-Help                                F4-Import form  F5-Mark      ▲
                                         F9-Jump to      F10-Continue

  Current location: A1: Sales Rpt
            ▼
          A         B       C       D       E       F       G       H
  ►1    Sales Rpt
   2    In mil $
```

Note

Moving Around Your Worksheet or File   Use the arrow keys to move the cursor on your worksheet or file. You can also click on **F9-Jump to** or press **F9** and type the cell address, field address, or row/column coordinates. Select **F10-Continue** or press **⏎** to jump to the specified cell, field, or character.

✦ **7** With the cursor in cell A1: Sales Rpt, click on **F4-Import form** or press **F4** to import the A1 cell identifier. Repeat steps 5,6, and 7 to import cells A2, A5, and A8 for the Footnote, X axis, and Y axis titles shown on the following screen.

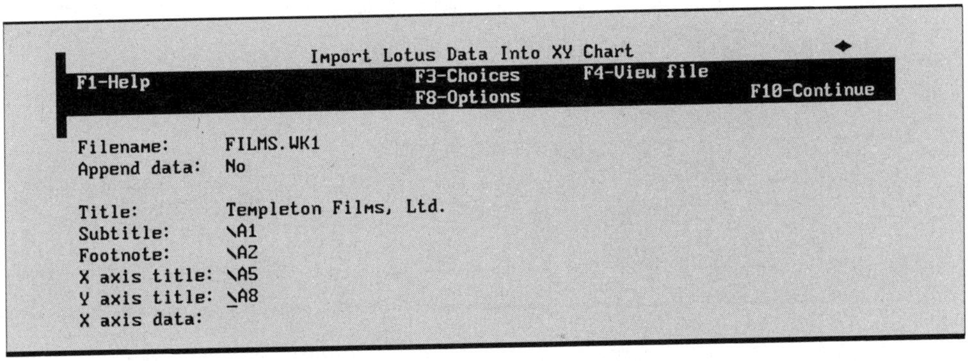

```
                    Import Lotus Data Into XY Chart        ◆
  F1-Help                       F3-Choices    F4-Uiew file
                                F8-Options                  F10-Continue

  Filename:     FILMS.WK1
  Append data:  No

  Title:        Templeton Films, Ltd.
  Subtitle:     \A1
  Footnote:     \A2
  X axis title: \A5
  Y axis title: \A8
  X axis data:
```

◆ **8**   To import a range of cells for the X axis data, place the cursor on the X axis data line and select **F4-View file** to display the worksheet.

◆ **9**   Move the cursor to cell C5, click on **F5-Mark** or press **F5** and move the cursor to cell F5 to highlight cells C5 through F5. To unmark a cell, press **F5** or **ESC**.

```
Current location: C5..F5: Q4
                                                            ▼
              A       B       C       D       E       F       G       H
       1   Sales Rpt
       2   In mil $
       3
       4                           1991
     ►5   Quarter              Q1      Q2      Q3      Q4
       6   Cost                16      26      30      18
```

◆ **10**   Click on **F4-Import form** to import your range of cells to the Import Data screen.

```
Title:        Templeton Films, Ltd.
Subtitle:     \A1
Footnote:     \A2
X axis title: \A5
Y axis title: \A8
X axis data:  C5..F5
```

◆ **11**   Move the cursor to Series 1 and type **\D4** at Series Names and **C8..F8** at Series Values.

	1	2	3	4
Series Names	\D4	Series 2	Series 3	Series 4
Series Values	C8..F8_			

٠ **12** When all the data has been imported, click on **F10-Continue** or press
F10 to display your XY Chart worksheet.

```
Title:     Templeton Films, Ltd.
Subtitle:  Sales Rpt
Footnote:  In mil $

                             ─ 1 ──    ─ 2 ──    ─ 3 ──    ─ 4 ──
Data │   X Axis
Pt   │    Name      1991      Series 2  Series 3  Series 4

1    │ Q1            53
2    │ Q2            56
3    │ Q3            47
4    │ Q4            40
5    │
```

٠ **13** Click on **F2-Show chart** or press F2 to view the current status of your
chart with the imported Lotus data. Return to your worksheet to edit
and enhance your chart as needed.

The following items contain detailed information on the various types of files
you can import into Harvard Graphics.

Importing Another Worksheet or File When you've imported one worksheet or file,
and want to import another one, display the Import Data screen. Select **F8-Options**
and **Select new worksheet** for Lotus and Excel, or **F8-Select file** for ASCII and
dBASE files, and then select the new file.

Importing Delimited ASCII Files When the ASCII Delimiters menu is displayed,
change the delimiters to match the ones in your file. To determine which delimiters are used in your file, display the Import Data screen and select **F4-View
file** to view your file. Make a note of your file's delimiters, and select **F9-Actions**
and then **Change delimiters** to return to the ASCII Delimiters menu.

Importing Named Ranges To import Named ranges into the Import Data screen,
click on **F8-Options** or press F8 and then click on **View range names** or press 2
to display a list of range names. Select the appropriate range name. Your selection appears on the Import Data screen.

Appending Data to the Current Chart   With the Append data option set to No, imported data overwrites existing data in the Import Data screen. When set to Yes, the imported data is appended to the last line of data.

Importing CGM Metafiles   To import a CGM metafile, you must first retrieve or create a chart. At the Main Menu, select **File** and **Import** and then **Import CGM metafile** to display the list of CGM metafiles in the Import directory. Select any CGM metafile for import to the current chart. You can then save the metafile as a symbol or chart.

For further details on importing specific files and data, consult your Harvard Graphics documentation.

♦ Exporting Harvard Graphics

Harvard Graphics can export charts to Professional Write picture files, Encapsulated PostScript (EPS) files, Hewlett-Packard Graphics Language (HPGL) plotter files, CGM metafiles, and PCX bitmap files. The following example uses an EPS file. The procedures for exporting Harvard Graphics charts to the other formats are basically the same.

The chart worksheet you created in the previous exercise should be displayed.

♦ **1**   Click on **F6-Main Menu** and **File** and then **Export** or press `F6` and `4` and `8` to display the Export pop-up menu.

```
 ▶ File          Apply templat│ ▶ Export Professional Write    1
   Output                      │   Export CGM metafile          2
                 Save chart    │   Export Encapsulated PostScript  3
   Presentation  Save as templ │   Export HPGL plotter file     4
                 Save as symbo │   Export PCX bitmap file       5
   Macros                      │
```

٠ **2**   Click on **Export Encapsulated PostScript** or press ⑶ to display the
Export As Encapsulated Postscript menu.

```
    Footnote:   In mi│  Export As Encapsulated PostScript
                                                                         ┌─── 4 ───┐
   ┌────┬─────┐    Directory:  C:\HG3\EXPORT
   │Data│ X Ax│    Filename:    _                                          Series 4
   │Pt  │  Nam│
   │    │     │    For use with:    Printer 1
   │ 1  │ Q1  │    Output quality:  High
   │ 2  │ Q2  │
   │ 3  │ Q3  │            │ 47        │            │
```

Note

Choosing the Right Printer Options   Printer options affect the appearance
of exported charts. Before you export a chart, set the correct printer options on
the Output to Printer and Printer Options menus. The Postscript printer driver
must be selected to export an EPS file.

---

٠ **3**   Enter the appropriate changes and filename on the Export As Encapsulated PostScript menu. Harvard Graphics automatically assigns an
.EPS extension to this file, and a .PWG or .HPP extension to a Professional Write or Hewlett Packard file.

٠ **4**   Click on **F10-Continue** or press ⒑ to export your file to the selected
file format and return to your chart worksheet.

٠ **5**   Click on **F6-Main Menu** and **Exit** and then **F10-Continue** or press ⒡
and ⒠ and ⒑ to exit Harvard Graphics.

Consult your Harvard Graphics documentation for more information on exporting
your charts.

Index

HARVARD GRAPHICS MENU BARS

Standard Function Keys

F1-Help	F2-Show chart		F4-Draw	F5-Mark
F6-Main Menu	F7-Spell/Text	F8-Options		F10-Continue

F1-Help	Displays context-sensitive help.
F2-Show chart	Displays current version of chart.
F4-Draw	Displays current chart on Draw screen.
F5-Mark	Marks blocks of text.
F6-Main Menu	Displays Main Menu.
F7-Spell/Text	Locates and corrects misspelled words.
F8-Options	Displays enhancement options.
F10-Continue	Executes an operation.

Pie Chart Function Keys

F1-Help	F2-Show chart	F3-Choices	F4-Draw	F5-Mark
F6-Main Menu	F7-Spell/Text	F8-Options	F9-Pie data	F10-Continue

F3-Choices	Displays options pop-up menus.
F9-Pie data	Modifies pie chart data.

XY Chart Function Keys

F1-Help	F2-Show chart		F4-Draw	F5-Mark
F6-Main Menu	F7-Spell/Text	F8-Options	F9-XY data	F10-Continue

F9-XY data	Modifies x axis data, enters and recalculates formulas and shows series statistics.

File List Function Keys

F1-Help		
	F8-Sort files	F10-Continue

F8-Sort files	Sorts files alphabetically.

Program Defaults Function Keys

F1-Help	F3-Choices	
	F7-Special characters	F10-Continue

F3-Choices	Displays options pop-up menus.
F7-Special characters	Displays list of special ASCII characters.